Equality, Reconciliation and Social Cohesion

The Inspiration of Sir William Deane

Editor: Frank Brennan SJ

Connor Court Publishing

Published in 2026 by Connor Court Publishing Pty Ltd.

Connor Court Publishing Pty Ltd.
PO Box 7257
Redland Bay QLD 4165
sales@connorcourt.com
www.connorcourt.com

ISBN: 9781923568822

Cover Design by Maria Giordano

The cover of this book includes a photo of a mosaic on the mural wall at the Australian Centre for Christianity and Culture in Canberra. The mosaic is an accurate reproduction of a painting by Hector Jandany from the Gija/Kija people in Warmun in the East Kimberley. The painting is entitled 'The Holy Spirit in our Land' and it depicts the white owl of the Kimberley. The painting was commissioned by Sir William Deane and Lady Helen Deane in 2005. They donated it to the National Gallery of Australia in 2008.

A year after his retirement as Governor General, Sir William was interviewed on the ABC Encounter program. He said: 'The main thing I noticed among indigenous Christians that I personally hadn't been conscious of to anything like the same extent among non-indigenous Christians, is the emphasis on the Holy Ghost, the Holy Spirit of our land, and of course it possibly goes back to the place of fire and water in indigenous life and in indigenous tradition. But once one moves from the Christian ethic of our indigenous people into their traditional culture, one has a great deal to learn no matter what one's system of beliefs may happen to be. And the most important thing I think that we have to learn is the way the past, all the way back to the Dreamtime, informs the present, and the way their lives are enriched by the past; all the time one finds in Indigenous communities that the knowledge and awareness of the past and of course where it hasn't been destroyed, the land, is part of the living present.'

Printed in Australia.

Books by Frank Brennan SJ

Too Much Order with Too Little Law

Land Rights Queensland Style

Sharing the Country

One Land, One Nation

Legislating Liberty

The Wik Debate

Tampering with Asylum

Acting On Conscience

The 2015 Gasson Lectures: Maintaining a Convinced and Pondered Trust

No Small Change: The Road to Recognition for Indigenous Australia

Amplifying That Still, Small Voice

The People's Quest for Leadership in Church and State

Observations on the Pell Proceedings

A Virtual Year: Homilies During Pandemic

An Indigenous Voice to Parliament: Considering a Constitutional Bridge

Lessons from Our Failure to Build a Constitutional Bridge in the 2023 Referendum

Pope Francis: The Disruptive Pilgrim's Guide

Edited Works by Frank Brennan SJ

Finding Common Ground

Reconciling our Differences

Discerning the Australian Social Conscience

Gerard Brennan's Articles and Speeches: Maintaining the Law's Skeleton of Principle (2 volumes)

Dedicated to William and Helen Deane,
Australia's First Couple of Reconciliation

Contents

Preface

It is 30 years since Sir William Deane commenced his term as Governor-General of Australia. During his five year term, he delivered almost 500 speeches. Many Australians are too young to remember Sir William's contribution to Australian public life. In the wake of the Bondi Massacre in December 2025 when two gunmen motivated by the ideology of Islamic State opened fire on a Hanukkah celebration killing 15 of their fellow citizens, our present Governor-General, Sam Mostyn, when delivering her Australia Day message for 2026 said: 'In searching for a message for this Australia Day during challenging times, I have looked for inspiration and I found it in the words of former Governor-General, Sir William Deane, who 25 years ago said Australia is a country of sharing, of mutual respect and acceptance, of concern for true equality, dignity, opportunity and hope for all Australians. He said Australians must walk together, talk together, care together and achieve together. In 2026, his message remains as relevant as ever.'[1] Her Excellency was right. That got me thinking that there was a need to make accessible Sir William's key remarks on equality, social cohesion and reconciliation.

I was privileged to work briefly as Sir William's Associate when he was a Judge in 1981. We became good friends. Sir William and his wife, Lady Helen Deane, each spoke at the 1997 Reconciliation Convention chaired by Patrick Dodson, the father of reconciliation. As Rapporteur at the Convention, I described them as the nation's first couple of reconciliation. As Governor-General, Sir William gave first priority to reconciliation between the First Australians and those of us who came later. Earlier as a High Court judge, he had been a judicial trailblazer for the principle of equality. As Governor-General he often spoke of the need for national inclusiveness or multicultural inclusiveness, the

[1] Governor-General's Australia Day Address to the Nation, 26 January 2026.

essence of which 'lies in a proper balance between respect for, and genuine tolerance of, the different national, racial, ethnic and religious backgrounds and cultures from which we come and the fundamental requirements of national identity, national unity and national standards'. He said that 'many principles and qualities have combined to enable and create the social cohesion of Australia's contemporary multiculturalism'. He listed 'equality of opportunity, equality of all before the law, our national concept of a "fair go", and our general tolerance of others'.

Finding that most of Sir William's speeches were not available, even in libraries, I approached him and asked permission to publish a selection of his writings and speeches. He agreed and trusted me to choose extracts from the vast collection of his speeches. This book is the result. I am very grateful to Sir William for making his observations freshly available at this difficult time when the nation is conducting a Royal Commission on Antisemitism and Social Cohesion. And I am indebted to Governor-General, Sam Mostyn, for providing a Foreword.

I have sorted the key lectures into 6 categories each with its own chapter: the land of the fair go; the ANZAC spirit and mateship; reconciliation and recognition; multiculturalism and social cohesion; religion and respect; and mourning and hope. Within each chapter, extracts are in dated order. In places, the extracts have been lightly edited, but not to change the sense. The chapter on reconciliation and recognition includes Lady Helen Deane's address at the 1997 Reconciliation Convention on 'Women and Reconciliation'. Each chapter commences with a brief introduction by me setting the context. Occasionally I quote from Sir William's letters to Buckingham Palace which have now been published by the National Archives of Australia.

Foreword

The Honourable Sam Mostyn AC, Governor-General

Having accepted Prime Minister Albanese's invitation to serve as Australia's 28th Governor-General, I sought the perspectives and experiences of all my living predecessors before being sworn into office. Sir William Deane's advice was simple, profound, and completely consistent with the character of his own term, and of his life's work. Sitting in his humble office in Canberra, he told me to put compassion at the centre of all my work. Compassion was the enduring nature of the five and a half years Sir William and Lady Deane spent at Yarralumla. It was threaded into every interaction, reception, visit, oration, and chance encounter. In embracing care, kindness and respect as the core of my term, I am always conscious of Sir William's extraordinary legacy and the wisdom he shared with me.

As a law student and young lawyer, I had read Sir William's High Court judgments. As Governor-General, I have carried with me his book Directions: A Vision for Australia. Reading the speeches in this volume, so thoughtfully gathered by Fr Frank Brennan SJ, it is impossible not to be deeply impressed by Sir William's clarity of thought and strength of purpose throughout his life. His work as Governor-General was focused primarily on three things: first, his commitment to the journey of reconciliation, and its demand for truth, honesty, and generosity; second, his celebration of our inclusive multiculturalism; and thirdly, his conviction that, as he so often said, the ultimate test of a democratic nation is how it treats its most vulnerable. From the outset of his term, he promised to be the champion of disadvantaged people, and by its conclusion, he measured his success by whether he had contributed, even a little, to Australia passing that national test of care and compassion. Everyone familiar with his time in office knows that Sir William achieved this purpose with his own ever-present compassion and grace.

As Governor-General, Sir William had the rare ability to embody both pride and grief in times of national mourning and memory. In commemorating the diggers or the firefighters, reflecting on our imperfect history, or finding the perfect words of comfort for the tragedies at Port Arthur, Childers, and Interlaken, he had a deep capacity for understanding human experience and nature at its worst, and honouring Australians' courage and kindness at its best.

Last December, Australia experienced an horrific antisemitic attack at Bondi Beach during a peaceful Hannukah by the Sea – the worst terrorist massacre our country has ever seen. At that time, I felt strongly that my place was beside those who were suffering. It was the role of the Governor-General, in that moment, to listen, to show kindness, and to stand in quiet solidarity with a grieving community, and with all Australians. In being present then, and afterwards reaffirming the essential care, kindness and respect that remain at the heart of our nation, I had Sir William's words with me.

Just this month, all of us at Government House were honoured by a visit from Sir William and Lady Deane. At 95, he is as warm, gentle, generous and articulate as he was 25 years ago, when he completed his time as our 22nd Governor-General. He was as clear as ever that the role of the Governor-General is to embody compassion, and to stand with the vulnerable in our community. It has been one of my greatest privileges to know him, and to learn from him. I hope that many generations of Australians will come to know him through the words and sentiments collected in this book.

27 May 2026

Government House

Yarralumla

Introduction

[Intro] William Deane – from Judge to Governor-General

William Patrick Deane was born in Melbourne on 4 January 1931. His parents moved to Canberra with William and his two older sisters in 1934. Deane later observed that 'in those Depression days, they had had little real choice but to leave home, relations and friends upon the transfer of the Commonwealth Patents Office where my father worked'. He went to kindergarten and primary school at St Christopher's Convent in Canberra. He recalled his first day at kindergarten in 1936: 'I ran away at the morning tea break and the occurrence, no doubt with some embellishments, become fixed in my mind through being recounted by family members over the years. It was only in late afternoon that I was eventually located asleep behind the old Capital 'Picture Theatre' (as we called it) diagonally across the road. Fortunately, those were much simpler times in terms of both crime and traffic and I don't think it really occurred to anyone that any serious harm might have befallen me.' Apart from that first day, he attests: 'My seven years in the primary school at St Christopher's were extraordinarily happy and rewarding.' He recalls: 'St Christopher's was rather unique even for its own times. Its pupils came from all parts of Canberra and from all sections of the community. There were children of the then Prime Minister, Mr Lyons. There were Ambassadors' children. There were the children of the wealthiest and the poorest of Canberra's families. There were children of different ethnic and cultural backgrounds. Yet in a period when the importance of our Australian multiculturalism and of the basic equality of our people was not generally recognised, I cannot recall ever encountering or observing any episode of discrimination or intolerance based on ethnic or social differences.'

For secondary school, he attended St Joseph's College, Hunter's Hill. in Sydney. The school was established in 1881. Deane is a very proud alumnus of the school, having been asked to propose a toast to the school at its 75th, 100th and 125th anniversaries. When proposing the most recent toast in 2006, he recalled how he had consulted one of his old teachers Brother Ligouri about what he should say for the first toast in 1956:

> After some thought, Brother Ligouri suggested that my theme should be the spirit of St Joseph's which he saw as one of courage and no compromise. Courage in terms of standing up for what is right. No compromise in the sense that to compromise truth is to harbour falsehood and to compromise principle is to lose it. I followed his advice. Now, 50 years on, I can do no better than emphasise the contemporary importance of that spirit which has inspired the mission of St Joseph's and of the Marists in all the years since the College was founded in 1881. And to express the profound hope that that spirit and the philosophy and standards of the Marists will continue to guide and inspire the College in the years to come.

After school, Deane attended Sydney University graduating in Arts and Law. After graduation, he worked in the Commonwealth Attorney-General's Department in Canberra before studying International Law in Europe. He was awarded a Rotary Foundation Fellowship which allowed him to study International Law at Trinity College Dublin (TCD) and The Hague Academy of International Law. In 1955 he was awarded the Diploma (*cum laude*) of The Hague Academy of International Law. Years later when awarded an honorary doctorate at Trinity College, he mused on why he chose this small university to study International Law. He said: 'My admiration for TCD sprang from the obvious. Namely, the extraordinary number of quite outstanding people whom such a comparatively small University, in so far as staff and student numbers were concerned, had managed to produce. Names that span almost all areas of human endeavour and achievement: world famous names from literature, politics, science, philosophy and law. But it also sprang from the far less obvious … the Australian names. People who, after studying here, migrated to Australia and contributed mightily to the development of so much that is best in my own country.'

He commenced work as a solicitor at the Sydney firm of Minter Simpson & Co, before being called to the Bar in 1957. He was appointed Queen's Counsel in 1966. In February 1977 Sir William was appointed a judge in the Equity Division of the Supreme Court of New South Wales. Subsequently in 1977, he was appointed a judge of the Federal Court of Australia and the President of the Australian Trade Practices Tribunal. In July 1982, he was appointed a Justice of the High Court of Australia. At the swearing in on 27 July 1982, Michael McHugh, President of the NSW Bar, described Deane who spent 20 years as a member of the NSW Bar as 'one of the most able counsel that the Australian legal profession has produced'. The President of the Law Council of Australia described him as 'a formidable lawyer with a high moral and professional integrity'. Justice Deane offered some observations on the oath he had sworn: 'The source of law and of judicial power in a true political democracy such as Australia is the people themselves: the governed: the strong and the weak, the rich and the poor, the good and the bad: 'all manner of people'.' He concluded: 'As a witness to that oath I have called upon the God in whom I profoundly believe. I shall honour it.' Deane served on the High Court until 10 November 1995. When his appointment as Governor-General was announced by Mr Keating on 21 August 1995, Sir William said: 'On my swearing in as a Justice of the High Court more than thirteen years ago, I pointed out that the source of all government authority and legitimacy in a true democracy such as Australia is the people. I then made a commitment to serve all the people of this country to the best of my ability as a judge of their highest court. I now extend that public and unqualified commitment of service to cover the office of Governor-General under our Constitution during the period of my appointment.' He was sworn in as Australia's 22nd

Governor-General on 16 February 1996 and served as Governor-General until 29 June 2001.

As a judge, Deane made very few speeches and he never gave interviews. He spoke publicly through his judgments. In a series of judgments he spoke eloquently and passionately about equality under the law and the need to put right past injustices.

Within his first year on the court, the High Court heard argument in the *Tasmanian Dam's case*. Deane had cause to comment on the effect of the 1967 referendum which expanded the Commonwealth Parliament's power to make laws with respect to Aboriginal people. Deane observed:

> As it became increasingly clear that Australia, as a nation, must be diminished until acceptable laws be enacted to mitigate the effects of past barbarism, the exclusion of the people of the Aboriginal race from the provisions of s 51(26) came to be seen as a fetter upon the legislative competence of the Commonwealth Parliament to pass necessary special laws for their benefit. The referendum of 27 May 1967, deleting the reference in s 51(26) and deleting s 127 altogether, was carried by an overwhelming majority of the voters in every State of the Commonwealth. The power conferred by s 51(26) remains a general power to pass laws discriminating against or benefiting the people of any race. Since 1967, that power has included a power to make laws benefiting the people of the Aboriginal race.[1]

In the 1985 decision *Gerhardy* v *Brown*, Justice Deane joined the majority ruling that a South Australian law requiring someone who was not a Pitjantjatjara person to obtain a permit before entering the Pitjantjatjara lands which covered one tenth of the state was valid. In reaching his decision, Justice Deane wrote:

> It would seem that the Aboriginal people had inhabited this country for at least forty milleniums before the arrival of the first white settlers less than two hundred years ago. To the extent that one can generalize, their society was not

[1] *Commonwealth* v *Tasmania* (1983) 158 CLR 1, 272-3.

> institutionalized and drew no clear distinction between the spiritual and the temporal. The core of existence was the relationship with and the responsibility for their homelands which neither individual nor clan 'owned' in a European sense but which provided identity of both in a way which the European settlers did not trouble to comprehend and which the imposed law, based on an assertion of *terrae nullius*, failed completely to acknowledge, let alone protect. the almost two centuries that have elapsed since white settlement have seen the extinction of some Aboriginal clans and the dispersal, with consequent loss of identity and tradition, of others. Particularly where the clan has survived as a unit living on ancestral lands however, the relationship between the Aboriginal peoples and their land remains unobliterated. Yet, almost two centuries on, the generally accepted view remains that the common law is ignorant of any communal native title or other legal claim of the Aboriginal clans or peoples even to ancestral tribal lands on which they still live (see *Milirrpum* v *Nabalco Pty Ltd* [2]). If that view of the law be correct, and I do not suggest that it is not, the common law of this land has still not reached the stage of retreat from injustice which the law of Illinois and Virginia had reached in 1823 when Marshall CJ, in *Johnson* v *McIntosh*,[3] accepted that, subject to the assertion of ultimate dominion (including the power to convey title by grant) by the State, the 'original inhabitants' should be recognised as having 'a legal as well as just claim' to retain the occupancy of their traditional lands.[4]

In 1992, Justice Deane wrote a joint judgment with Justice Mary Gaudron in the *Mabo* Case.[5] Six of the seven High Court judges recognised the existence of native title and ruled that such title could be extinguished by the states after 1975 only if they complied with the *Racial Discrimination Act 1975* (Cth). Deane and Gaudron wrote:

---

[2] (1971) 17 FLR 141.

[3] (1823) [1823] USSC 22; 8 Wheaton 543, at p 574 (5 Law Ed 2d 681, at pp 688-689).

[4] (1985) 159 CLR 70, 149-50.

[5] *Mabo v Queensland* (No 2) (1992) 175 CLR 1.

> If this were any ordinary case, the Court would not be justified in reopening the validity of fundamental propositions which have been endorsed by long-established authority and which have been accepted as a basis of the real property law of the country for more than one hundred and fifty years. And that would be so notwithstanding that the combined effect of Crown grants, of assumed acquiescence in reservations and dedications and of statutes of limitations would be that, as a practical matter, the consequences of re-examination and rejection of the two propositions would be largely, and probably completely, confined to lands which remain under Aboriginal occupation or use. Far from being ordinary, however, the circumstances of the present case make it unique. As has been seen, the two propositions in question provided the legal basis for the dispossession of the Aboriginal peoples of most of their traditional lands. The acts and events by which that dispossession in legal theory was carried into practical effect constitute the darkest aspect of the history of this nation. The nation as a whole must remain diminished unless and until there is an acknowledgment of, and retreat from, those past injustices. In these circumstances, the Court is under a clear duty to re-examine the two propositions. For the reasons which we have explained, that re-examination compels their rejection. The lands of this continent were not *terra nullius* or 'practically unoccupied' in 1788. The Crown's property in the lands of the Colony of New South Wales was, under the common law which became applicable upon the establishment of the Colony in 1788, reduced or qualified by the burden of the common law native title of the Aboriginal tribes and clans to the particular areas of land on which they lived or which they used for traditional purposes.[6]

There was no doubting William Deane's concern for the past injustices imposed on Aboriginal Australians. Reconciliation demanded equality under the law, putting right those past injustices insofar as that was possible.

6 (1992) 175 CLR 1, 109.

In *Dietrich v The Queen*,[7] Deane had the opportunity to reflect more broadly on equality under the law. Olaf Dietrich had been convicted in the Victorian County Court of drug offences in breach of the Commonwealth's *Customs Act 1901* (Cth). He was unable to afford private representation and failed to obtain representation at public expense. He appealed to the High Court. The Court did not find a right to counsel, but the court did order the suspension of all proceedings against Dietrich unless and until he could be represented by counsel. Justice Deane observed:

> It is true that, as has been mentioned, past practice in this country has been to force a person accused of serious crime to trial notwithstanding that, by reason of lack of means, he is unable to obtain legal advice or representation. That past practice and the approach to the poor and disadvantaged which it reflects have, however, long been inconsistent with the standards and circumstances of our community.[8]

In *Leeth v Commonwealth*,[9] another drug case, the question was whether s 4 of the *Commonwealth Prisoners'Act 1967* (Cth) was valid. It provided that a person convicted of a Commonwealth offence in a state court could be sentenced to a non-parole period consistent with that state's practice even though the practice varied from state to state. By a majority of 4-3, the High Court upheld the validity of the section. Deane joined Justice Toohey in a dissenting judgment espousing a constitutional implication of legal equality. They wrote:

> The common law may discriminate between individuals by reference to relevant differences and distinctions, such as infancy or incapacity, or by reason of conduct which it proscribes, punishes or penalizes. It may have failed adequately to acknowledge or address the fact that, in some circumstances, theoretical equality under the law sustains rather than alleviates the practical reality of social

---

[7] (1992) 177 CLR 292.

[8] (1992) 177 CLR 292, 336-7.

[9] (1992) 174 CLR 455.

> and economic inequality. Nonetheless, and putting to one side the position of the Crown and some past anomalies, notably, discriminatory treatment of women, the essential or underlying theoretical equality of all persons under the law and before the courts is and has been a fundamental and generally beneficial doctrine of the common law and a basic prescript of the administration of justice under our system of government. Conformably with its ordinary approach to fundamental principles, the *Constitution* does not spell out that general doctrine of legal equality in express words. The question arises whether it adopts it as a matter of necessary implication. In our view, several considerations combine to dictate an affirmative answer to that question.[10]

Justice Deane was a key member of the Mason Court which spelt out the implied guarantee of political communication in the *Constitution*. Once again, Deane wrote a joint judgment with Justice Toohey in *Nationwide News Pty Ltd* v *Wills*[11]. They said:

> The people of the Commonwealth would be unable responsibly to discharge and exercise the powers of governmental control which the *Constitution* reserves to them if each person was an island, unable to communicate with any other person. The actual discharge of the very function of voting in an election or referendum involves communication. An ability to vote intelligently can exist only if the identity of the candidates for election or the content of a proposed law submitted for the decision of the people at a referendum can be communicated to the voter. The ability to cast a fully informed vote in an election of members of the Parliament depends upon the ability to acquire information about the background, qualifications and policies of the candidates for election and about the countless number of other circumstances and considerations, both factual and theoretical, which are relevant to a consideration of what is in the interests of the nation as a whole or of particular

[10] (1992) 174 CLR 455, 486.

[11] (1992) 177 CLR 1.

> localities, communities or individuals within it. Moreover, the doctrine of representative government which the *Constitution* incorporates is not concerned merely with electoral processes. As has been said, the central thesis of the doctrine is that the powers of government belong to, and are derived from, the governed, that is to say, the people of the Commonwealth. The repositories of governmental power under the *Constitution* hold them as representatives of the people under a relationship, between representatives and represented, which is a continuing one. The doctrine presupposes an ability of represented and representatives to communicate information, needs, views, explanations and advice. It also presupposes an ability of the people of the Commonwealth as a whole to communicate, among themselves, information and opinions about matters relevant to the exercise and discharge of governmental powers and functions on their behalf.[12]

The head of the Department of Prime Minister and Cabinet had provided Prime Minister Keating with a list of prospective candidates for Governor-General when Bill Hayden was retiring. Keating saw no need for a list. He had his eye on Deane, especially in light of what he had written in the *Mabo* case. He interviewed Deane at the Lodge a couple of times and made his captain's call. He phoned Opposition Leader, John Howard, before making the announcement. Years later, Howard recalled, 'I told him it was a good appointment because I knew Bill Deane from university. He lectured me in Succession at the Sydney University Law School, and he was a very respected barrister. He was a Good Governor-General … I found him an eminently likeable, pleasant, easy person to deal with. There was no unnecessary pomp and circumstance.'[13] On Deane's last full day in office, Prime Minister, Howard, told Parliament: 'It is fair to say that he has brought to the discharge of his duties great personal commitment. He has displayed an unfailing interest in the place of the disadvantaged within Australian

[12] (1992) 177 CLR 1, 72.

[13] 'Cabinet papers: PM made captain's call on Deane', *The Australian*, 1 January 2018.

society. He has been very personally committed to the cause of reconciliation between indigenous and other Australians.'[1] Leader of the Opposition, Kim Beazley, told Parliament: 'He has made his mark in many ways as Governor-General–in more ways than most who hold that office. He has made his mark, really, as a voice and force for reconciliation in our community. I think it is safe to say that there has probably been no Governor-General of this nation who has so won the affection and trust of the indigenous and original community of Australia in the way in which he has. They have seen him as a champion of reconciliation and a champion of the right treatment of themselves. That response has been a marked feature of his Governor-Generalship.'[2]

In hindsight, Keating said: 'In the post-war years, I would say he is the one who brought great dignity to the post and whose Governor-Generalship was distinguished by his compassion, especially for those less well-off and most particularly the indigenous people, and that thoughtfulness and humility which characterised his personality and work.'

---

[1] Comonwealth, *Parliamentary Debates*, House of Representatives, 28 June 2001, 28868 (John Howard, Prime Minister).

[2] Comonwealth, *Parliamentary Debates*, House of Representatives, 28 June 2001, 28869 (Kim Beazley, Leader of the Opposition) .

1

The Land of the Fair Go

1.0 Editor's note

As Governor-General, Sir William Deane delivered an annual Australia Day address on 26 January. Each year he reflected on the state of the nation in light of the many travels and commitments undertaken the previous year by Lady Helen Deane and himself. He enjoyed speaking to volunteer groups who worked to assist people in poverty, especially those who were homeless. Having been a High Court judge, he had a great commitment to public education as the country prepared to celebrate the centenary of Federation. He often reflected on who we are as a people. In his 1999 Australia Day address, he told Australians that 'as we have developed, we have, as a people, become steadfast in our dedication to our free and democratic society: to our support of human rights; to the maintenance of international peace; to true equality and to the concept of "a fair go" for all Australians'.

1.1 The Opening of the National Conference of the Council to Homeless Persons, Melbourne, 4 September 1996

There are some words in our language which convey a sense of loss and desolation. 'Homeless' and its derivative noun 'homelessness' are two of them. As is often the case with such words, precise definition of the type which will permit identification by the application of the syllogism of formal logic is not really possible if, like the sociologist, one is concerned with substance rather than form. Some people who neither reside in nor have immediately available a home in the ordinary sense simply do not satisfy the sociologist's concept of homelessness. Thus, the multi-millionaire on an African safari between selling one mansion and deciding whether to acquire another might be described by a literalist as homeless. He is not, however, a homeless person for the purposes of the sociologist or, for that matter, of this conference. Homeless for those purposes requires, as an added element, a degree of social or economic disadvantage and special vulnerability or powerlessness.

Conversely, there are cases in which a person who has available to him or her the physical shelter of what is undoubtedly a house which the objective observer might describe as a home may, nonetheless, be homeless as a matter of ordinary common sense. The child who has run away from the parental home because of unbearable sexual or physical abuse provides a sad example of such a case. The parental house may be comfortable and immediately available but it would be to deny reality to say that the child was not, as a matter of substance, truly homeless. Those with direct caring contact with street children appreciate how senseless it can sometimes be to speak of restoring such a child to his or her 'family' or 'home'.

It is now a little over six months since I took up office as Australia's 22nd Governor-General. At the time my appointment was announced, Helen and I indicated that we were resolved to focus our activities, while I was Governor-General, upon the disadvantaged. We remain firm in that resolve. As you all know, the practical powers of the Governor-General are very limited and we realise that we can do little more than help draw public attention to the needs of the disadvantaged and to provide some encouragement to some of those who are working in the field on their behalf. With that in mind, we have visited, and will continue to visit, institutions and agencies providing services to the disadvantaged.

Perhaps the most important thing that has been brought home to us from those visits and personal contact is something which we already intuitively knew, namely, that the collective plight of the disadvantaged in this country constitutes a national problem of overwhelming dimensions. The unemployed, particularly the young unemployed; the Aborigines; the direct and indirect victims of drugs, including alcohol and nicotine; the seriously sick and physically impaired; the infants subjected to sexual and other abuse; the aged infirm; the mentally disturbed; the direct and indirect victims of gambling, largely State sponsored; the objects, even in a multi-cultural Australia, of racial discrimination and intolerance; those seeking rehabilitation after involvement in crime or imprisonment; the isolated and the acutely lonely: all these cry out for assistance or protection by Government instrumentalities and non-Government agencies or private individuals.

The problems which persons falling into those categories are likely to face are manifold. In their forefront, and often the gravest of all, is the crisis of homelessness. It is commonly encountered by members of each of the categories of disadvantaged persons which I have mentioned. I have seen estimates to the effect that, using a broad definition of homeless, there are upwards of 60,000 homeless people in Australia today. For my part, I wonder whether those estimates are, if a broad definition of homeless is truly accepted, anywhere near adequate.

Often, homelessness is a consequence of other disadvantage, such as poverty, drug addiction, physical or mental abnormality or sexual or other abuse. Conversely, when the crisis of homelessness does strike, it is likely to be itself a cause of other types of disadvantage: sickness, sexual or physical abuse, discrimination, isolation and loneliness, loss of self-esteem, even self-destruction. And where the problem of homelessness is not merely personal but reflects a community lack of adequate housing, the consequences will be communal as well as personal. Let me give an example.

The week before last, Helen and I visited the Aboriginal community at Maningrida in the top end of the Northern Territory. In many respects, it is an outstanding Aboriginal community. There is a hardworking local community council. There is a well run school. The problem of alcohol has been largely controlled. Petrol sniffing has been eliminated. And yet the health statistics of the indigenous residents of Maningrida are among the very worst in Australia. There, the Aborigines die at three times the rate per thousand per year of non-Aboriginal Australians. The death rate of the Maningrida Aborigines aged between 25 and 34 is approximately six times that of non-Aborigines. The disparity becomes even worse if one focuses upon particular areas of illness. Let me take one, rheumatic heart disease. That, as you probably know, is a disease which commonly results in profound damage to heart valves and often death in young people. Essentially, it is found only in economically or socially disadvantaged populations. It was last common in urban Australia 50 years ago. In a recent study by Dr Carapetis and Dr Currie of the Menzies School of Health Research, it was demonstrated that the incidence of rheumatic heart disease in Maningrida is possibly the highest ever recorded in the world, namely, 44/1000, that is, approximately one in 23. That is much higher than were the figures in this City at the worse stages of the Great Depression. Indeed, it is some six times higher than in Soweto. I pause to ask you to contemplate the public panic which would follow if it were disclosed that approximately one in every twenty-three of the citizens of this City was suffering from rheumatic heart disease.

There are several factors which combine to explain the health problems of Maningrida. One of the most important, and arguably <u>the</u> most important at least in so far as rheumatic heart disease is concerned, is the inadequacy of available Aboriginal housing. Recent figures indicate that, among the indigenous population, there are approximately six persons per room of each house in Maningrida during the wet season when disease is most likely to strike. In a situation where the ordinary residence consists of three or four bedrooms, that means that there are, on average, between 18 and 24 occupants of each house. And that in a situation where almost all residences have but one toilet. The reason for that over-crowding is not that the Aboriginal family entitled to primary occupancy wishes to share with two, three or four other families. We spoke to the Aboriginal elders, the visiting doctor and the resident Aboriginal health workers and have no doubt that they emphatically do not. It is because the available housing is hopelessly inadequate and the Aboriginal peoples have a habit, which non-Aborigines often deride, of sharing what they have with those in need.

To point to the overwhelming magnitude of the problems of homelessness in this country is not, of course, to deny that much is being done. Indeed, in this particular gathering, it would be wrong to fail to recognise just how much has been done and is being done in Australia. One must acknowledge the contribution which Governments are making to aid the extraordinary work of the many Australians who are devoting a significant part of their lives to aiding the homeless and other disadvantaged Australians. In that regard, I note that another of the lessons which Helen and I have learnt over the past six months is how humbling, yet encouraging, it is to come into contact with some of the many thousands of men and women, and in some cases children, who are selflessly serving our disadvantaged in homelessness and other areas. Moreover, the developments in the services for homeless people in Australia over the past twenty years have been such that it is now true to say that those services are now well in advance of what is available in most other parts of the world.

At the present time, a wide variety of services are provided through the jointly-funded Commonwealth/State Supported Accommodation Assistance Program ('SAAP') which was first established in 1984 and which has since functioned as a co-operative effort of Government and private aid agencies. A review of SAAP by a group of senior Government officials, in the second half of 1993, noted that the emphasis had been changing: from one that 'initially addressed the immediate needs of people who were homeless or in crisis, to one that provides post-crisis, transitional accommodation and support to assist towards independent living.' At that time, over eleven thousand people were accommodated each night in SAAP Services.

Welcome though those developments have been, the task ahead for those concerned to deal with the problem of homelessness remains a daunting one. Indeed, the extent of the available services of itself indicates the magnitude of the problem. There is so much that remains to be done. The numbers of our homeless seem to be growing. A breakdown in the 1993 review of the persons accommodated in SAAP Services in 1993 illustrates the widespread incidence of homelessness among the disadvantaged of our nation and the difficulties facing those who work to assist the homeless. Let me give some particulars.

Over half were under 35 years, with a higher proportion of younger women than men. Nearly one-third were children accompanied by one or both parents. Nearly a quarter were aged under 20. There was a higher than average representation of Aboriginal and Torres Strait Islander people. Some 12 per cent were in domestic violence services. The great majority were unemployed – a significant number second-generation unemployed. Between 13 and 15 percent had had some contact with mental health services in the previous five years. Between 17 and 30 percent had a drug or alcohol dependency, and 11 per cent had a physical or intellectual disability.

In the context of the increasing problem of homelessness in Australia, this First National Conference devoted to the subject is not only timely. It is overdue. The Council to Homeless Persons is to be congratulated for having initiated and planned it. All those who have worked so hard in its organisation and in the preparation of papers deserve our most sincere thanks.

The Conference's theme, 'Homelessness in the Lucky Country 1996-2000', with its combination of sad irony and future hope, is particularly apt. Donald Horne, who is commonly credited with coining the phrase the 'Lucky Country', was more than conscious of its irony as he asked why, in this country of such rich human and natural resources, there were so many poor and disadvantaged. He also, you will recall, asked why so many Australians knew or cared so little about the poor and the disadvantaged: why people don't care what goes on unless it directly confronts or interferes with them?

Those are questions which this Conference will necessarily address. In these days when, in a democracy such as ours, political action is so closely attuned to what the polls suggest to be popular opinion, it is increasingly imperative that those working for the disadvantaged be conscious of the fact that a primary goal must always be the creation or encouragement of a public expectation and insistence that a mature nation such as Australia will properly look after its disadvantaged. A related primary goal must also be the creation or encouragement of an awareness on the part of individual Australians that, while the assistance provided by Government and Government instrumentalities to the disadvantaged is absolutely vital, Government assistance can do only so much and must be supplemented by individual contributions of work, skill, dedication and, in many cases, companionship. In that regard, it is well to remember that the abiding wisdom of the patristic maxim that he who has failed to feed the man dying from hunger has truly killed him is directed to the individual and transcends mere notions of government welfare payments or services even when they are available.

1.2 Toast to Australia at the Australia Day Luncheon, Melbourne, 24 January 1997

Viewed from a European perspective and putting to one side Antarctica, Australia is the youngest of the world's continents. In another sense, it is perhaps the oldest. Long before it was actually 'discovered' by European navigators, the existence of the great unknown southern continent was a matter of European legend. The name 'Australia' itself has a long history. It was, of course, derived from 'Australis', the Latin for regions south of the equator, which was commonly used in all European nations in the 16th century and cropped up in various forms throughout the 17th and 18th centuries. As a distinguished predecessor of mine, Sir Ninian Stephen, has pointed out, it 'described the relatively unknown, the mysterious, down-under, which hapless Portuguese, Spaniards and Dutchmen had stumbled on, and sometimes been wrecked on, on their way to more fruitful lands'.

Even if one were to interpret 'Australia' as referring merely to the land mass itself, there would be no lack of grounds for superlatives. As this week's fires showed, our land can be harsh and dangerous. On the whole, however, it is both beautiful and generous. No doubt there are other places which can challenge individual aspects. But, at least for those of us who love it, there is simply nowhere on this earth that comes even close to equalling the totality – the vast mystery, the awesome beauty, the climate, the splendour, the resources and the sheer wonder – of the land and surrounding seas which are our country.

Australia is not merely the physical terrain. Primarily, it is the indissoluble Federal Commonwealth which is our nation. The preamble to the covering clauses of our *Constitution* makes that clear. The preamble also expressly tells us that that indissoluble Commonwealth is the people of the federating colonies who, humbly relying on the blessing of Almighty God, agreed to unite and thereby constitute it. It is the people themselves who became and remain our nation. Essentially, this toast to Australia is a toast to the Australian people, past and present. To all those who have made and make our nation what it is. To all those who have been and are Australia.

Our people come from all of the regions, races, cultures and religions of the world. Perhaps the greatest of all our nation's achievements is that, subject only to the continuing plight of our Aboriginal citizens, that diversity of origins, beliefs and backgrounds has been a source of strength rather than of weakness. The ethos which explains and underlies that strength and which has long enjoyed bilateral support in our national Parliament is that of multiculturalism.

Our multiculturalism does not mean that the habits, customs, cultures or traditions which particular Australians or their forebears have brought from overseas are immune from examination or reasoned criticism or control within Australia. It does, however, mean that, within the limits that are consistent with the overriding obligations and loyalties of Australian citizenship and with all the duties imposed by valid Australian laws, our citizens are entitled to expect and demand that the mutual respect and tolerance which are of the essence of multiculturalism should be encouraged and, in some circumstances, protected. The reason why that is so is that to undermine that mutual respect or to defy or deny that tolerance within our land is to defy or to deny the very basis of our Australian nation. Once it is recognised that we are, with all our cultural, ethnic and religious backgrounds, truly one people, one nation, it follows that whatever or whoever diminishes any of us diminishes our nation and us all.

You will all recall that in his Sydney address on his recent visit to Australia, President Clinton singled out our multiculturalism as 'a shining example' to the entire world of how people of different racial, cultural, ethnic and religious backgrounds can harmoniously come together as one nation.

Last week, I received a letter from the President in which he expressed Mrs Clinton's and his thanks for that visit. The President wrote in superlatives of Australia and of the Australian people whose hospitality continues to warm his heart, even as winter steadily takes over in Washington, DC, I add that the letter ended with a moving reference to this glorious land.

[H]ere in this 'glorious land' at this Australia Day luncheon I ask you to join me in celebrating our country, our nation and the people who constitute it.

1.3 Australia Day 1997 Address

It is now 11 months since I became Governor-General. Helen and I have moved from Moss Vale into Government House here at Yarralumla. We've opened up the house and gardens to the public as much as possible, and been fortunate to meet many Australians from all walks of life.

Our time here has been marked by occasions of both pride – and sadness – for our nation. Sadness at the terrible events at Port Arthur in April, the Black Hawk tragedy near Townsville in June, and the deaths on the beach near Margaret River in September. The occasions of pride, however, have been many, not least the success of our athletes at the Olympic and Paralympic Games in Atlanta.

Helen and I have made a number of visits to each of the States and Territories. There, too, we have experienced both sadness and pride. On the one hand, the visits have done much to heighten our awareness of the very large numbers of Australians who are facing great difficulties simply surviving on a day to day basis. We've seen the practical consequences of unemployment. Lack of jobs for young people, in particular, is an overwhelming social problem. It is destroying their self-confidence and self-esteem.

On the other hand, those visits have increased our pride in some of the many wonderful things about our country, including the selfless dedication and plain goodness of the thousands of ordinary Australians who work tirelessly to help those in need.

Today, I want to speak to you briefly about two things. The first is of deep concern. The second is uplifting. They should both be in the forefront of our minds on this Australia Day.

The matter which must deeply concern us all is the appalling state of health of the Aborigines. The facts that show the extent of those health problems are very depressing. They tell a tragic story of sickness, suffering, dying and death of fellow Australians.

Let me take the example of a newborn Aboriginal baby girl

and give you some plain facts about her future, if things don't change. On average, she can expect to live almost 20 years less than other Australians. She is three times more likely not to survive infancy. If she does survive until she is 15, she will be three and a half times more likely to die before she reaches 25. If she reaches 25, she will be six times more likely to die before the age of 34. Her prospects are even worse if we look at particular illnesses. For example, if she does become a woman, her chances of dying from a diabetes-related illness are 17 times greater than those of a non-Aboriginal woman.

Both sides of our national Parliament have accepted the importance of genuine reconciliation between the Aboriginal peoples and Australia as a whole. We must achieve it by the year 2001 if we are to avoid entering the second century of our nation as a diminished people. We won't achieve it until we reach the stage of basic justice and decency where the life expectancy of any Aboriginal baby is at least comparable to that of a non-Aboriginal one.

The second and, I'm happy to say, uplifting thing I would like to mention is our multiculturalism.

Apart from the Aborigines, we Australians are all immigrants or descended from immigrants. Our strength lies in our mutual tolerance. While we have our origins in all the regions and races of the world, we are united as a single nation. The ethos which underlies that strength and that unity is multiculturalism.

The essence of that multiculturalism is mutual respect and tolerance for all our different cultural, ethnic, national and religious backgrounds and lawful practices. We must be vigilant to defend it.

And that is not so much because we are concerned about what others may expect or think of us. It's because our multiculturalism is decent, just and right.

It is not only our Australian way. It is what we are.

May I suggest that, on this Australia Day, we reaffirm and celebrate our identity as a multicultural nation. I would also ask that we all, as Australians, resolve to address the two outstanding problems which face us, namely, unemployment particularly among our young people and the plight of our Aboriginal fellow citizens.

May God bless you all.

1.4 The Opening of the Mission Australia National Conference, Canberra, 10 February 1997

It is now a few days short of a year since I was sworn in as Governor-General. Some of you may recall that, at the time my appointment was announced, I made a point of saying that I hoped, during the period I am in office, to focus upon problems faced by the disadvantaged in our society.

Since then, Helen and I have tried to make good that undertaking. We have visited each of the States and Territories on a number of occasions. We have visited a very large number of Government and non-Government institutions serving the many categories of disadvantaged: the Aboriginal peoples, the unemployed, the direct and indirect victims of drugs, gambling, sexual and physical abuse; the homeless; the frail aged; the mentally disturbed; those who, even in multicultural Australia, are subjected to racial discrimination and intolerance; those seeking rehabilitation after involvement in crime and imprisonment, to identify but some. Those visits have served to confirm what we already instinctively knew, namely, that the collective plight of the disadvantaged is an overwhelming national problem. Indeed, the gap between the haves and the haves nots, the advantaged and the disadvantaged, seems to be widening rather than narrowing. There are, of course, a multitude of underlying causes. Undoubtedly, the most important is unemployment. Particularly youth unemployment.

Youth unemployment is commonly at a rate double that of general unemployment. In many localities, it is currently at levels exceeding 40 and 50 percent. In some places, second and even third generation unemployment among young people is commonplace. In many rural areas, it is undermining the whole fabric of community life and family relationships.

It is essential that our failure as a nation to provide adequate employment opportunities for our young people is not seen as merely an economic problem to be evaluated as a factor in some economic hypothesis and addressed only within the limits allowed by preconceptions of business efficiency. To the contrary, youth unemployment must be seen and addressed as an extremely important social problem which is marginalising a significant proportion of a whole generation of young Australians and having permanent destructive consequences with respect to their self-confidence, self-respect and self-esteem.. It is the most important problem facing our nation. And we cannot take the approach that its resolution lies simply in the hands of Government. It lies at least as much in the hands of private employers, both big and small. Hopefully, those employers will always be conscious of the fact that, both in formulating their commercial policies and in resolving the sometimes competing claims of young Australians and computers or machines, it is legitimate to take account of the national interest and human benefit in maintaining and increasing employment. Clearly, within the confines of what is possible in the context of requisite efficiency and competitiveness, the national interest will be much better served by preserving and expanding employment, particularly youth employment, than by subsequently devoting funds to help mitigate the consequences of its loss.

There is a danger in a social welfare society such as ours for ordinary people, including essentially good people, to take the approach that it is for the State to provide for, and look after, the needy or disadvantaged – and that, if welfare does not look after those in need, it is somehow their own fault rather than an occasion in which their fellow citizens are under a moral obligation to assist

It is true that the assistance provided by Governments and

Government instrumentalities to the disadvantaged is vital. Through it, the ordinary citizen contributes in varying degrees to the discharge of a duty dictated by basic consideration of decency and humanity.

Yet it is also true that our social welfare system is inevitably imperfect and inadequate. There are disadvantaged people for whom relevant Government assistance is either unavailable as a practical matter or insufficient. And even if adequate funds were available, that would still remain the case for, as you all know, there are many types of disadvantage which cannot be addressed by mere money but which require human assistance, human skill, human dedication, human companionship, human inspiration.

It is in this context that the contribution of the private welfare sector generally – and the work of the members of Mission Australia in particular – is of such tremendous importance.

No one acquainted with the non-government organisations serving the disadvantaged in Australia can fail to be conscious of the extraordinary goodness – and that is the only word – of those who serve in them. Many of those organisations conduct outreach programs of the various denominations of the Christian Church. Our visits to them have brought home to us with considerable force the fact that the Christian Church's mission of service and compassion for the sick, the needy and other disadvantaged is being jointly discharged throughout Australia by Christians of all denominations. Those involved in them demonstrate a Christian spirit which transcends the divisions between individual churches.

1.5 The Launch of 'Australian Poverty: Then and Now', Melbourne, 13 March 1998

It is most appropriate that the launch of this important book, *Australian Poverty: Then and Now*, is taking place at the University of Melbourne. For it was at this University in the 1960s that the seeds were planted which grew into one of the most influential Australian social sciences documents of the post war period – the 1975 Report of the Commonwealth Commission of Inquiry into Poverty, chaired by the late Professor Ronald Henderson.

Professor Henderson was the Foundation Director of the Melbourne Institute of Applied Economic and Social Research, as it is now called, between 1962 and 1979. As Dr John Nieuwenhuysen makes clear in his eloquent tribute in this book we are launching, Professor Henderson made an extraordinary contribution to the knowledge and understanding of poverty, unemployment and other disadvantage in this his adopted country. From the Melbourne Institute, with colleagues including John Harper, he initiated a series of pioneering studies which led to his appointment in 1972 to chair the Commonwealth Poverty Inquiry. The Henderson Report, as it came to be called when it was published in 1975, spoke to the conscience of the nation. For many, including myself, it represents a defining point in our country's appreciation and understanding of the spectre and implications of poverty in our midst. Professor Peter Saunders has accurately said of it:

> There can be few clearer examples of how, through carefully explained dissemination of its findings and implications, a piece of well-conceived and timely but independent social research can have a major impact on the public's awareness of the issues, and help mobilise support necessary for political action.

Sadly, and notwithstanding the quality of the 1975 Report and the extent to which the main thrust of its findings have been accepted, the problem of poverty in affluent Australia remains unresolved. Indeed, it is such a diverse and complex problem that it is unlikely that it will ever be completely solved. Nonetheless, one of the messages which emerge with startling and embarrassing clarity from the book that we are gathered to launch is that we can do so much more than we have in fact done since the publication of the 1975 Report. Indeed, read as a whole, the book does little to sustain even the complacency of an assertion that we have managed to stand still.

As has been pointed out many times, since 1975 in Australia – as in many overseas countries – unemployment has risen to heights that would have been regarded as unthinkable in the early 1970s. And there can be no doubt that unemployment has affected substantially the level, incidence and distribution of poverty in our society. Chapter 5 of this volume, by Professors Gregory and Sheehan, provides striking documentation of those things. It also addresses the question of the growth of social polarisation in the wake of unemployment. Indeed, whilst the link between poverty and unemployment that Ronald Henderson grasped still remains valid, the authors of this chapter entitled 'Poverty and The Collapse of Full Employment' argue forcefully that poverty in Australia in the 1990s 'is being systematically generated by trends within the economy and the labour market which show no signs of abating'. These structural changes, they point out, could not have been envisaged in 1973.

Another chapter, by one of the editors of this book, Professor Ruth Fincher, and Dr Maryann Wulff, underlines the relationship that has strengthened since 1975, between geographical location and the distribution of disadvantage.

Before taking up this job, Helen and I for many years lived in a New South Wales country town with a high level of unemployment, particularly youth unemployment. Since then we have made a point of visiting country centres suffering from particularly high levels of unemployment. I must say that I read with particular concurrence the conclusions of this chapter on the new 'spatial expressions' of poverty in contemporary Australia:

> … its pushing outward from central cities, the growing social polarisation within cities, the emergence of declining rural towns with large numbers of households on social security payments, declining industrial towns which have

> experienced severe cutbacks, and selected coastal regions of NSW and Queensland attracting large numbers of low-income people who are either in low-paid casual work or unemployed.

It almost goes without saying that it is of the utmost importance that social scientists continue to monitor the nature and degree of poverty in Australia, and to assess possible approaches and measures for its alleviation. That is not only important for the purposes of responsible government. It is also important for the purposes of responsible citizenship. None of us is entitled to take the approach that the problems of poverty and disadvantage in our country are exclusively the responsibility of government and that, if government aid to the poor and the disadvantaged is somehow unavailing, that is somehow their own fault.

Viewed as a whole, *Australian Poverty: Then and Now* constitutes an impressive study of the character, extent and distribution of poverty and disadvantage in our country. It also provides an essential insight into the nature and effects of efforts to address poverty and disadvantage in our country since the publication of the 1975 Henderson Report.

The book is not, of course, on the scale of the Poverty Report, which included a main volume, as well as 19 subsidiary ones. But in a relatively compressed coverage, it deals in its 16 chapters with many major topics: a general overview of the problem, employment, income, housing, education and health. It looks at the effects of poverty on particular groups such as indigenous people, migrants and homeless. And there is a telling chapter by Janet Taylor and Bishop Michael Challen on the voices of the poor. The names of the voices which sound across the past quarter of a century may be different. But the stories of disadvantage and need which they tell remain distressingly similar:

> You feel like you're shut out from the rest of the world because you can't afford anything.

When I accepted the appointment as Governor-General, I expressed the hope that I might help draw attention to the plight of the disadvantaged in our community. In the little over two years since then Helen and I have tried to fulfil that hope. We have visited an extraordinarily large number of government and non-government agencies serving the many categories of disadvantaged people in each of the States and Territories: the unemployed, the homeless, the frail aged, the direct and indirect victims of drugs, gambling, abuse and violence, to name but some of the obvious examples.

Those visits have served to confirm what we already instinctively knew, namely, that the collective plight of the disadvantaged is an overwhelming national problem. Indeed, the gap between the haves and the have nots, the advantaged and the disadvantaged, seems to us to be widening rather than narrowing.

This book, *Australian Poverty: Then and Now* provides scholarly confirmation of our general impressions. As the editors and authors wisely caution, poverty and disadvantage are extremely complex conditions to measure. It is certainly not possible to capture in a few statistical depictions the great diversity and intricacy of the measures.

But, at the very least, this work demands acknowledgment of the basic facts which it documents. It speaks not only to those entrusted with the exercise of government authority. It also speaks powerfully to the conscience of all Australians. As did the Henderson Report, it reminds us all that the ultimate test of our worth as a democratic nation is how we treat our most disadvantaged and vulnerable. As did the Henderson Report, it brings home to all who are prepared to listen and to learn that we in Australia have a long, long way to go before we can be satisfied about the results of that test. And, of course, as did the Henderson Report, it draws attention to the special problems of indigenous poverty – a stark aspect of the entrenched and heart-breaking mass of Aboriginal disadvantage which confronts and demeans our nation as a whole.

In conclusion, I wish to quote some perceptive words from the Foreword to *Australian Poverty: Then and Now*,[1] written by Dr Jean and Dr Davis McCaughey with which I profoundly agree. They say:

> The questions to be asked are: who are poor? What makes them poor? And how can their needs be met? The answer to the last of those questions is not simply charity. It calls for a change in attitude, for a re-assessment of the kind of society in which we want to live.

Or, put differently, it calls for a true assessment of the intrinsic worth of our society.

1.6 The Opening of Frederic House for St Vincent De Paul, Sydney, 25 March 1998

Like most jobs, that of Governor-General has its off days. Indeed, I must confess that there has been the odd occasion when Helen and I have woken up in the morning at Government House with the feeling 'What on earth are we doing here?' On the other hand, there are many days of pure magic when we know that there is nothing we would prefer to be doing. The best of those magic days are the days when we are privileged to participate, however marginally, in the work being done by so many Australians for the most disadvantaged and vulnerable of our community. Today is one of those days.

This building, named after the Society's Founder, Blessed Frederic Ozanam, will fulfil a great need in the lives of the 60 men who will come to know it as their secure, permanent and comfortable home. It will be a home where each man has his own bedroom and bathroom facilities; where each of the four main 'clusters' of rooms has a laundry, lounge, communal facilities and a kitchenette, although the main meals of the day will be eaten in the central dining room. It will be a home where the health of the residents will constantly be monitored; where special activities and interests are provided; where

[1] Ruth Fincher and John Nieuwenhuysen (eds), *Australian Poverty: then and now* (Melbourne University Press, 1998).

the care of those who live here is the first priority. A home, in short, where the individual dignity, privacy and independence of each of the men is respected, restored and maintained.

Obviously, Frederic House will meet a great need in the lives of its residents. But it will also meet an important need in the life of this city and of the Australian community as a whole. For the plight of the homeless – homeless men, homeless women, homeless young people – remains a substantial, indeed an overwhelming problem. And it is a challenge to each of us personally.

None of us is entitled to take the approach that the problems of poverty and disadvantage in our country are exclusively the responsibility of government and that, if government aid to the homeless and other disadvantaged is somehow unavailing that is somehow their own fault. We each have a moral duty to confront these problems. In terms of the parable of the rich man in St Luke's Gospel, who of us can deny that Lazarus lies hungry and in desperate need at our gate. Indeed, the plight of the homeless and the disadvantaged is a challenge to our own perceptions of the intrinsic worth of our society. For, surely the ultimate test of the worth of a democratic nation such as ours is how we treat our most disadvantaged and vulnerable.

The week before last, I launched the book *Australian Poverty: Then and Now*, edited by Professor Ruth Fincher and Dr John Nieuwenhuysen. Essentially, it is a study of the character and distribution of poverty and disadvantage, and the extent to which things have changed either for the better or the worse, since the publication of the Henderson Report in 1975.

The chapter by Peter Burke on 'The Poverty of Homelessness' points out that over the past two decades the prevalence of homelessness in affluent Australia has actually increased. In the early 1970s it was estimated there were some 3000 homeless men in both Sydney and Melbourne. By 1983 it was estimated there were some 40,000 people homeless, with a further 60,000 at risk.

It is true that there has been a substantial shift away from providing only basic institutional overnight services for the homeless, and towards longer term community-based housing and support – of which the Matthew Talbot Outreach houses provide an excellent example. But it is also true that over these last two decades the 'who' of the homeless have become much more diverse. Today's homeless people are younger and more evenly distributed between male and female than their 1970s counterparts. Indeed, Helen and I have spent a considerable amount of time with organisations helping homeless young people. Some of the youngsters who are assisted to a new sense of place, of home, of self-worth and self-confidence, are barely in their teens.

This project – Frederic House – is designed to help men at the other end of the age spectrum: the frail aged. The need for such a facility was clearly demonstrated by a 1989 client census of Persons in Supported Accommodation which disclosed that many people over the age of 60 in supported accommodation in New South Wales are frail and in need of a much higher level of care than that provided by existing centres. Indeed, their frailties and disabilities are such that they generally are in need of long-term care, yet many of them have to live in quite inappropriate surroundings lacking adequate support services. There are, in addition, large numbers of elderly people living in marginal accommodation, often with little or no family support, and in heart-breaking need of security, personal care, companionship and health and welfare services.

It is for 60 of these frail aged men that Frederic House has been built, as an extension to the services for the homeless provided by the St Vincent de Paul Society through the Matthew Talbot Hostel – now celebrating it's 60th Anniversary – and the outreach accommodation. As such, it is further evidence of the enormous contribution the Society makes every day towards fulfilling the basic needs of the marginalised and the disadvantaged. By doing so, it contributes mightily to the overall moral and social worth of our community.

1.7 The Launch of '*Australia – Land Of Achievement*', Sydney, 14 October 1998

'*Australia – Land of Achievement*'[2] is a celebration of the economic and commercial strengths and achievements of our nation. The book celebrates a number of our outstanding success stories. It defines our economic strengths as a nation and our advantages as a country with which, and within which, to do business. It also eloquently conveys, through both visual and written means, the wondrous beauty of the Australian landscape and the attractions of Australia as a tourist destination. In short, it is a much-needed Australian ambassador in the form of a book but with the qualities of eloquence, self-confidence, conviction and persuasion of an outstanding human ambassador.

In celebrating Australia and its people, the book focuses upon many of the achievements of our fellow Australians, individually and collectively, during the 98 years of our nation. It consistently makes the point that, overall, our political, economic and social institutions and systems set international benchmarks. It highlights the importance of Australia as a prime business, commercial, investment and tourist destination with an important role to play in the growing global economy. Through words and pictures, it states and demonstrates how our country is blessed with great beauty, with outstanding natural facilities and with extraordinary natural resources.

Among all the concurrent themes which run through '*Australia – Land of Achievement*' there is one which seems to me to particularly stand out. It is 'Strength in Diversity'.

As Max Walsh points out in the introduction, 'Australia has now become one of the most multi-racial and multicultural societies in the world'. The book emphasises the strength we have derived from our diversity in the context of our unity as a nation. As '*Australia – Land of Achievement*' makes plain, it is our multiculturalism, which enjoys support from all sides of mainstream politics,

[2] *Australia – Land of Achievement* (Focus Publishing, 1998).

which has, through diversity and mutual tolerance and respect, enabled us to build a unique and successful post-war business and human environment which offers a bridge between Asia and the west. In that regard, it seems to me to be of great importance that we Australians project to the other countries of our region how strong our commitment is to racial and cultural tolerance and respect which sustain that multiculturalism. '*Australia – Land of Achievement*', supported as it is by the Prime Minister, the Premiers and the Chief Ministers, will play a very important role in doing precisely that.

1.8 The Australian Day Council of New South Wales Luncheon, Sydney, 22 January 1999

At the outset, I acknowledge the traditional owners and thank their representatives for the message stick and gift and for their generous welcome to their ancestral lands.

Even if one were to interpret the 'Australia' we celebrate on Australia Day as referring merely to a geographic entity, there would be abundant grounds for the use of superlatives to describe it. No doubt there are other places which can challenge individual aspects. But, at least for those of us who love it, there is simply nowhere on this earth that comes even close to equalling the totality – the mystery, the beauty, the climate, the resources and the sheer wonder – of the land and surrounding seas which are our home.

But 'Australia' is not merely the physical terrain. Primarily, it is the indissoluble Federal Commonwealth which is our nation. The preamble to the covering clauses of our Constitution makes that clear. That preamble also expressly tells us that that indissoluble Commonwealth was and is the people of the federating colonies who, humbly relying on the blessing of Almighty God, have agreed to unite and to constitute it. It is the people themselves who became and remain our nation. In other words, 'Australia' is the sum of us all. All those who have made and make our nation what it is. All those who have been and are Australian.

Directly or indirectly, we Australians come from all of the regions, races, cultures and religions of the world. Perhaps the greatest of all our nation's achievements is the multiculturalism which has enabled that diversity of origins, beliefs and backgrounds to be a source of strength rather than of divisiveness and weakness. That multiculturalism enjoys bipartisan support in our national Parliament. Its essence is inclusiveness. It has enabled us to achieve national unity and to escape most of the old hatreds and old conflicts which have afflicted some of the lands from which we come. It not only sustains our nation. It symbolises what we are.

And we Australians – and our nation – have much else to remember and celebrate on Australia Day 1999 – the ninety ninth Australia Day, celebrated under that or some other name, since the establishment of our nation on 1st January 1901.

For the story of our nation in that time is a proud and blessed one. Only about half a dozen other nations can look back on a comparable period of democratic rule uninterrupted by foreign occupation or by dictatorship of the left or right. In material terms, we have been and are among the most prosperous nations of the world. And, as we have developed, we have, as a people, become steadfast in out dedication to our free and democratic society: to our support of human rights; to the maintenance of international peace; to true equality and to the concept of 'a fair go' for all Australians.

This Australia Day is also the last before the year 2000 and the second last before the centenary of our nation. It is not only a time to look back and celebrate. It is also a time to look to the future. To wish, to hope, to plan. To formulate our vision for our country and its people. And to face up honestly to any failures and to our lingering national problems.

As I think most of you know, I have, since I became Governor-General, sought to focus attention upon the plight of the disadvantaged. As we approach our second century as a nation, we Australians should all be conscious of the extent of entrenched disadvantage in our country. It is a great national problem. Indeed, Helen's and my constant contact with the disadvantaged and those who work with and for them leaves us in no doubt that the gap between the haves and the have nots in our affluent Australia is actually widening. If, as I believe, the ultimate test of our worth as a true democracy is how we treat our most vulnerable and disadvantaged, we Australians all bear an individual responsibility to do what we can to help our nation pass that test as it enters its second century.

And I have also, as Governor-General, sought to stress the importance of reconciliation between Australia's indigenous peoples and the nation of which they form such an important part. We have, in my view, made considerable progress towards that objective in recent years. There is, however, so much more to be done and to be achieved. And there are some plain truths which must be faced.

One of those plain truths is that we will not achieve true reconciliation until we are further advanced towards addressing the appalling problems of material disadvantage which oppress Australia's indigenous peoples. This is not an occasion to refer to those problems in any detail. It suffices to draw attention to the fact that an indigenous baby girl born in this country on Australia Day 1999 can, on current statistics, expect to live approximately 20 years less than a non-indigenous baby girl born on the same day. And the chance of her dying in infancy is three times greater than if she were non-indigenous.

Another of those plain truths is that we must – together – address the problems of the spirit faced by indigenous Australians: the loss, the emptiness, the lack of incentive and of self-esteem that have resulted from past dispossession, introduced diseases, and tragically mistaken, though often well-intentioned, policies. The problems of helping build trust and goodwill. And, as my wife stressed in her address to the 1997 Reconciliation Convention, the problems of communication between indigenous and non-indigenous Australians.

I conclude these comments with the message of reconciliation which I would inscribe if it were possible for me to send a personal message stick to every Australian on this coming Australia Day. That message would be a request that we foster and give effect to the qualities which will enable us to achieve true reconciliation within our land. Let me identify some of the most important of those qualities. There is the honesty to acknowledge both past injustices and the extent of the present disadvantage which has flowed from them. There are the vision and the determination to address that disadvantage and its associated problems of both the body and the spirit. There is the generosity to accept that weaknesses and problems such as alcoholism, domestic violence and inability to cope or to communicate effectively do not constitute justification for indifference or refusal to help but are, in truth, themselves part of an overall disadvantage which is entrenched in its nature and heart-breaking in its extent.

And finally, there are mutual goodwill and respect. They are of critical importance to the movement for reconciliation. Without them, we will never reach our ultimate objective of walking together as friends and true equals.

In truth, of course, those qualities of honesty, determination, generosity and mutual goodwill and respect are the very qualities which underlie so much of what is best in our nation and in our people. If we foster and give effect to them, we Australians will enter our second century as a nation as a truly united people. And we will together face the general problems of disadvantage in our midst and whatever other challenges the third millennium of our time may bring with justified confidence that we will meet them successfully and well.

1.9 Australia Day 1999 Address, 26 January 1999

It's now almost three years since I became Governor-General. In that time, my wife, Helen, and I have travelled extensively throughout Australia. We've had close contact with vast numbers of our fellow Australians from all walks of life and in all circumstances.

On this Australia Day, I wish to share with you some of our experiences and great pride in Australia and Australians. And I want to say something about my hopes for the future as we approach our second century as a nation.

Among the things that have impressed us most have been the courage and compassion of our fellow Australians in times of great tragedy … Port Arthur … the Black Hawk helicopter collision … the Thredbo landslide … the fire on HMAS 'Westralia' … the deaths of volunteer fire fighters. We've been overcome with admiration for those involved … the courage and sacrifice of many of the victims … the strength of the relatives … the dedication of those seeking to help and comfort… and the ability of Australians everywhere, particularly our service men and women and our rescue workers, to cope with crisis and emergency.

And we've been enormously impressed by the boundless concern and the plain goodness of all those Australians who strive to help the disadvantaged … giving and working quietly and without seeking public recognition or acclaim. The ultimate test of our worth as a truly democratic nation must surely be how we treat our most vulnerable. Those who work for the disadvantaged and those who support them do most to help us pass that test. In this United Nations International Year of Older Persons, I pay special tribute to those who help the elderly, particularly the frail aged.

And we've become increasingly conscious of the dedication of the countless Aboriginal and non-Aboriginal Australians who are working together for reconciliation. They're showing us all how much progress can be made by ordinary people of goodwill acting together. The road ahead to true reconciliation is a long and difficult one. It is, however, of critical importance to all Australians that we reach its end.

Perhaps most important of all have been the many thousands of young Australians we've met … at Government House or in other places such as refuges for street kids, the welcome home march in Sydney for the members of our successful Commonwealth Games team, Aboriginal and Torres Strait Islander communities, the recent Children's Summit in Canberra. Our contacts with them have made us increasingly aware of the uncertainties and disadvantage which some – too many – of them face. But those contacts have also made us extremely proud of young Australians generally … of their resilience, of their achievements, of the range of their interests, of their sense of fun … and of their lack of racial or other forms of prejudice.

They've helped bring home to Helen and me the importance of the multiculturalism which inspires and sustains our modern Australia. I'm often conscious of the contrast between the tolerance and breadth of vision of most of today's young Australians and the racial and religious intolerance which was so common in our country when I was a boy growing up in the 1930s and 1940s. One sometimes hears suggestions that multiculturalism is divisive. I disagree. I'm convinced that it is our multiculturalism which has made possible our national unity notwithstanding that we Australians directly or indirectly come from all the regions, races, cultures and religions of the world.

For me, multiculturalism means inclusiveness. Its essence is mutual respect and acceptance. It's enabled us to blend the many into a pretty harmonious whole without bringing to this new land old hatreds, old prejudices and old conflicts. It's contributed mightily to the mutual acceptance and respect which we've constantly observed among the young Australians we've met. And they've told us so.

Relief of disadvantage … reconciliation … the attitude of young Australia … multiculturalism. They share a common theme. And that theme provides the vision for the future of our country which I wish to leave with you on this Australia Day. It is a theme of caring ... of tolerance ... of concern for true equality, dignity, opportunity and hope ... for *all* Australians.

And the vision is not a vision of imposed uniformity but of true and worthwhile unity and mutual acceptance. Of Australians walking together, talking together, caring together, working together, achieving together. If we Australians consciously adopt and pursue that vision, we can face the challenges ahead with real confidence that we'll meet them successfully and well. And we'll enter the second century of our nation with the knowledge that, provided we are truly united, we will prosper together.

Good evening. And God bless you all.

1.10 The Conferral of an Honorary Doctorate, Trinity College, Dublin, 29 April 1999

During the time I was here, I was sometimes asked why I had chosen to come to TCD (Trinity College, Dublin) to study International law at a post graduate level. The honest answer to that question was not so much because of the Law School as because of the University itself. In saying that, I do not mean to be dismissive of the legal staff of the time. It was simply that, during student days in Australia, I had developed a very strong admiration for this particular University.

In one sense, my admiration for TCD sprang from the obvious. Namely, the extraordinary number of quite outstanding people whom such a comparatively small University, in so far as staff and student numbers were concerned, had managed to produce. Names that span almost all areas of human endeavour and achievement: world famous names from literature, politics, science, philosophy and law. But it also sprang from the far less obvious ... the Australian names. People who, after studying here, migrated to Australia and contributed mightily to the development of so much that is best in my own country. As Professor Jarlath Ronayne has pointed out, their names are, by and large, almost completely unmentioned and unremembered in the annals and histories of this their alma mater. Thankfully, it is not so in Australia where they are part of **our** history and where, thanks to Professor Ronayne himself and other scholars such as Professor O'Farrell, Sir Gerard Brennan and Alex Castles, their connection with this University is being increasingly appreciated and acknowledged. Let me pause to tell you a little about some of them and their influence. That influence was probably greatest in Victoria, the State of my own birth.

I set the context by reminding you that the first European settlement of Australia commenced in 1788 with the foundation of the then penal Colony of New South Wales. Five other Colonies – Victoria, Tasmania, Queensland, South Australia and Western Australia – were subsequently established. The six Colonies remained distinct until 1 January 1901 when they came together to constitute the Commonwealth of Australia.

Even before the Colony of Victoria was separated from that of New South Wales in 1851, the influence of TCD graduates there had been profound. The first three barristers to arrive in Melbourne – Brewster, Croke and Redmond Barry – were all graduates of this University. Two – Jeffcott and Therry – of the first three resident judges had likewise studied here. Between 1857 and 1935, there were four Chief Justices of Victoria. All were Irish and three of the four – Stawell, Higinbotham and Irvine – were TCD graduates. As were the first Victorian Solicitor-General and, among other leading Victorian judges and lawyers, Sir Robert Molesworth, one of the greatest of Victoria's – and Australia's – early judges. Needless to say, the influence of those TCD graduates upon the development of the law in Victoria was unbounded. That influence also had more tangible expression. As the present Chief Justice of Victoria, himself of Irish ancestry, pointed out to Her Excellency, President Mary McAleese, during her wonderfully successful visit to Australia last year, the Supreme Court library in Melbourne was originally designed with a flat roof, but by a sort of 'Hibernian conspiracy', it acquired a majestic dome 'for all the world the same as that atop the Four Courts in Dublin'.

The influence of TCD graduates in the early development of higher education in Victoria can be compared to their influence in the law. And the same can be said of the arts. The credit for the foundation of Victoria's first University, the University of Melbourne, belongs largely to Sir Redmond Barry, its first Chancellor. Much of the credit for the tradition of academic excellence which it established belongs to other Trinity graduates. The first Professors of Chemistry and Physics and the first Registrar were all TCD graduates. As was its most famous founding Professor, William Hearn, who was Dean of Law and held Chairs in modern history, literature and political economy.

Time precludes me from referring in detail to the part played by individual TCD graduates in the other Australian Colonies. There are so many names which could be mentioned. In South Australia, for example, Sir Robert Torrens was not only Premier but devised and introduced the new system of land title by registration which bears his name and which has revolutionised the law of property both throughout Australia and many other parts of the Common Law world. In addition to Victoria, TCD graduates served as Chief Justices in New South Wales, South Australia and Tasmania. In the mother Colony of New South Wales, another TCD graduate, JH Plunkett, did probably more than any other 19th century figure to advance the status and equality of his fellow Australian Catholics. As New South Wales Attorney-General, he also played a pivotal role in the establishment of Australia's first University, the University of Sydney.

Those TCD graduates in the antipodes – and I have mentioned but a few of them – exercised an extraordinarily potent liberalising influence upon the development of Australian institutions, Australian thinking and Australian political development. As Professor Patrick O'Farrell, himself a former Visiting Professor at this University, has pointed out in *The Irish in Australia,*[3] they were anxious not to repeat what they saw as mistakes which had been made on their side of the globe and were in the vanguard of the pursuit of law and order 'not simply because of their practical involvement as lawyers and judges, but as a salient article of their faith in a structured peaceful society as a cradle of civilisation and human values' including, I would add, the ideals of justice and true equality. They can claim a great deal of the credit for the democratic and egalitarian principles and convictions which came to be accepted and established throughout Australia and which now sustain our modern nation. That nation owes them, and this their University, a profound debt.

1.11 Australia Day 2000 Address, 26 January 2000

This Year 2000 Australia Day is a time to look back at the past and forward to the future. Back at our origins, our achievements, our successes and our failures. Forward to the challenges which lie ahead – including the critical challenge of preventing and healing harmful divisions within our society.

There are three strands of our Australian identity upon which we should particularly rely in facing that critical challenge.

The first is the national ethos of mutual acceptance and respect which binds us Australians together notwithstanding our diverse origins. That multicultural inclusiveness sustains our nation.

The second of these strands is what I think of as 'the spirit of ANZAC'. It takes us all the way back to the early hours of that day, almost 85 years ago, when the boats carrying the first 1500 young Australians were moving through darkness towards the Gallipoli shore. Last Anzac Day, at the deeply moving dawn service at Gallipoli, I tried to explain what that spirit means to us

[3] Patrick O'Farrell, *The Irish in Australia* (New South Wales University Press, 1986).

Australians: 'courage and endurance, and duty, and love of country, and mateship, and good humour and the survival of a sense of self-worth and decency in the face of dreadful odds'.

It also means mutual dependence. It is, as our great historian Manning Clark wrote, 'something too deep for words'. It inspires our nation.

Even at this moment, that spirit's being demonstrated by our fellow Australians who are serving – in our Defence Force, in police forces or in aid organisations – in hazardous peacekeeping and humanitarian operations in East Timor, in Bougainville and many other foreign places.

The third strand is the generosity and the sense of fair play that are so common between Australians.

During the almost four years that I've been Governor-General, my wife, Helen, and I have been overwhelmed by the generosity of the countless Australians who work – or give – to help those who are living below the poverty line or are in need of assistance. In times of national tragedy, we've been equally impressed by the willingness of ordinary Australians to stretch out the hand of assistance and comfort. That spirit of generosity is the great healing force of our nation.

We Australians enjoy tremendous natural advantages. Our country's among the most beautiful and resource rich on the globe. Currently, we're experiencing sustained economic growth. Yet the divisions among us – between the haves and the have nots and even the city and the country – give cause for concern. And while criticism and disagreement are hallmarks of true democracy, there's a real danger that an unjustifiable degree of distrust or denigration will damage our democratic institutions or discourage people from serving in them.

The three strands of our history and identity which I've mentioned – our multicultural inclusiveness, the spirit of Anzac and the generosity of ordinary Australians – will enable each of us, in our own way, to help heal those divisions and avoid that danger in the days ahead. They'll also help us realise a vision which I think we all share for our country: of Australians coming and staying together and supporting one another, in changing and often difficult times.

In the coming months, there are at least two national events which'll be of true significance in that regard.

In May, we will all have an opportunity to seek national consensus on the draft document which the Council for Aboriginal Reconciliation will present after years of work. With goodwill on all sides, we can reach that consensus. If we do, it will reflect the real progress which we've made in recent years. And, while there'll still be much further to go, we'll have reached an important milestone in the journey towards true and lasting reconciliation.

And then, in June, the Olympic Torch will arrive at Uluru – to commence its journey around Australia in the lead up to the Sydney Olympics. That journey will provide a wonderful opportunity for all Australians to come together in the months leading up to what should be a great world celebration of our nation and its people. Each of us, in our own way, can help make certain that it is.

The young Bendigo poet of Federation, William Gay, died some three years before his plea that Australians 'rise, united … And be one people' was fulfilled by the establishment of our nation on 1st January 1901. William Gay also wrote:

From all division let our land be free,
For God has made her one: complete she lies
Within the unbroken circle of the skies,
And round her indivisible the sea
Breaks on her single shore'.

As we approach the centenary of our Federation, my wish is that the prayer that our land be free of harmful division is also fulfilled. If it is, then the future will be one of untold promise, not only for our country but for all Australians.

Good evening. And may God bless you all.

1.12 The Lighting Of The Olympic Flame, Ancient Olympia, Greece, 10 May 2000

Today's inspiring ceremony in Olympia puts us in direct touch with the great ideals, history, and achievements of Greek civilisation.

The Olympic idea, an outstanding legacy of that civilisation, was born in this serene and ancient place, nearly 3000 years ago. From here, it has gone around the world and, despite the pressures and pace of our life at the beginning of a new millennium, the Olympic values of universality, peace, respect for others, human excellence, and fair play live on. Indeed, they have never been more needed.

This is a priceless contribution of Greece to the international community. It is therefore very fitting that the next time this ceremony takes place, it will be to inaugurate the Games in the country which gave them to the world.

The Olympic Flame is a powerful symbol of the Olympic values and of the unity of the world's peoples.

When we Australians receive the Torch from you, it will travel to the other side of the globe. Before arriving on our soil, it will have journeyed through our neighbourhood, the members of the Olympic movement of Oceania. It will give these countries, some of them very small and remote, a unique experience of the power and inspiration of the Olympic idea.

In Australia, the Flame will carry its message of inclusiveness and harmony throughout the length and breadth of our island continent, starting at Uluru, a place of great spiritual significance to our people, particularly indigenous Australians. As our enthusiastic, sports-loving people embrace the Torch, and feel the spirit of the universal ideals it represents, they will recall with deep gratitude its origins here in this great country.

1.13 The Opening of the Eungella SES and Dalrymple Rural Fire Headquarters, Eungella, Queensland, 23 October 2000

Over the more than four and a half years that I have been Governor-General, Helen and I have, on innumerable occasions, had close contact with Australia's emergency services, including our volunteer emergency services, in all parts of Australia.

There have been the times of senseless man-made tragedy, such as the awful killings at Port Arthur. There was the terrible loss of life in the landslide at Thredbo. There has been the devastation of flood in places as far apart as Katherine in the Northern Territory and Wollongong in southern New South Wales. There has been the terror of fire – in the bush in places such as Linton near Geelong in Victoria, where five Volunteer firefighters lost their lives, near Lithgow in New South Wales where two Volunteer firefighters were killed and, more recently, in the Ku-ring-gai National Park near Sydney where seven firefighters were killed or gravely injured. And, of course, there has been the tragedy of fire in city and town, such as the recent nightmare of death and destruction at Childers in this State.

In all those – and in countless other – circumstances, we have been conscious of, and deeply moved by, the dedication, the bravery and the sacrifice of our emergency workers, particularly the thousands upon thousands of volunteer workers. They give with extraordinary generosity of their abilities and of themselves and risk so much in the service of their communities.

Again, on many occasions, we have heard detailed and inspiring stories of the heroism of volunteer emergency workers in the course of Investiture ceremonies in Canberra where awards are made in our Australian system of Honours and Awards. And we have always been conscious of the fact that inevitably heroism often goes unacknowledged and even unknown.

Today, we pay tribute to the volunteers who comprise the Eungella SES, the members of the Rural Fire Brigade and, through them, emergency service volunteers in all parts of Australia. Our nation owes you all collectively an immense debt. This shed which we are opening for the Eungella SES Group and Rural Fire Brigade is symbolic of countless other basic emergency service premises in all parts of our nation. The volunteers here are representative of the hundreds of thousands of such volunteers spread throughout all parts of Australia. There are, for example, some 85,000 volunteers in Emergency Services in Queensland alone, which is roughly three times the total Australia-wide number in our regular army.

On a wider plain, of course, the small SES and Fire Group here at Eungella can be seen as representative of all of the vast army of millions of volunteers who, reflecting the essential goodness of ordinary Australians, work for those in need of assistance throughout Australia. Next year, as you all know, we celebrate the Centenary of the Federation which brought our nation into being. We will also be celebrating the United Nations International Year of Volunteers. Accordingly, it is particularly appropriate at this time that we are conscious of the extraordinary worth of the work of all our volunteers and of its importance to the well being of our nation. Both the Commonwealth and State Governments, including the Queensland Department of Emergency Services, will be coordinating a range of activities throughout next year recognising the importance and huge diversity of the contributions made by volunteers to our national life both in our cities and in our rural and regional communities.

In recent weeks, we have seen an unforgettable demonstration of that worth and importance first at the Sydney 2000 Olympic Games and now the Sydney 2000 Paralympic Games. It is true to say that no one is entitled to more credit for the wonderful success of those Games than the volunteers who brought intelligence, courtesy and friendship to everything they did. Indeed, it is those volunteers who have ensured that the Sydney Olympic and Paralympic Games will be remembered as not only the most successful but also the friendliest ever held.

1.14 The Launch of 'Forging the Nation' Exhibition, Australian War Memorial, Canberra, 26 October 2000

It is most appropriate that this Exhibition – *Forging the Nation* – begins its travelling life here at our Australian War Memorial. The Exhibition plainly invites those who visit it to reflect not only on our history but also on our basic identity as a people. And there is no building in the world which is a better place for such reflection than this, our national shrine. As some of you know, I have, on a number of occasions in the past, expressed my personal conviction that the Tomb of the Unknown Soldier in the Hall of Remembrance just behind us is the true heart of our nation. The Unknown Australian Soldier who rests there continues in death to serve: by enriching our commitment to peace and by symbolising – and reminding us of – the sacrifice of all those who died or suffered for Australia in time of war.

Looking back at its first century, it is noteworthy that, apart from the significant bombing of the north and the intrusion of some Japanese submarines into Sydney Harbour during World War II, our nation has never been subjected to hostile military attack or known the footstep of an enemy soldier. We have, throughout the history of our Federation, been one of the world's nations most devoted to peace. Yet, as this Exhibition reminds us, our history and our identity have to a large extent been defined by war.

The Exhibition focuses on the first 20 years of our Federation. In the years leading up to 1914, the impression conveyed seems to me to be largely one of national trappings, including I might say Governor-General trappings, without much real substance of heart or spirit. Then came the pivotal event of this period for the new nation: the First World War – the Great War that was to end all wars. As the Exhibition makes plain, the suffering and loss of that war, which affected nearly every Australian family, was accompanied by – indeed was even a source of – real national pride and emerging national identity. Pride in the achievement of our young nation and its soldiers. Pride in the conviction that death and suffering had not been in vain. Pride in what has, since the disaster of Gallipoli, often been seen as 'the Spirit of ANZAC'.

That 'Spirit of ANZAC' was quickly accepted by Australians as the lynch pin of our national identity. Though born from the doomed campaign at Gallipoli, it is not really about loss at all. On Anzac Day last year, at the deeply moving dawn service at Gallipoli, I tried to explain what that spirit means to us Australians: 'It is about courage and endurance, and duty, and love of country, and mateship, and good humour and the survival of a sense of self-worth and decency in the face of dreadful odds.'

It also means mutual dependence. It is, as our great historian Manning Clark wrote, 'something too deep for words'. Born in the time frame of the Exhibition, it still inspires our nation, some eight decades on.

Obviously, the Centenary of Federation is a time when we should look back and appreciate the history of our nation. Our achievements, our successes and our failures. It is, of course, also an occasion for understanding and confronting, rather than burying or evading, the problems of the present. In that regard, a frank and intelligent understanding of our history of our land before Federation and of our nation since is a prerequisite of understanding and effectively addressing any entrenched disadvantage or divisions that currently reflect that history. For the past is absorbed into the present and the future. It stays to shape who we are and what we do. That means, of course, that an Exhibition such as this has much to teach us about the present, as well as the past.

1.15 The Unveiling of the Lucinda Memorial – Centenary Of Federation Monument, The Spit, Sydney, 27 October 2000

This Memorial marks the Centenary of our Federation and the start of the new millennium by means of two components – a replica mast of the Paddlewheel Steamer Yacht *Lucinda* and an assemblage of 2001 rocks gathered from all over the Commonwealth of Australia and its Territories.

In a superficial sense, a Lucinda Memorial can be related more to the year 1891 than to the Centenary of Federation since it was at Easter in that year that the *Lucinda* sailed past this point bearing the leading lawyer delegates to the 1891 Constitutional Convention. The fame of the *Lucinda* and its importance to our nation lies, however, in the great contribution which the work of those who sailed in her in the course of that voyage made to the Constitution which became the compact of Federation of the people of the six Australian Colonies and under which our nation became established on 1 January 1901. Accordingly, this Memorial to the *Lucinda* is an ideal Centenary of Federation project.

Again, it might be suggested that the monument would be more appropriately erected up the coast on the shores of Broken Bay or the Hawkesbury River where the *Lucinda* spent two of the three days of its critical Constitutional voyage. Again, I think that suggestion would be superficial and wrong. On the Good Friday and Easter Saturday of that important week-end, the passengers on the *Lucinda* included the great draftsman of our Constitution, Sir Samuel Griffith, as well as Barton, Kingston and Downer. The person whom I consider to be the primary architect of our Constitution, Andrew Inglis Clark, had however fallen ill with flu. He did not join the party until the Sunday when the *Lucinda* was here in Middle Harbour. It is much more appropriate that a Lucinda Memorial be erected at a spot where both Griffith and Clark had been members of the working party on board than at a spot where one of them had been absent.

We all know, of course, of the importance of Sir Samuel Griffith in our nation's history.

The part played by Andrew Inglis Clark in the framing of our Constitution has not been as widely acknowledged as it should have been. This is probably because Clark never became a truly national figure in the way that Griffith did. Some time after the Sydney Convention of 1891, he became a Justice of the Supreme Court of Tasmania. Sadly, he was never appointed a Justice of the High Court. Yet his claim to be accepted as the primary architect of our Constitution seems to me to be irresistible.

Inglis Clark's draft of a complete Constitution had been widely circulated before the 1891 Sydney Convention. It was, to a large extent, a selection of provisions from the United States and Canadian Constitutions, the Constitutions of the Australian Colonies and the *Imperial Federal Council of Australasia Act* of 1885. Nonetheless, it was the primary plan of what was ultimately built. Equally important, Inglis Clark's draft Bill demonstrated that the intelligent and careful selection and adjustment of provisions from those earlier instruments could combine and reconcile the English scheme of constitutional monarchy within the Westminster system and the American scheme of the distribution of government powers and strict separation of judicial from legislative and executive power.

My enthusiasm for this Lucinda Memorial should be apparent from what I have already said. There is one other matter which I would mention today. It is that this gathering today is for the unveiling of the Lucinda Memorial is not only an appropriate component of the celebration of our Centenary by reason of the importance of the visual image of the *Lucinda* in the story and framing of our Constitution. It has a perhaps less important claim to be so regarded by reason of a factor of some particular relevance to me. This week-end we celebrate the Centenary of the establishment by Letters Patent, on 29 October 1900, of the Office of Governor-General which I hold. I can think of no better place for the current Governor-General of Australia to celebrate the Centenary of that component of the establishment of our nation than here at this beautiful place where some of our leading Founding Fathers of our nation worked so effectively on our nation's Constitution so many years ago.

1.16 The Centenary of the Proclamation of Federation, Centennial Park, Sydney, 1 January 2001

We come together to Centennial Park to commemorate the proclamation of our Federation, at this place, one hundred years ago.

Together, we represent all Australians, across all States and Territories.

We also represent, as their heirs and beneficiaries, the four million people of the six Australian colonies who, 'relying on the blessing of Almighty God', came together as the Commonwealth of Australia on the First of January 1901.

We represent the generations of Australians, of so many different backgrounds, whose work in peace and sacrifice in war have built our country over the past century.

And we represent, especially through the young people and families here, the hopes and dreams of what Australia can be, in this generation and the generations to come.

So this gathering of Australians, including the nation's constitutional and political leadership, symbolises the continuity of our history.

It also symbolises our democracy which is the cornerstone both of our nation and of these celebrations.

The strength and vigour of that democracy is based upon the inclusiveness of our society – the extent to which we ensure that no group or section of Australians is excluded from full participation in the benefits, opportunities and responsibilities of our national life. In that regard, on today of all days, we should be mindful of how our Constitution originally excluded the Aboriginal peoples of our country from both the national census and the power of the Parliament to make special laws.

That exclusion was remedied by the overwhelming vote of the Australian people in the 1967 Referendum which can now be seen as the real start of our search for true and lasting reconciliation.

That search is, in turn, part of a larger continuing journey together of all Australians – to be one people; strong in our unity; rich in our diversity.

Before Federation was achieved, a young Australian poet, William Gay, a schoolteacher from Bendigo, called upon his fellow-citizens to 'rise, united and be one people.'

Sadly, William Gay died, three years before his vision could be fulfilled.

Now, as we enter the second century of our nationhood, his words, which were adopted by Alfred Deakin, have a renewed sense of purpose:

> From all division let our land be free,
> For God has made her one: complete she lies,
> Within the unbroken circle of the skies,
> And round her, indivisible, the sea,
> Breaks on her single shore.

1.17 The Opening of the Centennial Ceremony, Centennial Park, Sydney, 1 January 2001

The opening words of the national anthem we have just sung tell us to rejoice.

And so we should. For we have much to celebrate as we recall the coming together, exactly one hundred years ago today, of the six Australian colonies to 'be one people' – in the words of our first Prime Minister, Edmund Barton, 'a nation for a continent'.

We all remember our gratitude and pride in Australia during the recent Olympic and Paralympic Games. We bring that same grateful pride to this celebration of our nation's 100th birthday.

Grateful pride in the land itself: this matchless continent, its islands, its surrounding seas. For those of us who love this 'wide brown land', there is nowhere else on earth that comes even close to its ancient majesty, its mystery, its varied beauty and its sheer wonder.

Grateful pride in the commitment to democracy under the rule of law, which created our nation and which has deepened down the century. We have sealed it by sacrifice in war. We have maintained its tenaciously in peace. Few other nations can look back on a century of democratic rule, unbroken by dictatorship, military coup, civil war or conquest.

And, above all, grateful pride in our Australian people who, as our Constitution makes plain, are our nation. All those who have been and are Australian. And what they were and are: their decency, their generosity, their sense of fair play; their spirit of ANZAC.

And their mutual respect and acceptance which underlie our greatest achievement, namely, the way we are making our diversity, of origin, race, culture and belief, a source of national strength and unity rather than a cause of weakness and division.

So let us rejoice and be grateful for all the achievements of our past and for this day.

At the same time, let us be honest and courageous about the failures and flaws which mar those achievements and which together we can address and overcome.

The damage we have done to the land, its rivers and coasts, notwithstanding our love of its beauty.

The unacceptable gap between the haves and the have-nots, in this land of the 'fair-go' for all.

How far we still have to travel on our journey towards genuine reconciliation between Australia's indigenous peoples and the nation of which they form such a vital part.

Conscious of all these things, let us re-dedicate Australia to the ideal of unity, under freedom, democracy and the rule of law, which brought our Commonwealth into being, one hundred years ago.,

And, in this Centennial Park, on the ancestral land and meeting place of the Eora, Gadigal and Tharawal peoples, let us look to the future, and dream of what it might hold for our nation.

Let us walk together into that future with honesty, vision and determination, with Australian generosity of spirit, and with Australian goodwill and fair play.

Thereby we will truly, in the best and fullest sense, 'Advance Australia Fair'.

1.18 The Opening of the Exhibition '*Belonging: A Century Celebrated*', State Library of New South Wales, Sydney, 3 January 2001

The evocative word 'belonging', in the context of a celebration of our first century as a nation, is a challenging title for a major exhibition. It invites an examination of who and what we Australians and the nation we constitute are: where we have been and where we are going, our characteristics and qualities, our strengths and weaknesses, our inclusiveness and exclusiveness.

This Exhibition – *Belonging: A Century Celebrated* – has succeeded in meeting that challenge. That is not surprising since it is staged for the Centenary of Federation by four of the principal Institutions holding our national documentary heritage – the National Archives, the National Library and the State Libraries of New South Wales and Victoria.

The Exhibition has much to teach and to interest us about our past as it invites us to think about what it has meant to belong and not to belong in this country during the twentieth century. Equally important, it has much to tell us about the present and the future. For what is past is absorbed by – and helps shape – what is and what will be.

There is a need for caution in making generalisations about belonging and not belonging at the time of the establishment of our nation one hundred years ago. There are, however, a few generalisations that can be made.

One is that, in 1901, if you were completely white (in the sense of ancestry rather than all over), British and of free settler descent, came from a Christian background and used the word 'home' to refer to a country on the other side of the world, you certainly had all the qualifications necessary to officially belong. If you had all those qualifications and had the added advantage of being an adult male, you may have even been a delegate at a Constitutional Convention.

On the other hand, if you were black and your ancestry stretched back for 40, 50 or 60 thousand years in this ancient continent, you most certainly did not officially 'belong' in the new nation. To the contrary, the Constitution expressly ordained that 'aboriginal natives' were not even 'to be counted' in 'reckoning the numbers of people of the Commonwealth'. And that notwithstanding that, as this Exhibition makes plain, you belonged to your country in a way that many still find difficult to comprehend, let alone understand.

Between those two extremes, there lay a myriad of possible, probable and even near certain belongers and non-belongers.

Our first century as a nation has transformed our national identity. There remain, of course, some divisions. But, as the Exhibition illustrates, there has emerged, particularly in the last three or four decades, a nation whose people, directly or indirectly, come from all the regions of the world and in which mutual acceptance and respect are progressively making our diversity of origin, race, culture and belief a source of national strength and unity rather than a cause of weakness and division.

That is not, of course to deny that we still have a considerable way to go before we reach the stage where it could accurately be said that all Australians truly 'belong', or feel that they 'belong', to their nation, to their local community or even at all. It is, however, to recognise the great progress we have made towards forging a truly inclusive nation in which at least the starting point is that if you are Australian, you belong.

'*Belonging*' explores these and other more particularised issues in an engaging fashion – sometimes challengingly, some-times sorrowfully, sometimes light-heartedly and sometimes comically. At times it confronts us. At times it praises us. At times it gently pokes fun at us. At times it delights us. At times it evokes sadness and even shame. But always, it should cause us to think … and to see ourselves a little more clearly. And, hopefully, it will succeed in encouraging and helping all who visit it in Sydney, in Melbourne or elsewhere in this Centenary Year to face and answer the question of what sort of nation they would like to belong to in the twenty first century.

Each visitor to the Exhibition will form his or her own assessment of the comparative importance of particular aspects. I mention but two of them which will be of enduring significance to me personally. One is the importance of place, landscape and physical environment in the context of belonging – not just for indigenous Australians but for Australians generally. The other is the reminder of the injustice suffered by many completely loyal Australians who were interned during the World Wars because of a suspicion of disloyalty by reason of ties with one or other of the nations with which Australia was at war.

1.19 Australia Day 2001 Address, 26 January 2001

This is my fifth Australia Day message. It's also my last as my time as Governor-General ends this June. That time has been an immensely happy one for Helen and me. We're profoundly grateful to our fellow Australians for their friendliness, kindness and encouragement.

This evening, I want to share with you some of our impressions and experiences over the last five years.

During that period, we've been most deeply affected by the occasions of great tragedy in which we've been closely involved. Invariably, we've been overwhelmed by sadness and sympathy for the victims and their relatives and by admiration for the dedication and skill of those engaged in rescue efforts or supporting activities.

Indeed, we've been constantly impressed by *all* who work, or give, to help the disadvantaged and those in special need. In this United Nations International Year of Volunteers, I pay special tribute to our volunteers. To all who voluntarily give of their time and themselves to help others.

And Helen and I've been increasingly encouraged by those striving for genuine and lasting Aboriginal reconciliation. We've also been humbled by innumerable instances of reconciliation at a personal level which we've been privileged to share. The road ahead remains a difficult one. But we are convinced that our country can ultimately reach its end.

Looking back, my most unforgettable memory is of Gallipoli on the Anzac Day before last. As dawn broke and the Last Post sounded over Anzac Cove, we stood in Ari Burnu Cemetery surrounded by Australians and New Zealanders, including many young backpackers. The feeling of reverence, of sadness for young Australian lives lost so far from home and of pride in Australia and its people was simply overwhelming.

And there've been countless other occasions and events. For example, within the last four and a half months, the Sydney 2000 Olympics and Paralympics and the Centenary of our Federation brought us Australians together in ways which we'll always remember.

We've met some inspiring individuals over the last five years. They include Australians who have dedicated themselves and their lives to the service of others. They also include some of the many thousands of young Australians we've met in a vast variety of circumstances. Those young Australians have made us more aware of the challenges, difficulties and uncertainties which can confront our young people in the modern world. But they've also made us extraordinarily proud of young Australians generally and confident about Australia's future.

Looking to that future, let me repeat the theme and vision for our country which I've sought to convey in each of my Australia Day messages while I've been Governor-General. That theme is one of caring … of mutual respect and acceptance … of concern for true equality, dignity, opportunity and hope … for all Australians. And the vision is one of Australians walking together, talking together, caring together, working together, and achieving together. If we Australians can consciously adopt that theme and hold fast to that vision, we can face all the challenges ahead with real confidence that we'll meet them successfully and well.

Finally, on this Australia Day, I'm reminded of some words of Louise Haskins, once quoted by King George VI, which seem to me to be of particular significance to those of us who believe in a God as we stand at the beginning of our second century as a nation and the third millennium of our time:

And I said to the man who stood at the gate of the year:

> *'Give me a light that I may tread safely into the unknown'.*
>
> *And he replied: 'Go out into the darkness and put your hand into the hand of God.*
>
> *That shall be to you better than a light and safer than a known way'.*

Good evening and thank you all.

1.20 The Joint Commemorative Meeting of the Parliament of the Commonwealth of Australia and the Centenary Commemoration Ceremony, Melbourne, 9 May 2001

At the outset, I acknowledge the Wurundjeri people on whose ancestral land we are privileged to be gathered.

I have received the following message from Her Majesty The Queen:

> I extend to all of you gathered in the Royal Exhibition Building in Melbourne, especially to the Senators and Members of the House of Representatives through whom all the people of Australia are represented on this historic occasion, my congratulations on the one hundredth anniversary of the Commonwealth Parliament. Since the ninth of May, 1901, when my grandfather, commissioned by, and in the name of, my great-grandfather, opened the first Commonwealth Parliament, Australia has established and nurtured one of the best parliamentary democracies in the world. I have every confidence that that democracy will continue to flourish in the centuries ahead.

I have also received the following message from Her Majesty Queen Elizabeth The Queen Mother:

> I offer my congratulations to the Commonwealth Parliament on its Centenary. I remember so well our visit in May 1927 when my husband opened the provisional Parliament House in Canberra and how touched we were by the warmth of the welcome we received.
>
> I have such fond memories of my visits to Australia and I send to all Australians my best wishes for happiness and prosperity in the years ahead.

On this day in this magnificent building in 1901, our nation's central democratic institution, the Parliament of the Commonwealth, came alive.

Throughout the following century, that Parliament has been the focal point of our national political life ... the place and the means whereby national laws are made, national governments are controlled, national aspirations are articulated and pursued and national questions are debated and determined.

Over the years, the overwhelming majority of our Commonwealth parliamentarians have served Australia with dedication and integrity. As a nation, we have known a century of democratic rule, uninterrupted by military conquest, civil war or dictatorship of the left or right. Truly, we have much to celebrate as we look back on the first century of the life of the Parliament and of the democracy of which it is the keystone.

At the same time, we must look to the future and to the challenges which lie ahead. For the strong and vibrant democracy, which we have inherited, must never be taken for granted.

One challenge is for our democratic institutions to remain stable and yet be responsive enough to meet the aspirations and expectations of the changing Australian community. Those expectations include: the expectation that, in the context of our multicultural diversity, the Parliament will be truly representative of all the people; the expectation that the elected representatives of all Australians will work to heal any divisions in our society and, in particular, to achieve true and lasting Aboriginal reconciliation; the expectation that the voices of the disadvantaged will be heard; the expectation that our natural environment will be protected and preserved for future, as well as present, Australians.

All of us who are privileged to hold public office, be it elected or appointed, owe a duty of trust to the present and future generations of Australians to put the pursuit of the common good above personal gain or ambition. As we celebrate the Centenary of the first meeting of our national Parliament, let us be conscious of that duty and of the basic fact of our democracy, namely, that the ultimate source of all government power and authority in this land is the people – all the people – of our Commonwealth.

God bless Australia.

2

The Anzac Spirit and Mateship

2.0 Editor's note

William Deane's father, Cornelius Aloysius, served in the 58th Australian Infantry Battalion during World War I and was awarded the Military Cross. It was only when Governor-General that William read the citation for his father's gallantry: 'For the conspicuous gallantry and devotion to duty during operations near Bayonvillieres and east of Harbonierres on the 8th and 9th August 1918. Lieutenant Deane was in command of a company in the attack and led his men through a very thick fog with remarkable skill... he found when the fog had lifted a portion of the attacking troops in front had lost direction and that a gap existed in the front line. He led his men into this gap, capturing two officers and 54 other ranks. ...On the 9th August he led his company against a nest of enemy strong points full of machine guns east of Harbonierres, which he captured in turn. Although his casualties were heavy, 38 per cent of his company being out of action, he finally captured a large German headquarters and mopped the same up, 18 officers and 250 other ranks being taken prisoner. Throughout the whole operation he displayed remarkable courage and fine leadership, inspiring the greatest confidence in all ranks under his command.'

William hung a framed copy of the citation in his Yarralumla office. As Commander in Chief, he reverently attended services honouring the service of our military. A highlight of his Governor-Generalship was attendance at the dawn service at Gallipoli on Anzac Day 1999. In the last year of his term as Governor-General, he attended the Anzac Day service at Balibo in East Timor. He wrote to the Queen saying: 'Your Majesty may be interested to know that I travelled to East Timor a couple of weeks ago to spend the Anzac Day (25 April) with the members of our Defence Force serving with the United Nations Peacekeeping Force there. The dawn service at Balibo where most of our army personnel are stationed and which is very close to the Indonesian border was extraordinarily moving and quite unforgettable. Equally unforgettable, though for contrasting reasons, was the sheer devastation of the capital, Dili. The great majority of the major buildings have either been raised to the ground or stand as shells which have been partly restored by boards over windows and corrugated iron where the roof once was. The East Timorese are extraordinarily gentle people but the resentment over the killing and devastation must be immense.'

2.1 Remembrance Day, Australian War Memorial, Canberra, 11 November 1996

It is now 19 minutes until the clock reaches the hour of eleven. At that hour, on this day, 78 years ago, the guns of war finally fell silent along the Western Front, and the killing and maiming of a generation of our young men ceased as the Armistice began.

The tragedy of the Great War for our nation and our people did not, however, end with the silence of the guns. So many young lives remained destroyed – unlived and unfulfilled. So many dreams remained unrealised. The wounded still suffered. The bereaved still grieved or were yet to learn of their loss.

Across Australia, as in other parts of the world, ordinary people took stock of the carnage and resolved that the deaths, the suffering and the awful loss would not be in vain; that the Great War would be the war to end all wars; that they would always remember those who had died or suffered in the cause of peace. 'Look down', wrote the soldier poet Siegfried Sassoon, 'Look down, and swear by the slain of the War that you'll never forget'.

And so, at the eleventh hour of the eleventh day of the eleventh month of 1919, the first anniversary of the Armistice, our nation stopped to remember. Throughout the land, in schools, in workplaces, on the street and in the homes, Australians stood still and observed two minutes silence.

There was hardly a family which had not been touched by the Great War. Australia as a whole mourned for what had been lost and for what would never be.

But there was also pride. Pride in the achievement of our young nation and its soldiers. Pride in the conviction that death and suffering had not been in vain. Pride in the knowledge that Australians, with origins in all the regions of the world, had truly become a nation: one people who would remember. That was expressed in many ways but perhaps none so poignantly as on the headstones of the Australian soldiers buried in war cemeteries in France.

On the grave of Private James Reid, aged 26, who died in 1916, his parents wrote:

> It's just our James
> But he'll never be forgotten.

On the grave of Private Gar, aged 25 and also killed in 1916, the even more simple words:

> He died for Australia.

We now know that the Great War was not the war to end all wars. Within 20 years our servicemen and women again were called to fight, first in the cause of freedom and decency and then in desperate defence of our own land. At Milne Bay and Kokoda our troops for the first time anywhere turned the tide. And finally, we and our allies prevailed.

Again there was grief, and pride, and gratitude. Again we prayed that there would be no more war. But then there was Korea, ... then Malaya ... and then Vietnam. And there was conflict in the Gulf and in the course of United Nations peace-keeping operations, in circumstances of real danger which called for strength, determination and dedication.

Today, the Great War has become World War I. And Armistice Day has become Remembrance Day. Yet we, particularly our young who hold the future in their hands, must honour and renew the pledge to remember made so often on behalf of us and our nation on this day in the past.

So it is that Remembrance Day is now a day on which Australia and Australians pause and remember the sacrifice of all those who have died or suffered in Australia's cause in any war or conflict in which Australia, as a nation, has been engaged. And it is the day on which, in their memory and in their honour, we, as individuals and as a nation, renew our commitment to peace.

Each of us in this place is conscious of our nearness to the Unknown Australian Soldier in the War Memorial's Hall of Memory. For me, his tomb has become the true heart of our nation. The Unknown Australian Soldier who rests there continues in death to serve: by enriching our commitment to peace and by reminding us of the sacrifice of all those who died or suffered for Australia in time of war.

After this ceremony, let us each take a poppy or some other flower and lay it on that tomb. By that act, we will observe and renew our pledge to remember and our commitment to peace. And we will keep faith with their memory..

Here at the heart of the land they loved.

2.2 The Launch of 'A Nation at War', Australian War Memorial, Canberra, 21 May 1997

As we all know, the proud tradition of Australian official war history began with CEW Bean. As official historian of Australia's part in the 1914-18 war, he oversaw a 12 volume series, of which he wrote 6 himself. These books in their distinctive covers – 'the colour of dried blood' – were widely acclaimed in Australia and overseas.

Gavin Long continued the tradition with the official history of Australia's involvement in the 1939-45 war, a 22 volume series. Robert O'Neill then wrote the two volumes of official history of Australia's involvement in the Korean War. These series were similarly praised.

Charles Bean and Gavin Long wrote as journalists and official war correspondents before becoming war historians. Since then official historians have been academically trained in that field. Robert O'Neill and Peter Edwards, the current official historian, studied in Australia and at Oxford, where each was a Rhodes Scholar. Dr O'Neill is now the Chichele Professor of the History of War at Oxford. Dr Edwards is the Executive Director of the Australian Centre for American Studies at the University of Sydney.

All of these historians have enjoyed the privilege of unfettered access to Australian Government records and have been assured of publication without political or official censorship.

Today we are gathered to launch the 6th volume in the 4th series of Australian official war histories. The series covers Australia's involvement in three conflicts between 1948 and 1975 – the Malayan Emergency, the Indonesian-Malaysian Confrontation and the Vietnam War. In short, it is the story of Australia's experience of the Cold War in Southeast Asia.

This latest volume tackles the most controversial aspect of a highly controversial subject – Australian politics, society and diplomacy during the Vietnam War, from the commitment of the first battalion of Australian troops in 1965 to the fall of the Republic of Vietnam in 1975. The title, *A Nation at War*,[4] has a double meaning. Australia as a nation was involved in the war in Vietnam. At the same time, within the nation, Australian society was becoming increasingly divided over the wisdom and morality of that involvement. Historians and readers who take an interest in dissent and social change sometimes disregard the importance of politics and diplomacy and vice versa. This book combines social, political and diplomatic history.

Dr Edwards traces the changing moods of public opinion and the differing levels of public opposition, resistance and defiance during

[4] Peter Geoffrey Edwards, *A Nation at War: Australian politics, society and diplomacy during the Vietnam War 1965-1975* (Allen and Unwin, 1997).

the period of our involvement in the war and its aftermath. He discusses the qualities of Australian Prime Ministers and other political leaders. He suggests that Vietnam revealed major flaws in some highly regarded politicians, while bringing out unsuspected strengths in some with lesser reputations. He also analyses the significance of certain incidents and episodes which had a major political impact at the time and have had an enduring effect on popular memory.

On Australia's foreign relations, the book describes Mr Harold Holt's efforts to argue that Australia's future lay in Asia, using terms that would wrongly be considered new when they re-surfaced in the 1980s and 1990s. The author also records the vicissitudes of the Australian-American relationship, from Prime Minister Holt's celebrated statement that Australia was 'all the way with LBJ' and Prime Minister Gorton's declaration to President Nixon that Australia would 'go Waltzing Matilda' with the United States to the subsequent tensions between Washington and Canberra over the size of the Australian commitment and, after the withdrawal of Australian forces, Prime Minister Whitlam's letter of protest over the December 1972 bombing of Hanoi which led Nixon to group `Australia with Sweden as his least-favoured Western governments.

By combining these social, political and diplomatic dimensions, Dr Edwards presents us with a comprehensive but highly readable account of Australia in this critical period.

In such a controversial area, it is inevitable that there will be readers who disagree with at least some of the book's judgments and conclusions. Nevertheless, we can agree that the book, and the series of which it is part, demonstrate a combination of historical scholarship and literary skills of which Dr Edwards, his colleagues in the Official History Unit and the Australian War Memorial as a whole can be justly proud.

The period covered by the fourth series is longer than that covered by any previous official war history. It encompasses some of the great themes of recent Australian and international history – the political and military dimensions of the Cold War, the decolonisation of the European empires, the social changes of the 1960s and 1970s. Dr Edwards and his colleagues have skilfully contended with vast quantities and a great diversity of source material, including literally kilometres of official files and sources in the United States, the United Kingdom, France, Vietnam, Malaysia, Singapore and Indonesia.

In *A Nation at War* this wealth of material has been turned into a fascinating and scholarly narrative. Dr Edwards has taken great care to ensure that, in dealing with one of the most turbulent and controversial periods in Australian history, he has remained non-partisan. Several historians with expert knowledge of the subject but with widely differing perspectives have already commented on the independence, fairness and balance of the book's judgments.

As official historian and general editor of the series, Dr Edwards has overcome many obstacles to bring the series to fruition. Notwithstanding the Memorial's limited resources, he was able to recruit to his team distinguished historians from the Australian Defence Force Academy, the Australian National University and the Air Power Studies Centre. He has guided that team in the production of a series which has received remarkably consistent praise in reviews; and at a time when timeliness is assessed as keenly as quality, the volumes have appeared at a commendable rate, one each year since 1992. In the process, Dr Edwards and his colleagues have spoken to schools, universities, historical societies and other community groups, as well as writing articles for academic and popular journals.

What do we learn from this book? One of its central arguments is that Australia had little option but to support the United States in Vietnam in 1964-65, given the regional situation and Australia's dependence on American support; but that by 1968-69 the international position had changed considerably. Dr Edwards argues

– plausibly, I think – that Australia missed a major opportunity to reassess its policies and to withdraw its troops, especially the conscripts, from the war. Had that been done, many of the painful divisions in Australian society in the early 1970s might have been avoided.

Much of this volume relates directly to contemporary issues. We cannot fully understand such vital questions as our relationship with Asia, our alliance with the United States, and the changing nature of Australian society, without examining our recent past. Those who were committed to either side of the Vietnam debate will find much to reflect upon, while those with no personal experience of the Vietnam War will learn a great deal from this book about how Australia came to be the country it is today.

Perhaps most important, the story of the Vietnam War and its aftermath reminds us of how much our nation, through its elected governments, demanded of those whom, by a macabre lottery, it sent to fight and sometimes die in a far off land and how slow it was to adequately acknowledge their service and their sacrifice.

One of the respects in which the Vietnam War differed from other wars in which Australia has been involved is that, in other wars, our service men and women returned in triumph to the enthusiastic recognition and thanks of a grateful nation. Our service men and women who returned from Vietnam in the later years returned to an increasingly divided nation. Each of the battalions which served in Vietnam marched through an Australian city on its return. Otherwise, many Vietnam veterans felt that they received little or inadequate recognition or acclaim for the sacrifices they had made in the service, commonly the compulsory service, of their country. To many returning from Vietnam, Australia and Australians seemed ungrateful for their service and indifferent to the subsequent effects of that service and of that ingratitude upon their health and lives. It was only with the Welcome Home march in Sydney in 1987 and the opening of the Vietnam Memorial here in Anzac Parade that, hopefully, that impression was largely dispelled. In the result, it cannot be too strongly stressed that Australia's debt to many who served in our country's forces in Vietnam is immeasurably greater than it would have been if that service and its effects had been properly acknowledged at the time. The failure to acknowledge it adequately at the time is something which, I think, all fair-minded Australians now regret.

2.3 The Graduation Parade of the Australian Defence Force Academy, Canberra, 11 December 1997

The Australian Defence Force Academy (ADFA) is the principal training establishment for officers in the Australian Defence Force. Its objectives are to provide a military education and training to develop the professional abilities and the qualities of character and leadership required of officers in our Defence Force and, consistently with that military training, to provide a balanced and liberal education.

The almost 300 graduands who are on parade today have satisfied the heavy demands imposed by those objectives and have successfully completed all the requirement of the ADFA courses. That is a truly outstanding achievement.

Those of you who are graduating today – the graduating class of 1997 – are completing three years of study and experience in the Combined University and Tri-Service atmosphere which is so special to the Australian Defence Force Academy. For each of you, today's Parade marks the passing of an important milestone in your career. For some, that career will be a lifetime of committed service in the Australian Defence Force. For others, it will embrace a period of military service followed by a subsequent career outside the Defence Force. Regardless of what path your particular future career may take, your time at ADFA, with the combination of tertiary qualifications from one of the nation's leading universities and the military training and skill which can only be derived from a great Military Academy, will stand you in good stead for the rest of your lives.

As you know, the Academy has existed for only 12 years. In an important sense, however, it is much older since it incorporates the experience, the knowledge and much of the traditions of the Service training establishments which preceded it and the standards, the loyalties and the great history of the branches of our Defence Force which those older establishments existed to serve. In addition, the Academy shares in the standards, the learning and the traditions of one of Australia's leading Universities.

Inevitably, at times, there have been and will be tensions between the role of the ADFA as our main Military Academy and its role of providing a liberal University education. Long experience in this country and elsewhere has, however, demonstrated that military training and discipline and a liberal tertiary education are not inconsistent with one another. To the contrary, they complement each other and, in combination, provide an ideal basis for the qualifications, attributes and qualities of discipline, leadership, loyalty and honour which our Defence Force has in the past and must in the future demand of its officers. Nonetheless, the task of striking the proper balance between the two roles is not always an easy one. That proper balance must, however, be struck. And it must be struck in a way that recognises that the essential function of the Academy is to provide its graduates with those essential qualifications, attributes and qualities and thereby equip them to undertake the obligations of leadership in our nation's Defence Force. As a mark of respect to Air Vice Marshall Beck who is retiring and in fairness to the graduands, I think I should say that, from my own knowledge of ADFA and its graduates and graduands, I am confident that the Academy is striking the appropriate balance and is succeeding in discharging its functions as our country's most important Military Academy in a way and with results of which Australia can be justly proud.

Each graduating class is faced with differing contemporary

challenges. Yours relate to a peacetime environment with increased emphasis on United Nations service. Our military leaders must be informed about the complexities of international relations and their effect upon national defence. Our service personnel must adjust to the social dynamics of our nation, including full appreciation and acceptance of the contemporary role and complete equality of women in society in general and the services in particular. You must be flexible and capable of adapting to change, particularly in this age of technology. You will be part of our Defence Force at a time when it is undergoing the most significant structural change of the modern era.

In the result, the years ahead will demand much of you as officers in our Defence Force. But you will have much to sustain you. You will have the knowledge that the work you do is of critical importance to your country and to all its people. And you will have the strength and pride that comes from being part of a Defence Force which has, throughout the history of our nation, served Australia superbly well.

2.4 The Launch of '*Sacred Places: War Memorials in the Australian Landscape*', Canberra, 17 November 1998

It was only five years ago, on the 75th Anniversary of the Armistice that brought the First World War to an end, that the remains of an Unknown Australian Soldier who had died in that war were laid to rest in the Hall of Memory here at our Australian War Memorial. It was an occasion at once symbolic and deeply moving in the dignity of its ceremonial. It was, as Professor Inglis observes in this splendid new book *Sacred Places: War Memorials in the Australian Landscape*,[5] an occasion in which the ritual marked the true completion, in a spiritual sense, of the national memorial, in the National Capital, to *all* Australians who have served and died in their nation's wars.

---

[5] Kenneth Inglis, *Sacred Places: War memorials in the Australian landscape* (Miegunyah Press at Melbourne University Press, 1998).

And it did so in a way that transcended the formal and the ceremonial. For what was wonderful about the burial of the Unknown Australian Soldier was the way in which its meaning was so spontaneously understood and accepted by the Australian people. It spoke to something deep and abiding in the hearts of men and women everywhere. Some 50,000 people placed wreaths and flowers on the open tomb in the three-and-a-half days before it was sealed. While waiting in a queue to enter the Hall, they discovered you could wedge the wire stem of a red Remembrance Day poppy between the bronze tablets in the cloisters bearing the names of the Roll of Honour. Soon, as Professor Inglis remarks, 'the walls became more densely splashed with scarlet as people on their way to and from paying respect to the Unknown Soldier, made their own personal gestures in memory of the known, from brothers, husbands and fathers killed in Vietnam, to great-uncles two world wars away'. For, as the then Prime Minister, Mr Paul Keating, eloquently observed, the Unknown Soldier was and is 'all of them'.Those gestures and that perception would have profoundly gratified the great war historian, CEW Bean, who conceived this place as a combined museum, repository and shrine – unlike any other in the world. Half a century after the Australian War Memorial was opened in the midst of a *second* World War, Professor Inglis writes that the Hall of Memory 'was welcoming at last the sentiment of reverent recollection CEW Bean had always wanted it to harbour'.

It is, in the main, that spirit of 'reverent recollection' that has led Australian men and women to erect some 4000 memorials to those who have served and fought and died in our wars over the course of the present century. Memorials that can be found everywhere from the capital cities and their suburbs, regional centres and country towns to the smallest rural hamlets and wayside halts. Memorials whose nature ranges from the monumental – the cast or carved soldier generally at repose, the obelisk, column or cenotaph – to the utilitarian – memorial hall, fountain, swimming pool, entrance gates or avenue of trees. Memorials that may stand prominently upon a hill or in a garden or in a busy thoroughfare, but almost always on common – usually civic – land. Memorials that, until the decision to return the bodies of service personnel killed in Vietnam, were surrogates for the funeral stones denied the loved ones left to mourn at home. Memorials that with simple, spiritual though not specifically religious texts – commonly LEST WE FORGET, from Kipling's *Recessional* – enable people to lay their own thoughts and feelings with their tributes. Memorials, too, that unlike those in other parts of the world, very often list the names of the survivors as well as the dead – certainly from the First World War.

They are war memorials that are omnipresent in the Australian landscape, although until recently they have largely been ignored by cultural and architectural historians. Professor Inglis, in this thorough, scholarly, accessible and altogether handsome book, has corrected that omission. Now, he remarks, 'the interrogation of war memorials has become a vigorous branch of cultural history' both for what they tell us about the people and communities who made them and also for what, remembering the response to the burial of the Unknown Australian Soldier, they have to tell us about our society today.

There are few memorials to the colonial conflicts of the 19th century – certainly almost none, at least of an official kind, to the Aborigines who were slaughtered in the 'Black Wars' of that period. It was not until the South African War that the history of war memorials in this country finds its proper beginnings: it is then that we see the first stone trooper appear, the first references to 'the fallen', the first listing of the names of the living as well as the dead. Yet the Boer War touched the lives of few Australians. The young Australian nation remained, in the words of Ernest Scott, 'unruffled by war'. Or, in the words of Bernard O'Dowd, 'a prophecy waiting to be fulfilled'.

All that was to change with the landing of the Anzacs at Gallipoli on 25 April 1915. As Professor Inglis observes, 'the days of 'She is not yet' were over'. It may well be, as Bean was to say, that the real meaning of Gallipoli was 'the discovery of the character of the Australian men'; but the Great War as fought at the Dardanelles, on the Western Front and in the Middle East was to touch virtually every Australian man, women and child. Ken Inglis estimates that every second extended Australian family was bereaved by the war. That nationwide loss gave rise to the extraordinary 'war memorial movement', as he calls it, of tributes in stone and marble and brick that were to transform the Australian landscape.

Each memorial has its own history. Professor Inglis and his team have spent the past 15 years studying and recording those histories in the pages of this book and on a comprehensive inventory lodged in the Australian War Memorial. The individual histories display some recurring themes: for similar questions were faced by people across the country. Where would the memorial be? Who would pay for it? What form should it take? Should the opening be a civil or religious ceremony, or some combination of both? In some places, the questions were only settled after considerable local conflict ... 'like going into battle with Germany again' as *The Mudgee Guardian* reported. In other places they were settled amicably, such as at Thirroul whose stone soldier, unveiled on Anzac Day 1920, was described by DH Lawrence in the pages of his novel *Kangaroo*: '... small and stiff and rather touching ... a real township monument'.

The monument at Thirroul recurs as a *leitmotif* throughout *Sacred Places*, standing for all township monuments: its construction, opening, its place in the local Anzac Day ceremonies, its move in more recent times to a park away from the busy traffic, and the fact that lately the numbers of people attending the Dawn Service have actually been increasing. The third last photograph in this beautifully illustrated book is of two young Australians visiting the Thirroul monument with their Lebanese grandfather to see the name of their Anglo-Australian grandfather who was killed in Libya during the Second World War. Such is the place still occupied by war memorials in today's multicultural Australia. In that regard, it is worth noting that at the head of Anzac Parade – of what Professor Inglis calls our 'sacred way' in a phrase from classical antiquity – stands the Australian Hellenic Monument and, opposite, the Ataturk Memorial Gardens with its inspired words from the defender of Gallipoli and founder of modern Turkey: 'You the mothers, wipe away your tears ...'.

On approximately half of all the First World War memorials in the Australian landscape the names of local soldiers who survived are inscribed together with those who were killed. That is, as I said, a most unusual practice in other countries. It reflects the fact that, as Monash consistently stressed, the Australians were *all* volunteers – the only sovereign country whose combatants by 1918 could be so described. As Professor Inglis points out, the practice also underlined 'with appalling regularity' the awful fact that about one in five of the men who went to war from that place never came home.

It was different with the Second World War. True, far greater numbers of men and women were involved in the armed services and in civilian war work. It is true that some Australian cities were bombed and that for the first time conscripted men fought outside Australian soil: but the number of deaths, at around 30,000, were half those of the First World War. In many cases the names of those who died were added to the existing monuments, but generally speaking the separate memorials to the forces of the Second World War took a utilitarian form. As the Canberra poet, Geoff Page, writes:

> The next bequeathed to us
> Parks and Pools
> But something in that first
> Demanded stone

Monumentality may have been out of fashion. But it had returned

– albeit in contemporary form – by the time the memorials were raised to those who served and died in Korea, Malaya and, especially, Vietnam. Indeed, Professor Inglis remarks that the Australian Vietnam Forces National Memorial is 'the most impressive monument' along Anzac Parade. In some places, moreover, the memorials to Australians who had fought in Vietnam were actually made by Vietnamese people who had come to Australia as refugees from that war. And, of course, the lottery which compelled service and the perception of contemporary ingratitude that marked the Vietnam War have, in retrospect, added a special significance and sadness to the monuments to those who died.

Ladies and gentlemen, there is so much more I could say about this truly outstanding book if time permitted. One might, for instance, discuss at length why it is that we are seeing such an extraordinary renaissance of interest in Anzac Day and our country's military past by today's generation of young people – not only here in Australia but also by those who visit in great numbers – many of them young backpackers – the peninsular at Gallipoli and the old battle fields of the Western Front. Is it simply nostalgia? Or affection and admiration for ageing veterans? Or family tradition? Or a sense of national identity and patriotism? Or does the pride and anguish we feel for those who fought and suffered and who are remembered on our war memorials touch some deeper well-spring of honour and sacrifice and commitment to the peace they gave us?

I cannot answer such questions in any comprehensive way. I can only say that such depths of national emotion were touched on that Remembrance Day in 1993 when the remains of the Unknown Australian Soldier were laid in the Hall of Memory. And they have not abated since. For me, his tomb has become the true heart of our nation. I believe – as CEW Bean would doubtless hope – that it will remain so at least for the foreseeable future. Here in the heart of the land they loved.

And here is undoubtedly the most appropriate place in the world for us to be gathered today for the launch of '*Sacred Places: War Memorials in the Australian Landscape*'. For just as the Unknown Soldier is all of those who served and died in all our wars, this Memorial in our National Capital is *the* national monument and tribute to them all.

2.5 The Dawn Service, Anzac Cove, 25 April 1999

Just before dawn, on that first Anzac Day 84 years ago, the boats carrying the 1500 men who would make the first landing were moving through darkness towards these shores. All was silent, save for whispers of apprehension and the splash of oars.

Ahead of them, two searchlights briefly pencilled the sky, then disappeared. Still silence. The leading boats touched the beach. The first Anzacs leaped out. A yellow beacon flared to the south and a single shot was heard. Then several more. And as the boats further out came in, the fire broke upon them from the heights above us. The silence and the waiting were over. And the key, as one of the Anzacs was later to say, 'was being turned in the lock of hell'.

All the demons of war were let loose as the day wore on. Some men died in the boats and on the beaches ... many more in the bitter fighting up on the ridges ... through scrub and ravines towards the third ridge. There were the sounds of gun fire and of bombs. And of the screams of combat, of suffering and of death. And occasionally through it all, so we are told, there came the voices of young soldiers singing: 'Australia will be there'. And, in at least one instance, 'This bit of the world belongs to us'.

By the evening, 16,000 men of the Australian and New Zealand Army Corps had landed here; of them some 2000 were dead or seriously wounded. And the Turkish defenders had forced the advance back to the second ridge – from which position, despite some small gains at huge cost, nothing essentially changed over the next eight months.

There are now no living Anzacs who were here on that first day. The last survivor, Ted Matthews, an Australian signaller, died in December 1997. There are only a few remaining of the Anzacs who subsequently served here during the Gallipoli campaign. The last New Zealander, Doug Dibley, a stretcher-bearer, died a little more than fifteen months ago. The fourth last Australian, Frank Isaacs, died in Perth only this month. So few left who experienced – who can personally recall – the long months of stalemate, of attack and counter-attack on pieces of hillside that were given soldiers' names – Plugge's Plateau (behind us), Quinn's Post, MacLaggan's Ridge, Johnston's Jolly. Yet the story of those months, and of all that they involve, lives in our national histories and collective memories.

For ANZAC is not merely about loss. It is about courage, and endurance, and duty, and love of country, and mateship, and good humour and the survival of a sense of self-worth and decency in the face of dreadful odds. These were qualities and values the pioneers had discovered in themselves in what were, for Europeans, the new lands of Australia and New Zealand. They were tested here and on the ancient battlefields of Europe for the first time in the Great War. They were not found wanting.

This was not the ANZACs' bloodiest campaign of that war. The casualties in France overwhelmed those of Gallipoli. But it was the *first*. And it was heroic even in failure. And what makes it unique is that it was here the people of our countries – Australia and New Zealand – found their nationhood. 'Before the war who ever heard of ANZAC,' said their Commander-in-Chief, the British General Sir Ian Hamilton. 'Hereafter', he added, 'who will ever forget it?'

The campaign failed, but the men were not defeated. There is a crucial difference. In a triumph of daring and initiative, over 35,000 ANZACs were evacuated during eleven December nights, with barely a casualty. With their boots muffled, the last of them came down from the heights to the beaches on 20 December, and into the boats that took them in darkness and silence back to the waiting ships.

But their dead – our dead – remained behind. Here on the other side of the world from the lands they loved: over 2,700 New Zealanders and over 8,100 Australians. For many who were leaving that was the unbearable tragedy. In words which I quoted at Ted Matthews' funeral, one of them wrote:

> 'Not only muffled is our tread/To cheat the foe,
> We fear to rouse our honoured dead/To hear us go.
> Sleep sound, old friends – the keenest smart
> Which, more than failure, wounds the heart,
> Is thus to leave you – thus to part'.

Yet we are *not* apart. While this is Turkish land, it has become a sacred site of *our* nations. And we are united with those young ANZACs who were left here so long ago. Not only while we are here, honouring them and all that they bequeathed us. But also – constantly – in their and our homelands so far away. For there as well as here, their spirit walks abroad. To challenge, to guide and to inspire. For as long as we remember. For as long as our nations endure.

No one can express all that this day means to us Australians and New Zealanders. It is, said Australia's great historian Manning Clark, 'about something too deep for words'. But in the stillness of the early dawn, and in the silence that will settle once more along this shoreline, we feel it in the quiet of our hearts. The sense of great sadness. Of loss. Of gratitude. Of honour. Of national identity. Of our past. Of the spirit, the depth, the meaning, the very essence of our nations. And of the human values which those first ANZACs – and those who came after them – embodied and which we, their heirs, must cherish and pass to the future.

May they rest with God.

2.6 The Service at the Lone Pine Memorial, Gallipoli, 25 April 1999

There are other beautiful and evocative cemeteries at Anzac for the Australian dead. But none holds a more honoured place than Lone Pine. The other nations that fought at Gallipoli – Turkey, Britain, France, New Zealand – all have their special battle-grounds where commemorative services are held today. But this Memorial and this Cemetery are where *we* Australians turn.

From here, we look down to the sea and marvel at how far they had come 'in a raked boot-scrambling roar', as the poet, Les Murray, put it, 'to the heights of thyme and rosemary'. We look up and realise how far they had to go. The position was first taken by Australian troops, then lost to a Turkish counter-attack, soon after the April landings. A solitary pine tree grew here, and the diggers called the place 'Lonesome Pine' from a popular song. For the Turkish soldiers, it became *Kanli Sirt* – or Bloody Ridge – after their dreadful losses here in May of 1915.

The soil became even more bloody during the Australian assault on the Turkish trench system and the fearful struggle below ground over four days in August. Seven Victoria Crosses were awarded; but there were over 2,000 Australian and 5,000 Turkish casualties.

So seared upon the Australian consciousness was Lone Pine, that it became our principal memorial here on Gallipoli. It contains the graves of soldiers who died throughout the campaign: from the beginning to the end, the known and the unknown. For here, too, are commemorated over 4,200 Australians and 700 New Zealand soldiers who have no identified grave or who were buried at sea. Among them, private James Martin who died on a hospital ship. He was, we believe, only 14 – though he said he was 18 – perhaps the youngest of all the Anzacs to die here.

Such was the magnitude of suffering at Gallipoli that we can comprehend it only through the individual. Private CA McAnulty killed even as he was writing home to Melbourne from Lone Pine: 'I've pulled through alright so far, just got a few minutes to spare now'. Private John Simpson, 'Murphy' Simpson – the man with the donkey – fatally wounded after so many days – 'all day every day' – heroically and ever cheerfully carrying water up and wounded men down – 'one man a trip' – through the hell fire of Shrapnel Valley. 'They sing, they cheer, they smoke their cigarettes', said John Monash, 'even when so badly hit as to have to be carried on a stretcher'.

And there was the respect that the ANZAC and Turkish troops came to feel for each other – as opponents, as soldiers and also as men – here on the heights of Gallipoli. And Turkish soldiers also lie beneath the soil here at Lone Pine. As we mourn our own countrymen – and of course our brothers from New Zealand – who died here, we also remember and honour all the other soldiers, Allied and Turkish, who died in the course of the Gallipoli campaign. And we express our thanks for the fact that this Peninsula, which the Turkish authorities on the initiative of President Demirel are developing as the Gallipoli Peace Park, is a sanctuary of peace and a constant reminder of the power of reconciliation.

Outside the Australian War Memorial in Canberra is the Ataturk Memorial Garden, named after the Commander of the Turkish forces on Gallipoli and the father of modern Turkey. It is the only memorial to a former enemy on Anzac Parade. It carries the immortal words of Kemal Ataturk that are inscribed at Anzac Cove (and which were read at the Dawn Service there this morning). Words addressed to the mothers, urging them to wipe away the tears for their dead sons. 'After having lost their lives on this land, they have become our sons as well'.

From the Ataturk Memorial Garden in Canberra, you look across Anzac Parade to an Aleppo Pine, planted in 1934 from a cone taken by a soldier from the logs above the Turkish trenches here, and sent home to his mother in memory of another dead son. Seedlings from that tree now flourish in many places – including back here in its native soil at the Lone Pine Memorial and Cemetery.

Other seeds were planted. As the ANZACs left, Padre Walter Dexter, who had been denied his request to stay here to tend the graves of his dead mates, scattered wattle seeds. He desired, as he said, that 'a bit of Australia shall be here'. The wattles didn't survive. But his desire was fulfilled in any event. For not only 'a bit', but an essential part, of Australia will always be here … with the graves, the bodies, the memories and the spirits of the young Anzacs who were left behind. Here in this sacred site in the annals of our nation.

Let us all, as we walk among these graves on this 84th Anzac Day, listening to the wind in the pine trees, looking across the scarlet-poppied slopes to the 'heights of thyme and rosemary', remember the extent of our debt to our fellow countrymen who died here so many years ago. And, on this our national day of honour, let us recall not only those young Australians who gave their lives in our nation's service here at Gallipoli, so far away from their and our homeland, but also all who have died for our country on other battle fields of the First World War, in the Second World War, in Korea, in Vietnam and in other places. And let us all be conscious of the whisper of things 'too deep for words' that can be heard here in this place by all who have true love of our people and our country in their hearts.

2.7 The Opening of the 60th Anniversary of the Siege of Tobruk, Brisbane, 7 April 2001

Time passes more and more quickly as one gets older. I'm sure that it seems quite extraordinary to most of you that, next Tuesday, it will be sixty years to the day since the 10 April 1941 when the Siege of Tobruk began. Incidents from the approximately 8 months which followed are no doubt still indelibly etched in your minds. For those months, from the 10th April until early December, saw unfold one of the greatest chapters in the military history – indeed the history – of our nation. That chapter tells a story of courage and skill, of heroism and sacrifice, of determination and endurance and, of course, of victory for the besieged. It is a story of which not only those who have the honour of being 'Rats of Tobruk' but all Australians are rightly proud.

There are of course significant differences between the Australian stories of Gallipoli and Tobruk. For one thing, they were in different wars. For another, Gallipoli was an epic of Australians seeking to take enemy held territory while Tobruk was a saga of Australians under siege. Again, Gallipoli was a tragic miscalculation which ended in failure while Tobruk was a great victory for the allied cause – a victory which contributed mightily to subsequent allied victories, including the Second Battle of El Alamein which saw the tide of war begin to turn.

Yet Gallipoli and Tobruk have much in common. Both stretched from April to December. In both, our Australian soldiers were required to fight, and often to die, on the other side of the world from their homeland and loved ones. Both were marked by grim determination, selfless sacrifice and deeds of great heroism. Both ended in troop withdrawal. In both there were exhibited to the full the qualities which go to make up our Anzac spirit. At Gallipoli on Anzac Day 1999, I attempted to identify some of them: 'courage, and endurance, and duty, and mateship, and good humour, and the survival of a sense of self worth … in the face of overwhelming odds'.

And the story of the Australians at Tobruk in 1941, like that of the Australians at Gallipoli in 1915, has resounded over the decades to become part of our national identity. At Gallipoli, in 1999, I paid tribute, on behalf of the Australian people, to all the ANZACs of 1915. This evening, at this 60th Reunion, I am privileged, again on behalf of the Australian people, to pay tribute to all the Rats of Tobruk of 1941.

The six decades since 1941 have taken their toll. Inevitably, the passage of time and the vast distances of our land have imposed difficulties and strains upon the wartime bonds which united our Australian Rats of Tobruk throughout those unforgettable 242 days. Yet, those bonds persist and friendships endure across time and space. I have no doubt that those bonds and friendships will be refreshed and strengthened by this Reunion and that they will continue to enrich and sustain you after you have dispersed.

Brave memories. Brave deeds. Brave men. Your achievements shine in the military annals of our nation. I join you in remembering and honouring all your fellow Rats of Tobruk who died either at Tobruk or subsequently for the allied cause during the war or who have died in the postwar years. And I thank you and all the other living Rats of Tobruk for your service in our nation's cause in those years that are gone and wish you every happiness today and for all the days to come.

2.8 The Anzac Day Dawn Service, Balibo, East Timor, 25 April 2001

None of us Australians here at Balibo this morning, as the Anzac Day dawn breaks over East Timor, could fail to be overwhelmed by feelings of pride and of sadness.

Pride in our homeland in this Centenary Year of the Federation which established our Australian nation. Pride in our Defence Force which has, throughout the one hundred years of our nation's life, served it so well in conflict and in peace. Pride in the present members of our Defence Force currently serving in other foreign places in peace-keeping/peace-monitoring roles – in the Middle East; in Sinai; in Mozambique; in Bosnia; in Kuwait; in Ethiopia; in Sierra Leone; in Bougainville. Pride in all of you, the members of our Defence Force serving our nation here in East Timor. Your service is of immeasurable importance to Australia and all its people. And in the best traditions of our nation's military forces, stretching all the way back to that first Anzac Day 86 years ago and beyond.

On this morning in this place, we are especially conscious of all the Australians who died in the Timor region in the cause of freedom in World War II, including all those whose whereabouts are unknown. They sacrificed everything fighting to protect our homeland against aggression. We are conscious also of all the Timorese who died or suffered helping our Australian soldiers.

On this Anzac Day in our Centenary Year, we mourn and pay tribute to all the servicemen and women who, during the life of our nation, have died in the course of its service – in the Boer War, in World War I, in World War II, in Korea, in Vietnam and in other conflicts or in peace-keeping duties. I name among them Corporal Stuart Jones who was killed by an accidental firearm discharge here in East Timor since last Anzac Day. Mindful of the ANZAC ties which have bound our country to New Zealand in times of war as well as peace, we honour all who have died while serving in the forces of our constant friend and ally, New Zealand. And, mindful also of the ties which bind our country to East Timor, we honour all the people of this land who have died in the cause of freedom in recent times.

Let us be mindful of them all. Of how much they gave. Of how much they lost. Of lives destroyed and unfulfilled. Of dreams unrealised. And, as we remember them and their loss, let us renew our determination to work for peace.

May they all rest with God.

2.9 The Anzac Day Service at Dili Cathedral, Dili, East Timor, 25 April 2001

For us Australians, Anzac Day is sacred to the memory of all our countrymen and women who have died while serving in our nation's military forces ... whether in war or other conflict or in peace-making or peace-keeping endeavours. And on this day we also remember and honour all those who have served in our nation's forces and have since died. We remember them and we honour them.

Two years go, at this time on Anzac Day, I stood in Lone Pine Cemetery at Gallipoli where many of the Australians who died during the Gallipoli Campaign, from April to December 1915, are buried and where over 4,200 Australians and 700 New Zealand soldiers who were buried at sea or have no identified grave are commemorated. Until today, that day, which started with a Dawn Service at Anzac Cove, was by far my most memorable one as Governor-General. This day, with a Dawn Service at Balibo with our Australian troops and now this service in Dili Cathedral with so many fellow Australians, is for me of comparable significance.

Being here today, with our serving Defence Force personnel, has reinforced for me the continuity of the spirit of Anzac notwithstanding that the focus has changed from warfare and conflict to peace-making and peacekeeping. At Gallipoli, I tried to explain what that spirit means to us Australians: 'courage and endurance, and duty and love of country, and mateship, and good humour and the survival of a sense of self-worth and decency' regardless of the odds. It also means mutual dependence. It is, as our great historian Manning Clark wrote, 'something too deep for words'.

Like Gallipoli, the Island of Timor, while being foreign soil, has a special place in the history of our Australian nation. For on this island our Australian soldiers fought and died in the defence of freedom during the Second World War, with many still missing, presumably lying in unknown graves. Today, on this Anzac Day in this Cathedral, we honour and mourn them all. And we pay tribute on behalf of all Australians to their courage and their sacrifice. After this service, I shall be travelling to Dare where I will lay a wreath in their honour, on behalf of all Australians, at the Sparrow Force Memorial.

The memory of our soldiers who died inevitably reminds us Australians of all those East Timorese who so heroically helped them. The close relationship between the Australian people and the people of East Timor reaches back over the decades to those dark days. It has been reinforced in more recent times by the service of so many Australians, including military personnel and police force members, in peace-making and peacekeeping efforts.

Last September in Sydney, I was privileged to represent Australia at the Opening Ceremony of the Sydney 2000 Olympic Games. One of the most emotional moments of the whole Opening Ceremony was when the announcer introduced the three representatives of East Timor in the March of the Athletes. The stadium erupted in a roar of support which was only equalled by the welcome given to our Australian athletes. A little more than a month later, the great Olympic Stadium again erupted when, in my closing speech at the Paralympic Games, I mentioned how all Australians had rejoiced to see the East Timorese take their place in the international sporting family. I mention these things for the reason that, while my visit here has primarily been to spend Anzac Day with our Australian Defence Force personnel and other Australians serving in East Timor, I want it also to symbolise the enduring friendship between the Australians and East Timorese people.

In February 1997, Jose Ramos-Horta called on me at Government House in Canberra. At the end of his visit, he gave me a replica of an East Timorese hut. During the more than four years which have passed since that time, that hut has been prominently displayed in the study at Yarralumla. Throughout the days of killing and devastation, it stood there as a reminder of the heroism and suffering of the East Timorese people. In the days that have followed, it has stood as a symbol of hope for the future of the emerging nation. I brought it with me to East Timor to be here in this Cathedral at this service. You can see it on the Sanctuary.

So on this Anzac Day, we Australians honour and pay tribute to all our fellow countrymen and women who have died in the military service of our country in the Timor region or elsewhere or who have died since such service. We also remember and pay tribute to all who have died in this land in the cause of freedom either during the Second World War or in more recent times. And mindful of the Anzac ties which have bound our country to New Zealand in times of war as well as peace, we honour and pay tribute to all who have died while serving in the forces of our constant friend and ally New Zealand.

May they all rest with God.

2.10 Anzac Day Message 2001

Today is my sixth and last Anzac Day as Governor-General. I am spending it with our troops in East Timor.

Being there will reinforce for me the continuity of the spirit of Anzac. Two years ago at Gallipoli, I tried to explain what that spirit means to us Australians: 'courage and endurance, and duty and love of country, and mateship, and good humour and the survival of a sense of self-worth and decency in the face of dreadful odds'. It also means mutual dependence. It is, as our great historian Manning Clark wrote, 'something too deep for words'.

This year we are celebrating our country's achievements over the century since Federation. The Anzac spirit has been evident through the years right back to the beach at Gallipoli. Recall just some of the anniversaries that fall this year. Ten years since the dispatch of Australian naval personnel in the Gulf War. Fifty years since the Battle of Kapyong in Korea. Sixty years since the capture of Bardia in Libya by the Australian 6th Division. Sixty years also since the siege of Tobruk, the sinking of HMAS *Sydney* off the Western Australian coast with tragic loss of life, and in December, 60 years since the outbreak of war with Japan in which some 17,000 Australians would pay the ultimate sacrifice. Nor should we forget that 14 years before the Anzacs landed at Gallipoli, on the very day of our Federation, two companies of the Queensland Mounted Infantry Regiment were involved in hostilities in South Africa, sustaining the first Australian casualties in the Boer War.

The tradition of Anzac is a long and proud one. It inspires our nation. In this our Centenary of Federation Year, let us express our pride and gratitude for the contribution and sacrifice made by the members of the armed forces, those serving and those who have gone before. And in this our second century, let us pursue tolerance and mutual understanding and rededicate our country to the cause of peace.

3

Reconciliation and Recognition

3.0 Editor's note

Writing to Queen Elizabeth on 7 August 1997, William Deane said, 'Progress towards reconciliation between Australia's indigenous peoples and the nation as a whole remains slow. It is, however, being made.' He went on to inform Her Majesty: 'An independant member of Parliament (Ms Pauline Hanson) has been making intolerant and ignorant remarks which have proved divisive domestically and done considerable damage to Australia's image in some of our neighbouring Asian countries.' After One Nation did well in the 1998 Queensland election, winning 11 seats, Deane wrote at some length to the Queen on 26 June 1998. He outlined the concerns of rural voters during difficult economic times and went on to say: 'In such a rural environment, it is perhaps not surprising that the party which can make completely unfunded promises and invoke latent resentment towards particular sections of the community, such as Asian migrants and Aborigines, should have obtained a level of support which had not been anticipated by most politicians and political commentators. For example, One Nation has adopted a policy of abolishing all native Aboriginal title to land notwithstanding the fact that existing Commonwealth legislation or constitutional constraints preclude the valid implementation of such a policy by either the Queensland or Commonwealth parliament. Unfortunately, the increased level of support for such a party with such policies puts real pressure on the mainstream conservative parties to depart from the standards of decency and tolerance which would otherwise have been accepted as being beyond question.' By 30 September 1998, Sir William was predicting 'that the One Nation Party will win one or two places in the Senate but will otherwise lapse into insignificance'.

In preparation for the royal visit to Australia in March 2000, Sir William wrote at considerable length to the Queen four days before her arrival offering 'some comments about some aspects of the current political and social scene in this country'. The topic to which he devoted most attention was Aboriginal reconciliation. He wrote:

> As Your Majesty may know, this year is the final year of the ten-year life of the Council for Aboriginal Reconciliation, whose chairwoman, Ms Evelyn Scott. Your Majesty will meet on Monday, 20 March. It is intended that on 27 May the Council will be delivering to me and others, and making public, its final text of a possible document of reconciliation. In the course of this year's Australia Day address I said:
>
>> In May, we will all have an opportunity to seek national consensus on the draft Document which the Council for Aboriginal Reconciliation will present after years of work. With goodwill on all sides, we can reach that consensus. If we do, it will reflect the real progress which we've made in recent years. And, while there'll still be much further to go, we'll have reached an important milestone in the journey towards true and lasting reconciliation.
>
> Much of the discussion of reconciliation has turned on the Prime Minister's firmly held view that it is not appropriate for the political leadership of this generation to make any form of official apology for events in the past for which they bear no direct responsibility. More recently the focus has been on suggested inconsistency between the Prime Minister's statement on election night in 1998 that he would work towards achieving lasting reconciliation by the end of this year and his recent statement that he now considers it undesirable to concentrate on dates and that he does not believe that the target of the end of this year is, in any event, a realistic one. Some of the discussion also turns on differing emphases placed on providing for the health, housing and other physical needs of indigenous communities as against dealing with the psychological

and spiritual elements that are also the subject of the movement towards reconciliation. Although it is of course the case that reconciliation would be on a different path if the Prime Minister had different views relating to it, commentators can exaggerate the issues. Indigenous leaders have indicated their preparedness to move beyond the apology issue and only yesterday the deputy chair of the Council, and Australian of the Year, Sir Gustav Nossel, said the members of the Council 'are not going to die in a ditch or be seriously diverted from the grave purpose which unites us here by this question of the apology'.

The focus on indigenous issues has also been sharpened by the recent suicide in gaol in Darwin of a young Aboriginal from Groot Island imprisoned for minor theft. The suicide has drawn attention to the mandatory sentencing laws of the Northern Territory and Western Australia which operate to remove any discretion from judges in dealing with property offences. However minor the theft and regardless of personal circumstances, a finding of guilt on a third occasion leads automatically to imprisonment. It has a disproportionate effect on the Aboriginal population and, as we know from the Royal Commission on Aboriginal Deaths in Custody established in the late 1980s, suicide by Aboriginals in prison is all too common. Whether those laws are inconsistent with Australia's international obligations as a signatory of UN Conventions such as that dealing with the rights of children has been reported as being considered by the UN High Commissioner for Refugees following a request to the Secretary-General, Mr Kofi Annan, by the Leader of the Opposition. The laws have been criticised by many, including former Prime Minister, Malcolm Fraser, and former Chief Justices, Sir Harry Gibbs, Sir Anthony Mason and Sir Gerard Brennan. The Commonwealth Parliament could legislate to override the mandatory sentencing laws, quite simply in the case of the Northern Territory using its plenary powers relating to territories, and more controversially in the case of Western Australia using the external affairs power. Although many in the Government, including the Prime Minister, are not in favour of the mandatory sentencing laws, whether the

> Commonwealth should so intervene raises sensitive issues of Commonwealth-State/Territory relations. The matter will come to a head before long as the Opposition and Australian Democrats are expected to combine to pass a Private Members Bill in the Senate and there is speculation about some Government Members crossing the floor in support of passage in the House of Representatives.

After National Reconciliation Week 2000, Sir William wrote again to the Queen: 'On Saturday, 27 May, there was a large ceremony at the Opera House in the course of which the Council for Aboriginal Reconciliation presented its Declaration Towards Reconciliation to 14 national leaders including myself, the Prime Minister and the Premiers and Chief Ministers of all the States and Territories. The ceremony was marred by very noisy shouting and interjections while the Prime Minister was speaking which made it impossible to hear what he was saying for a large part of his speech. Otherwise it was very impressive. On the Sunday, the largest March that has been held in Sydney for very many years took place over the Harbour Bridge to show support for Aboriginal reconciliation. Somewhere between 150,000 and 500,000 people are estimated to have marched. It would seem that halfway between those two figures (ie 300,000) is probably a correct estimate. Yesterday a similar march of tens of thousands of people took place in Brisbane. For the moment, the subject of Aboriginal reconciliation is in the forefront of political discussion. Unfortunately, the plight of indigenous Australians remains as desperate as ever.'

The defeat of the 2023 Voice Referendum makes a revisiting of Sir William's insights all the more necessary.

3.1 The Launching Of 'The Tent Of Meeting', Canberra, 8 November 1996

This is a natural and traditional meeting place. The name 'Canberra' itself is, as you probably know, an anglicised version of an Aboriginal word metaphorically referring to the plain between the mountains. Before the Europeans came, indeed when I was a boy living in this city, this site looked down over the Canberra plain through which the Molonglo River flowed. Out there to the right was and is Pialligo, Aboriginal for 'meeting place'. In pre-European times, a number of Aboriginal tribes would meet on spots such as this during their journeys across the region to the mountains. Among other things, they met for the annual Bogong moth hunting expeditions. Now, of course, Canberra has assumed a different importance in our modern Australia as a 'meeting place' for the representatives of the whole nation.

The temporary tent to be erected today on this site is intended to be seen and used as a meeting place. It will, we all hope, also be a forerunner of a permanent National Centre for Australian Christianity and Culture. Its underlying theme is one of reconciliation. The essence of reconciliation is genuine tolerance, understanding and respect. Hopefully, the meetings of people and minds that will take place here will encourage reconciliation between different segments and sections of our country: reconciliation, in fulfilment of the modern ecumenical movement, between the various denominations of the Christian Church; reconciliation between our nation and the Aboriginal peoples who constitute such an important part of it; reconciliation between all the Australian people regardless of their racial, ethnic or religious backgrounds or cultures.

Apart from the Aborigines, we Australians are all immigrants or descended from immigrants. Our strength is that, while we immediately or more distantly came from all the regions and all the races of the world, we are united as one people, one nation. The approach, the ethos and the conviction which underlie that strength and that unity, and which have long enjoyed bipartisan support in the Australian Parliament, is that of multiculturalism. That is a long word. However one precisely defines it, its essence is respect for, and genuine tolerance of, the different national, racial, ethnic and religious backgrounds and cultures from which our citizens come. All our citizens are and must be subject to the overriding loyalties and obligations of their Australian citizenship and their duties under valid Australian laws. Subject to those obligations and duties, however, they are entitled to cherish with affection, with respect and with pride, the habits, customs, cultures and traditions which they or their forebears have brought from the lands or regions of their birth. Multiculturalism does not mean that those habits, customs, cultures or traditions are immune from examination or reasoned criticism within Australia. It does, however, mean that, within the limits that are consistent with the overriding obligations and loyalties of Australian citizenship and with all the duties imposed by valid Australian laws, our citizens are entitled to expect and demand that the mutual respect and tolerance which are of the essence of multiculturalism should be encouraged and, in some circumstances, protected. The reason why that is so is that to undermine that mutual respect or to defy or deny that tolerance within our land is to defy or to deny the very basis of our Australian nation. Once it is recognised that we are, with all our cultural, ethnic and religious backgrounds, truly one people, one nation, it follows that whatever or whoever diminishes any of us diminishes our nation and us all.

In recent months, it has at times seemed that tolerance and mutual respect were under attack in our country and that, notwithstanding the very nature of our community, multiculturalism itself was being assailed. It has also, at times, seemed that the facts relating to the past history and present plight of the Aborigines in our land were being distorted and that the critical importance of reconciliation between our nation and the Aboriginal peoples who form part of it was being denied. We owe it to ourselves and to our country to ensure that any such attacks and distortions or denials are never allowed to prevail, or to create the impression that they are prevailing, over the basic qualities of decency, mutual respect and tolerance upon which our multicultural nation was built and which still underpin it.

Let those of us who are gathered here today resolve that the Tent of Meeting on this site, and the National Centre which will follow it, will make an important contribution to the preservation and advancement of those national qualities and, through them, to progress towards the ultimate goal of true and informed national reconciliation.

3.2 The Australian Reconciliation Convention, Melbourne, 27 May 1997

One of the remarkable things about the debates at the Constitutional Conventions which preceded the establishment of the Australian nation on 1 January 1901 is the almost complete absence in them of reference to the country's indigenous peoples. As I read the record of those debates, there is only one example of anything even approaching a serious expression of interest or concern about the Aborigines. Significantly, it is to be found in the comments of a New Zealand delegate, Captain Russell, at the 1891 Sydney Convention. Having expressed the view that New Zealand's relations with the Maoris must be left without 'interruption' and that questions of native title were 'of very grave moment' in that Colony, he is recorded as saying:

> And so, in the colonies of northern Australia, you yourself may yet find that you have difficulties unforeseen to cope with. It is true that the native races of the more settled portions of Australia have given you but little trouble, and you have dealt with them summarily, but possibly when you go to northern Australia you will find there a race more resolute and more difficult to deal with.

The only recorded reaction to those comments was a monosyllabic 'no' from Mr Playford, a South Australian delegate. Captain Russell responded to that reaction by saying that he bowed 'to the wisdom and experience of those who have already had to deal with them'.

New Zealand was not represented at the subsequent debates in Adelaide, Sydney and Melbourne in which the final form of the *Constitution* was settled without any substantive discussion either of the circumstances or future of the Aboriginal peoples or whether it was or was not desirable that the new Commonwealth be entrusted with any responsibility in relation to them.

Looking back to the last decade of the nineteenth century, one can do little more than speculate about why it was that the founders of our nation paid no regard in the Constitutional debates to the plight of the Aboriginal peoples of the various Colonies or to whether some provision for their welfare or interests should be made in the Charter of the new nation which they were framing. By and large, those founders were otherwise good and decent men. Yet they appear to have simply ignored the tragedy of the circumstances of the new nation's indigenous people and any responsibility of the new nation to address or resolve their problems.

Those were, of course, times in which assumptions of white, or sometimes, white British, superiority were matters of basic conviction or even loyalty and in which racial intolerance and disdain were the entrenched norm. In that context, if one must speculate about explanations for the absence of any real discussion of the Aboriginal peoples or their plight or legitimate claims, the most likely explanation is not ignorance or unawareness of what was, by then, the terrible circumstances of our continent's indigenous peoples. It is that there was an unspoken consensus that, putting to one side those Aborigines who were assimilated, the Aborigines were a disappearing problem which could simply be ignored. In that regard, let me digress to quote two intelligent contemporaneous observers of the Australian scene. The first is the English novelist Anthony Trollope who, during 1871 and 1872, visited all of the Australian Colonies and is said to have probably seen 'more of them than any other traveller had done up to that time'. He was lionised by local society and exposed to the views of those in positions of authority. His conclusion about the Aborigines was:

'Of the Australian black man we may certainly say that he has to go. That he should perish without unnecessary suffering should be the aim of all who are concerned in the matters.'

The second is Captain Wharton FRS, writing in 1893 as editor of a transcription of Cook's log book. In a passage quoted by Gaudron J and myself in our joint judgment in *Mabo v Queensland*, he wrote of the Aborigines:

> .. although treated by the coarser order of colonists as wild beasts to be extirpated, those who have studied them have formed favourable opinions of their intelligence. The more savage side of their disposition being, however, so very apparent, it is not astonishing that, brought into contact with white settlers, who equally consider that they have a right to settle, the aborigines are rapidly disappearing.

Whatever be the true explanation, the *Constitution*, as adopted, contained but two references to the Aboriginal peoples of Australia. Both had their origin in the work of those who gathered on the Queensland Government steamer, the *Lucinda*, over Easter 1891 in the course of the Sydney Convention. Both were dismissive or negative in nature.

The first reference excluded 'the Aboriginal race in any State' from s 51(xxvi)'s grant of legislative power to the Commonwealth Parliament to make laws with respect to 'the people of any race ... for whom it is deemed necessary to make special laws'. There was no discussion at all about that exclusion in the course of the Convention debates.

The other reference to Aborigines in the Constitution was s 127's instruction that, '[i]n reckoning the numbers of the people of the Commonwealth or of a State or other part of the Commonwealth, aboriginal natives shall not be counted'. On two occasions, there was some cursory discussion of that provision in the Convention Debates. That discussion, brief though it was, discloses some confusion among the delegates about its effect. Upon analysis, however, s 127 was clearly of general application. In particular, it applied both to the provisions dealing with numbers of parliamentary representatives and to the provisions dealing with financial responsibilities and entitlements. Not surprisingly, the section came increasingly to be seen as a constitutional declaration of the essential worthlessness and irrelevance of Australia's indigenous peoples. Indeed, viewed against the background of the times and the indifference displayed in the Convention debates, that is precisely what it was.

Constraints of time preclude me from tracing in any detail the emergence of demands for constitutional amendments both to remove s 127's directive that Aboriginal natives be not counted in reckoning the numbers of the Australian people and to confer legislative competence upon the Commonwealth with respect to their welfare. I shall confine myself to a brief outline of some central facts and events.

In 1911, after the Commonwealth took over responsibility for the Northern Territory, a distinguished deputation of scientific, commercial, religious and political men urged the Prime Minister, Mr Fisher: to appoint forthwith, a Commission of Inquiry, with a view to the drawing up of a comprehensive scheme for dealing with all the native obligations of the Commonwealth; to establish a separate Department of Native Affairs; and to introduce such legislation as would secure the welfare of the Aborigines in the Northern Territory. Their urging was unproductive.

In 1929 and 1930, numerous submissions were made to the Royal Commission on the Constitution to the effect that the Commonwealth Parliament should possess legislative powers to make laws with respect to Aborigines. In the 1931 Report of the Royal Commission, a majority rejected those submissions. However, in a strong dissent, a minority accepted them pointing out that it was the responsibility of the nation as a whole to care for the nation's indigenous peoples regardless of the particular State or Territory in which they happened to live.

Thereafter, the campaign for amendment of the provisions of the

Constitution referring to the Aboriginal people intensified. War intervened in 1939. The fact that thousands of Aborigines enlisted and fought in the Australian forces during the war served to underline the validity of the Aboriginal claims. When, in 1944, the Australian Government sought, through a referendum, to obtain additional legislative competence for the post-war period, it included, among the 14 heads of legislative power which it sought, the power to make laws with respect to the welfare of the Aboriginal peoples. The then Leader of the Opposition, Mr Menzies, indicated support for the grant of that particular legislative power but explained that, in circumstances where a single affirmative or negative vote was required to be given in respect of all fourteen heads of power, the Opposition was constrained to advocate a negative answer to them all. In the result, the referendum was defeated and s 127 and s 50(xxiv) remained unqualified.

It was in the late 1950s that the cry for recognition of the legitimate claims of the Aboriginal peoples of Australia assumed the dimensions of a national crusade. In 1957, a film showing the terrible plight of Aborigines affected by nuclear experiments in Central Australia was shown to a horrified audience in Sydney. In the same year, the petitions seeking constitutional amendments commenced to flow. Thereafter, the focus of the crusade became firmly fixed on the removal of s 127 from the *Constitution* and the conferral upon the national Parliament of legislative power with respect to the welfare of the Aboriginal peoples. There were, of course, other objectives in the fight for indigenous equality and justice. Thus, in 1965, there set out from Sydney University, under the leadership of Charles Perkins, a bus-load of 'freedom fighters' who dramatically challenged the practical segregation of Aborigines in public places and facilities in a number of New South Wales towns. In the following year, 1966, Vincent Lingiari led a walk-off by the Gurindji workers on Wave Hill Station in a strike which won wide popular support around the nation and which marked the commencement of the Aboriginal land rights movement. Nonetheless, the immediate and central objective was constitutional reform.

Over the years leading up to 1967, there were many organisations, notably FCAATSI, and many thousands of individuals who, in one way or another, joined in the crusade. It would be impossible to list them all. The leaders included Aborigines such as Pastor Doug Nicholls, Pearl Gibbs, Oodgeroo Noonucal, Charles Dixon, and Joe McGuinness. They also included non-Aborigines such as Charles Duguid, Shirley Andrews, Don Dunstan, Gordon Bryant, WC Wentworth, Barry Christophers, Jack and Jean Horner and those two remarkable women, Faith Bandler and Jessie Street. And, as those around me demonstrate, they included many others, both Aboriginal and non-Aboriginal.

Ultimately, when the petitions had become a torrent and popular support had become an avalanche, the Parliament enacted legislation providing that the question whether s 127 and the exclusion of Aborigines in s 51(xxvi) should be deleted from the Constitution should be submitted to the Australian people. The referendum was held on this day exactly 30 years ago. The result was overwhelming. In all, an affirmative answer to the question was given by well over 90 percent of those who voted – 5,183,113 to 527,007 – and by a majority in every State of the Commonwealth. No other constitutional referendum in the history of this country has been carried by such a majority. In that regard, it is relevant to mention that another proposal submitted for determination at the same time in relation to repeal of the constitutional nexus between the numbers of the two Houses of Parliament was roundly defeated.

What, one is inevitably led to ask, is the present significance of that referendum whose 30th anniversary we celebrate today? That question can be answered in terms of legislative power. More importantly, it can be answered in terms of social and political significance.

In so far as legislative power is concerned, one occasionally reads suggestions that the effect of the exclusion of 'the Aboriginal race in any State' from s 51(xxvi) was merely to exclude the making of laws with respect to Aborigines from the scope of the grant of legislative power contained in that particular sub-section while leaving completely unaffected the more general legislative powers conferred by the many other sub-sections of s 51 of the *Constitution*. If that suggestion were correct, the deletion of the exclusion was of little importance. With due respect, however, the suggestion is misconceived. It ignores the well-known principle enunciated by Dixon CJ in *Attorney-General v Schmidt* and confirmed as recently as 1990 by a unanimous High Court that:

> ... when you have ... an express power, subject to a safeguard, restrictions or qualifications, to legislate on a particular subject or to a particular effect, it is in accordance with the soundest principles of interpretation to treat that as inconsistent with any construction of other powers conferred in the context which would mean that they included the same subject or produced the same effect and so authorized the same kind of legislation but without the safeguard, restriction or qualification.[6]

In other words, the effect of the exclusion of 'the Aboriginal race in any State' in s 51(xxvi) had been, while it remained, to prevent the enactment, under any of the heads of Commonwealth power, of a law which could properly be characterised as a law with respect to the Aboriginal race in any State. That meant that, while the exclusion remained, the Commonwealth lacked legislative power to make any law designed for the special benefit of the Aboriginal people in any of the States. In contrast, once the exclusion was deleted, the Commonwealth, under s 51(xxvi), possessed plenary legislative power to make any special laws which it deemed necessary for the welfare of the Aboriginal peoples.

From the wider social and political point of view, the significance of the carriage of the 1967 referendum is beyond

---

[6] (1961) 105 CLR 361, 371-2.

measure. It marked the first great turning point in the relationship between Australia's indigenous people and the nation of which they form such an important part. Its removal of s 127 constituted an overwhelming rejection by the Australian people as a whole of past notions that the Aboriginal peoples were somehow inferior or worthless. In the context of the referendum campaign and of what had been said on both sides of politics, the removal of s 51(xxvi)'s exclusionary clause rightly and unambiguously placed on the national Parliament primary responsibility in respect of the nation's indigenous people. In that regard, those who make much of the fact that a legislative power does not necessarily carry with it responsibility for making legislative provision ignore the enduring practical significance of a referendum in which an unprecedented majority of the Australian people made clear that they saw the primary responsibility for the Aboriginal peoples as thereafter being that of the Commonwealth Government. Perhaps most important for present purposes, the joint campaign of indigenous and non-indigenous Australians in support of the referendum and its carriage by more than 90 percent of the people constituted a first major step along the road to true reconciliation.

In the euphoria that followed the passage of the referendum, it might have seemed to some that reconciliation had been achieved. Looking back, we now know how mistaken any such belief or hope would have been. In 1967, the policy of removal – often forcible removal – of Aboriginal children from their parents, their families and their people was still being actively implemented in some parts of the country. Let me pause for a moment and say to my Aboriginal fellow Australians how profoundly sorry I personally am that those things were done. In 1967, as now, the health and living conditions of most Aborigines were appalling. In the Northern Territory, the Wave Hill strike continued. As did Aboriginal exploitation. The legal and factual fallacy of *terra nullius* was still mistakenly seen as the law of the land. In many places, legal and practical discrimination and segregation of

Aborigines remained. Yet, notwithstanding all those things, the plain fact remains that, on 27 May 1967, the sparks struck by many individuals in different parts of our country became a flame which continues to burn and which will reproach all Australians for so long as we remain unreconciled.

May I conclude with a plea? I think most of you are aware of how conscious I am of the current plight of Australia's indigenous people: among other things, of the appalling state of Aboriginal health,unemployment, particularly youth unemployment, education, living conditions, lack of self-esteem. Of how much there is to cause discouragement and distress. As I pointed out in the inaugural Lingiari Lecture last August, those terrible problems are the present consequences of past oppression and injustice. We will not achieve true reconciliation unless and until we address and resolve them at least to the extent that it can be seen that we are making real progress towards the position where the future prospects of an Aboriginal baby are comparable to those of a non-Aboriginal one. Nor will we achieve true reconciliation unless we address the problems of the spirit as well as those of the body. Yet, on this anniversary of the 1967 referendum, I ask you to pause and look up to that which is positive. To acknowledge the positive things that have been done and achieved since 1967. And to realise that one of the great advances of the last 30 years has been that the bond between those Australians who participated in the crusade leading up to the 1967 referendum has expanded to encompass vast numbers of Australians, both indigenous and non-indigenous, who now, in their different ways, are committed to pursue the cause of true justice and equality for our country's indigenous peoples. If those of us who are convinced of the rightness and urgency of that cause, look round and appreciate the depth of our mutual commitment to it and to one another, we will gain the confidence, the strength and the wisdom to speak more quietly, more tolerantly, more constructively and more persuasively to our fellow Australians who are yet to be convinced. And if we reach out to touch one another's hands, we will demonstrate to all Australians that we can, in the words of that old man of the Gurindji people, walk forward together as friends and equals. If we do those things, we can be certain of one thing: that is that, however difficult the road to true reconciliation may be, we will ultimately reach its end.

3.3 'Women and Reconciliation', Address by Lady Helen Deane at the Australian Reconciliation Convention, Melbourne, 27 May 1997

Let me commence by acknowledging the Kulin Nation upon whose ancestral lands we are gathered.

There are times when hurtful and harmful things are said and done which raise questions about our commitment to the achievement of true reconciliation between our nation as a whole and the Aboriginal and Torres Strait Islander peoples. Nonetheless, there is, I feel, broad national acceptance of the proposition that the achievement – somehow, somewhere – of such reconciliation must be in the forefront of our national objectives and aspirations.

To identify, accept and make a commitment to an objective or aspiration is, however, but a beginning. The road to reconciliation is a very difficult one. But it is not closed. Clearly, however, we will not reach its end unless and until there exists the necessary level of mutual tolerance, understanding and respect. The focus of my comments this afternoon is upon how we can help reach that level of mutual tolerance, understanding and respect through communication between indigenous and non-indigenous women.

I have a profound belief that women are now ready to work towards reconciliation in the way that women can collectively approach most of life's significant challenges. By sitting down together, by identifying with each other's problems and valuing each other's strengths, by listening, and by finding practical ways to offer support, by hard and unselfish work and by quiet leadership and influence.

My essential message is this: reconciliation must ultimately reflect consensus; consensus about past maltreatment and injustice; consensus about present disadvantage flowing from that past maltreatment and injustice; consensus about the minimum which we must in partnership do to redress it; and consensus about the future.

Necessarily, the basis of any such consensus lies in communication; communication which allows us to set aside prejudices, some of them deeply held and familiar, and which encourages us to work towards finding common ground.

For my part, I am committed to doing what I can to support the achievement of reconciliation – if possible, by the centenary of the establishment of our nation on 1 January 2001. I believe that commitment is shared by many other non-indigenous women. In my case, it has largely flowed from what I have learnt and am learning of the history, the problems and the hopes of indigenous people, especially the women. I now know that, while there may be some room for disagreement about the extent, there is simply no room for denying the facts, and the injustice, of the past killing and the past oppression, including the taking of the children, of the Aboriginal peoples. I also know that, in a context where the life expectancy of an Aboriginal baby is almost 20 years less than that of a non-Aboriginal one, there is little room for denying the terrible extent of the present disadvantage and plight of the Aboriginal peoples.

Until I moved with my husband to Government House 16 months ago, I was like most Australian women in that I'd had very little contact with indigenous women. By and large, I suppose I was affected by the same kinds of uncomfortable stereotypes and images that influence many other Australians. Since then, I have had the opportunity of visiting a number of Aboriginal communities and meeting many Aborigines. I note that the leading Aboriginal women I have met include some who are role models not only for other Aboriginal women but for Australian women generally.

I have learnt many things from those visits and that contact. Among them is that a major obstacle to reconciliation is apprehension and reluctance about face-to-face communication.

Meaningful communication and personal associations overcome the exaggerated sense of difference which flows from ignorance. So I have become increasingly conscious, through communication and listening to the stories of Aboriginal women, that their concerns and aspirations are very similar to my own. Indigenous women are concerned about the welfare of their families, about having hope for the future, about stopping their children from getting into trouble. What indigenous women want for their families and communities – good health, effective education, a minimum standard of housing, safety, self-respect, a sense of place and purpose – is very much the same as what I want for my own family and for those who are close to me.

The erosion of indigenous culture, in many cases, has left women picking up the pieces of their communities – taking on key roles, mostly unpaid, as carers, counsellors, organisers and advocates. They aspire, like all women, to full equality of opportunity, to be treated with respect and protected from exploitation and violence and to have the diversity of their roles and responsibilities recognised and valued. Especially as the performance of Aboriginal girls in the classrooms commonly outstrips that of the boys, they are aware that the guidance and the future of their people lie increasingly in their hands. Most are wary and many are distrustful of non-indigenous women. Few identify with us. Like most of us, however, almost all respond to an extended hand of friendship.

I believe that if we women can understand those things a bit better, if we can adjust our own attitudes and show a little more tolerance and concern, we can go a long way towards resolving any antagonisms, apprehensions or distrust which may exist between us. Communication at the public level seems so often to be competitive and angry. Once women sit down together and communicate at the community or personal level, finding that common ground will no longer seem so difficult.

Indeed, I am convinced that the barriers to communication between non-indigenous and indigenous women at the private level have already started to come down. There is a growing wish among women to communicate and an increase in their ability to do so. There is a growing awareness among women that communication between them is possibly the most effective way to change the relationship between all of us Australians and to create a context in which true reconciliation may become a practical reality rather than an ambitious and largely theoretical dream.

Over the last couple of months, in particular, women's organisations and individuals across the country have mobilised their considerable networks in a nationwide discussion on women and reconciliation. Stimulated through a project of the Australian Institute of Women's Research and Policy at Griffith University and the Council for Aboriginal Reconciliation, more than 20 national, regional and professional women's groups have been involved in activities leading up to this Convention.

Meetings have been arranged, booklets and flyers and petitions have been produced, and I understand that the phones between organisations have been running hot.

But, primarily, this first phase of what I hope will develop into a major campaign has provided opportunities for women to meet, to talk and to listen. We women can help each other in many ways. But we must start with the realisation that there is so much that we can learn. And so many things which we must face up to.

The written history of our nation has been largely silent on the relationship between non-indigenous and indigenous women. The story of that relationship is not a happy one. Thus, it was often women who implemented the policies, often tragically well-intentioned, that separated Aboriginal children from their families. More generally, one must, looking back, express regret that more women did not actively oppose or speak out against so many other things which were done to indigenous people over so many years.

There were, of course, from the beginning, the shining exceptions – some known, many unknown. I'm sure that a number of speakers over the next couple of days will emphasise the importance of sharing history. And stories will be told, I hope, of some of the non-indigenous and indigenous men and women who have striven, since the very beginning, to promote justice and equity.

Listening to those stories, and to Aboriginal women who can speak of the legacy of their past suffering and grief, will hopefully provide the basis upon which we can move on together in friendship towards true mutual understanding, respect and equality.

Overall, the Griffith University and Reconciliation Council project highlights five central themes which have come up time and time again. These are:

- firstly, the need for women to provide forums for indigenous women – indeed for all women – to `get to the truth'. Of course, there are many truths when it comes to re-telling tales of the past, but it is clearly important that women be invited to tell their own stories, and to be heard;
- secondly, the importance of women encouraging tolerance in their children;
- thirdly, the role that non-indigenous women can play in helping indigenous women to know their rights, and thereby, gain self-esteem;
- fourthly, the importance of encouraging indigenous women to participate in decision-making activities at a community level, including local government and school boards, and all manner of community advisory bodies; and
- fifthly, the overwhelming need for more education about indigenous history and cultures, within schools, and also within professional and community organisations.

The power of storytelling as a vehicle for communication and reconciliation has been a major thread in the women's project. It has provided the raw material for women to see into each other's lives. And to ask questions not only of one another but of themselves. For example, how would I have felt if I had sent my children to school one day and found that they had been taken from me forever when I went to pick them up? How would I feel to have lost my mother, my community and my language? How would I feel to know that, whatever I say and whatever I do, I am likely to face ignorance and prejudice from some sections of society.

It is this personal sharing of everyday experience that puts the current situation of many indigenous women into some context – the health problems, the education difficulties of their children, the often atrocious living conditions, the effects of alcohol and drug abuse and violence. It's not that we non-indigenous women haven't or hadn't heard the statistics. But hearing the women's stories face-to-face transforms those statistics from empty figures into a human reality.

We women and our organisations must seize and take advantage of the present widely felt longing for true reconciliation. The communication must continue and the stories must be told. We must identify with one another. We must reach a consensus about the nature and extent of indigenous disadvantage and plight and the establishment of an effective partnership and effective programs to address and resolve them. If we do these things, the voices of women, and there are enough of us, will make a difference.

My hope is that through the women's project, and through this convention and its aftermath, we will be able to establish a forceful coalition of women's groups to further the process of reconciliation at a personal and community level.

We must not let the momentum be lost.

3.4 The Opening of New Premises for the Bangarra Dance Theatre, Sydney, 11 June 1997

Bangarra represents something truly wonderful, exciting and very special about this country of ours. Through their dance, contemporary Australians are able to enter the ancient, and in a sense timeless, Aboriginal worlds of our continent. And yet, as the critical responses to its work reveals, Bangarra has also developed a new language of dance through which contemporary urban Aboriginal people are able to express themselves, their ideas and their spirits. Drawing particularly on the culture and dance of the Yirrkala community, the Company has fused the traditional aspects of Aboriginal and Torres Strait Islander life with modern choreography and movement to create a style that is innovative, electrifying and truly Australian.

It has been said that Bangarra represents the experience of the rising generation of indigenous people: the young, largely living in the cities, who know and have experienced the enduring consequences of past injustice. Those young people are, through the power of their art, transforming that knowledge and experience into a rich, emotional and creative form of expression that is hopefully entering the consciousness of our nation. Even while they are confronting and portraying stories of great heartbreak, their vision and their talent teach those who are prepared to watch and listen that the human spirit is able to rise above despair. At the same time, the fire of Bangarra helps light the difficult road towards true reconciliation. In that regard, I personally believe that the fact that Aboriginal art is now speaking so powerfully to us all as Australians – through dance, through music, through the iconography of traditional and contemporary painting – is an important positive indication that somehow, somewhere, we will ultimately – and together – find the end of that road.

I notice that, in the spring edition of the Bangarra Newsletter last year, Stephen Page expressed the hope that, just as Australians have begun to recognise the value of indigenous culture through the arts, so they will also recognise and support the basic needs and rights of Aboriginal and Torres Strait Islander people in their daily lives. That is a hope which I believe the great majority of Australians share.

Clearly enough, as all of us – both indigenous and non-indigenous – who are joined in the quest for true reconciliation know, we will not achieve it until we address and resolve the current plight of the indigenous Australians – as regards, among other things, health, unemployment, particularly youth unemployment, education and living conditions. We must first reach the stage where we are at least approaching the position where the life expectancy and future prospects of an Aboriginal baby are comparable to those of a non-Aboriginal one. But, equally clearly, we have no real prospect of reaching that stage unless we also effectively address the terrible problems of the spirit as well as those of the body.

In the eight years since its foundation, the Bangarra Dance Theatre has done much to identify and help resolve those problems of the spirit which are a living legacy of what was done and lost in the past. Equally important, Bangarra has, through the magic of its performances, become a powerful instrument for inspiring both non-indigenous and indigenous Australians to come together and to seek real equality and true and lasting reconciliation. I have no doubt that, from the security of its new home, Bangarra and its members will continue to stir and speak to the longing within our hearts for all those things.

3.5 Eulogy For Dr HC 'Nugget' Coombs, St Mary's Cathedral, Sydney, 14 November 1997

Even as a boy in Western Australia, Nugget Coombs had been sympathetic and attentive to the voices of indigenous Australians. But it was not until his retirement from the Reserve Bank in 1968, and his appointment as Chair of the Council for Aboriginal Affairs by Prime Minister Holt – as a 'job with a challenge' following the 1967 referendum – that he seriously devoted himself to Aboriginal issues. They became, and remained over the next three decades, the principal focus of his life and work. He began as the public servant instructing what should be done. Nonetheless, as a young Gallarwuy Yunapingu had made clear to him, he was quickly accepted by the Aborigines as their friend. He stayed to listen. To live with Aborigines as friends and equals. To learn from them. And to argue passionately for their welfare. And for their right to be different. Different in their human, material and spiritual relationships – to each other and to the land and its resources. To be part of and have equal access to non-Aboriginal society if they chose; but also, as he put it, 'to be able to conduct their society in accordance with their ways of thinking, educate their children in relation to that and to conduct their own ceremonies'.

Each of us, in his or her own way, has much to learn from the wisdom of what Nugget Coombs had to say and from the lessons which he taught. If we do learn, we will, hopefully, make further progress towards the fulfilment of his vision for his country and his country men and women. That vision was essentially one of reconciliation, multiculturalism and the protection and enhancement of our environment. It was concisely expressed by him on Australia Day in 1982 in words which concluded:

> an intimate love of the Australian earth itself which will, for Aboriginal, for European, and for Asian Australians, provide the emotional bond uniting us in a shared identity which offers both community and respected independence. If we achieve that love and realise the pleasure in diversity ... we may all come to *enjoy* being Australian which would, I believe, be more important than *proud* of being Australian.

Mr John Coombs QC has told me that his father had a habit of asking his children over the dinner table: 'What have you done that's memorable today'? If one asks that question about Nugget

Coombs and his life, the answer is surely 'Almost everything'. If one takes his achievements in any one of the different roles he played in our national life over more than 60 years separately, he was an outstanding Australian in each of them. When one takes his achievements in all of those roles cumulatively, it is apparent that he was, by any measure, a truly great Australian.

May he rest with God.

3.6 The Receiving of an Honorary Doctorate of the Queensland University of Technology, Brisbane, 24 May 1999

Some of you may recall that, when my appointment as Governor-General was announced, I indicated that my wife, Helen, and I hoped, during my period in office, to focus our efforts upon the disadvantaged in our country. At the same time, we indicated that we hoped to do what we could to further the cause of a just and lasting reconciliation between the Aboriginal people and the Australian nation, of which they form such an important part. In the more than three and one-half years since then we have made no secret of the fact that we believe that the achievement of such reconciliation should be one of our country's most important objectives as we move towards a new millennium and our second century of nationhood.

There are, of course, many issues involved. There are matters of the spirit and of spiritual healing which must be addressed if our country's Aboriginal peoples are successfully to overcome the consequences of past dispossession and oppression. On the threshold of those matters is, of course, the basic requirement that our nation as a whole honestly and frankly acknowledges the now incontrovertible facts of our history.

And there are matters of the body – the plain fact that on almost every measure of material well being – in health, welfare, housing, community services, employment, – indigenous people are greatly disadvantaged as against the rest of the Australian population. In that regard, it is unnecessary to do more than quote one plain statistic: an Aboriginal baby born in this country today has, on present figures and on average, a life expectancy of almost 20 years less than that of a non-Aboriginal baby. Think of that: almost 20 years. And the statistics indicate that the discrepancy is still widening.

In each of the areas of disadvantage which I have mentioned, education provides an essential ingredient of successful resolution. There are two aspects of that. The first is better access to full educational opportunities for Aboriginal people themselves. The second is more effective education for the broader community about Aboriginal perspectives, approaches, achievements and problems so that there will, in time to come, be new understandings and a better general recognition of the innate worth of Australia's indigenous peoples and of the extent of the present consequences of past oppression and injustice. In particular, that there will be wider understanding of the fact that problems such as alcoholism, domestic violence and inability to cope or to improve or to communicate effectively do not constitute justification for indifference or refusal to help but are, in truth, themselves part of an overall disadvantage which is entrenched in its nature and heart breaking in its extent.

These days, it is sometimes difficult not to feel discouraged – even depressed – about the slow course of the reconciliation process. Certainly, the path ahead is steep and long and full of obstacles and progress is much slower than I, at least, had hoped for. On the other hand, when one moves closer to those who are also on the journey – when one looks at the myriad projects and institutions where indigenous and non-indigenous Australians are working quietly and helpfully together to further the cause of understanding and equity, of which this University provides but one example – one realises how much has been and is being achieved away from the gaze of the public eye. It is then that one realises that, however far we may have to go on the road to reconciliation, one should occasionally look back and appreciate how far we have travelled. If we do that, those of us who are convinced of the rightness and justice of the cause will speak more quietly, more tolerantly, more constructively and more persuasively to our fellow Australians who are yet to be convinced. For, if we who are convinced do that, I remain hopeful that, however long and difficult the road to true reconciliation may be, we will ultimately reach its end.

3.7 Receiving the Draft Document For Reconciliation, Sydney, 3 June 1999

As the Council for Aboriginal Reconciliation has made plain, it is not necessary for everyone to agree with every sentence or word of the Draft Declaration. Hopefully, however, we do all share the hope that this Draft Document will be the basis of a sincere and constructive round of public consultation and discussion from which there will emerge a nation fully committed to the basic principles of justice, fairness and equality which light the road to true and lasting reconciliation.

The achievement of such reconciliation between indigenous Australians and the nation of which they form such an important part is one of our most important challenges as we approach the second century of our Federation. This Draft Document will play a significant role in helping us meet that challenge. For those of us who are already united in the cause of reconciliation, it will be a source of encouragement and renewal. I share the Council for Aboriginal Reconciliation's hope that it will also serve as a means for Australians generally to give expression to shared aspirations and ideals.

Finally, I make a plea to all Australians – indigenous and non-indigenous. It is that the search for reconciliation be marked by generosity and goodwill on all sides and be free of mere point-scoring and of personal attacks. In that regard, it is important that, in the process of consultation and dialogue that flows from the Draft Document, those of us who are convinced of the rightness of the cause of reconciliation recognise that we will only speak persuasively to our fellow Australians who are yet to be convinced if we speak quietly, reasonably and constructively. That way, and only that way, we can walk together, talk together, care together and achieve together.

If we can do those things, we can be confident that, however long and difficult the road to true reconciliation may be, we will together ultimately reach its end.

3.8 The Opening of the Conference of the Association of Heads of Independent Schools of Australia, Melbourne, 29 June 1999

Looking at your Conference program, I was particularly interested in the themes and subject matter of your Social Issues Day on Thursday, 'Daring to Reconcile'. It is a subject which invites attention to many areas which must inevitably broaden perspectives – multiculturalism and diversity in the school community; the plight of the disadvantaged and the marginalised; the need for tolerance and understanding; for those of us who are Christian, the importance of the ecumenical movement within the Universal Christian Church; and, of course, the great national goal of reconciliation between the Aboriginal and Torres Strait Islander people and the Australian nation as a whole of which they form such an important part. All of these topics – multiculturalism, tolerance, the disadvantaged, the search for Christian unity and for mutual respect and understanding between all religions – are, as many of you know, of great moment to me. But today, I would like to focus my remarks on reconciliation between our nation and its indigenous peoples, and to reaffirm my conviction that the need to effectively address the material and spiritual disadvantages resulting from past dispossession and oppression remains one of the most important challenges facing us Australians as we enter a new century – our second as a nation – and a new millennium.

So far as the material disadvantages of indigenous people are concerned, they are now much more widely known and acknowledged. They include: the inadequacies of much Aboriginal education; the vastly higher than average levels of Aboriginal unemployment, particularly youth unemployment; the deficiencies of Aboriginal housing; the problems of water supply and infrastructure in many Aboriginal communities; and above all the appalling problems relating to Aboriginal health.

It is sometimes said that statistics lie. They do not lie when they identify the extent of those health problems. Nor can those statistics be discounted as bare figures without human content. They tell a story of present human sickness, suffering, dying and death which can be traced to past dispossession, oppression and injustice. It is unnecessary that I do more than quote one of those statistics. It is that an Aboriginal baby born in this country today has, on present figures and on average, a life expectancy of some 18 years less than that of a non-Aboriginal one. And the statistics actually indicate that the discrepancy is still widening. Clearly enough, we will not achieve true reconciliation unless and until we address those problems and resolve them at least to the extent that it can be seen that we are making real progress towards the position where the future prospects of an Aboriginal baby, in terms of health, life expectancy, living conditions and self-esteem, are at least within the same area of discourse as the future prospects of a non-Aboriginal one.

My wife, Helen, and I were in the Northern Territory last week, and saw something of the terrible inroads that disease and premature deaths have been making among the people of Bathurst and Melville Islands – the Tiwi Islands – as they have in Aboriginal communities throughout Northern Australia. Dr Wendy Hoy, of the Menzies School of Health Research in Darwin, has spoken of an epidemic of hypertension, type 2 diabetes, cardiovascular and renal disease evolving among Aboriginal people. Deaths from heart attack and stroke, from diabetes and kidney disease are at rates many times greater than for non-Aborigines – in places up to 15 times greater – and they have been getting worse. For instance, deaths from diabetes, from heart attack and stroke among Aboriginal women in the Northern Territory tripled during the 1980s, and renal failure rates have been doubling every three to four years. The Tiwi Health Board pointed out recently that, of the 2300 people on the Islands, there were only 14 people aged over 70. No wonder they spoke of the Tiwi having 'the worst chronic disease levels of any group in Australia, and possibly any other country'.

That is the sad news. But there is also a good news story. It is that, through the Tiwi Health Board, through the 'Tiwi For Life' program, through the Co-ordinated Care Trial under the auspices of Government, through the great work undertaken by Dr Hoy and the Renal Centre, and above all through the effort and commitment of the people of the Islands to become involved with their own health programs in their own way, the Tiwi people have, in my view, at last reached the turning point.

I do not presume to speak about the impact of dispossession on the *spiritual* lives of indigenous Australians, other than to acknowledge its depth and to express the hope that, through the reconciliation process, a reclamation and a redemption has at least begun. And to note that, the legacy of that dispossession has also had an effect on the spiritual dimension of the Australian community as a whole, both indigenous and non-indigenous as witness the emotional impetus and breadth of the reconciliation movement at the grass roots level in the last few years. Let me illustrate the point by two examples of reconciliation in action. The first is a ceremony which Helen and I attended at Yirrkala in the Gove Peninsula last Thursday.

Between 1932 and 1933, five Japanese and three Europeans were killed by Aborigines in the Peninsula's Caledon Bay area. Not surprisingly, there was an extreme reaction by Government sources and the wider non-indigenous community. Watching events from Mapoom Mission – later to be immortalised by Midnight Oil in their 'Beds are Burning' song – was a young Anthropologist, Donald Thomson, who explained what had happened in terms, later confirmed as accurate, of aggressive and unlawful intrusion on traditional lands and unprovoked abuse, including rape, of indigenous women.

In time, an Aboriginal man, Takeara, was convicted by a jury and sentenced to death by the Supreme Court in Darwin for the murder of one of the Europeans. That was despite the fact that the effect of the evidence was that McColl had handcuffed and raped Takeara's wife and emptied his revolver at him when he sought to intervene. Three sons of the Aboriginal leader of the area, Wongo, were also arrested and convicted. They were sentenced to life imprisonment.

Donald Thomson obtained the backing of a number of community leaders associated with the University of Melbourne and was finally requested by the Commonwealth Government to go to the area to seek to restore peaceful relations. Before going, he visited the three sons of Wongo in Fannie Bay Jail in Darwin and was entrusted by them with a message stick to their father which he delivered to Wongo. In discussions with Thomson, Wongo explained how the killings had all occurred in the defence by his people of their women and their traditional land. He handed to Thomson, as representative of the Government, a second message stick, explaining that the marks inscribed upon it represented 'himself sitting down quietly and maintaining peace among his people'. In his subsequent report to the Commonwealth, Thomson made representations to obtain the release from jail of Wongo's three sons. His suggestion was accepted and, early on Sunday morning 28 June 1936, Thomson took custody of the three men at

Fannie Bay Jail and travelled with them to Arnhem land where they were re-united with Wongo at Yirrkala. In the meantime, Takeara's conviction had been quashed by the High Court of Australia which ordered his immediate release.

The story is remarkable in many respects. I tell it partly because the delivery of the second message stick by Wongo to Thomson as a representative of the Commonwealth Government and the subsequent release of Wongo's three sons seem to me to constitute one of the first incidents of true, albeit localised, reconciliation between indigenous people and our nation as a whole after the devastation of so many years of dispossession and oppression. The main reason that I recount the story is, however, that it seemed to me that the ceremony at Yirrkala only last Thursday was a final component of that instance of reconciliation.

The ceremony was attended by indigenous and non-indigenous people from all parts of the Gove Peninsula. There were seven Aboriginal speakers, including Gatjil Djerrkura, the Chairman of ATSIC, and Galarrwuy Yunupingu, the Chairman of the Northern Land Council, who both come from the area. They all spoke of reconciliation and of the importance not only of reconciliation but also of national unity. The central point of the ceremony, which involved much traditional dancing and formality, occurred when Mrs Dorita Thomson, the widow of Donald Thomson, handed to me, as Governor-General, the two message sticks which had remained in the Thomson family's possession after Donald's death in 1970 – the one from Wongo's sons to their father and the other from Wongo to the representative of the Commonwealth Government. In turn, I entrusted the message sticks to the last living son of Wongo. He accepted them with great dignity on behalf of all the people of the area. There were tears among some of the Aboriginal people present. It was one of the rewarding moments of my life.

There have been countless other example of reconciliation at a personal or local level which I have personally experienced in the three and one-half years since I became Governor-General. The second which I would mention this morning is that of the 'Captive Lives Exhibition' – which was staged in the National Library of Australia in Canberra in 1997. It is currently in Perth, from where it travels to the Australian Museum in Sydney in August, and subsequently to regional Queensland, northern New South Wales, and finally to western Victoria.

The 'Captive Lives Exhibition' is, if measured merely by reference to size or cost, scarcely a major one. But the story which it tells and the manner of the telling combine to make it a profoundly moving experience of national, indeed universal, significance and importance. It is the story of nine essentially gentle and trusting Aboriginal people who were enticed from their homes on Palm Island in North Queensland in 1883 by an American entrepreneur and exhibited as 'uncivilised savages' in Barnum and Bailey's circus and in fair grounds and dime museums in the United States and subsequently in Europe. Within a year one of the nine – a young man of about 21 who had acquired the name of 'Tambo' – was dead. His even younger wife and other companions were prevented from according him the ceremonial rites traditionally seen by their people as essential for the release of the spirit. His body was in fact sold to the owner of a dime museum, mummified and put on display. Within a year of Tambo's death, a further five of the human exhibits, including his young widow, were dead. Within another two years the remaining three were lost to history, presumably also dead.

Remarkably, a little over five and a half years ago, Tambo's mummified body was found in the basement of a Cleveland funeral parlour. His identity was ascertained by an Australian, Mrs Roslyn Poignant, who was at the time fortuitously in the United States researching the story of the group. In February 1994, on the 100th Anniversary of his death, the young man called Tambo was laid to rest in his native soil. Thereafter, Mrs Poignant devoted herself to collecting materials for what was to become the Captive Lives Exhibition. The opening was attended by Elders of the Palm Island community and the young man's collateral descendants. It culminated in a formal joint imprint of hands by the representatives of the indigenous peoples, by me as Governor-General and by others associated with the Exhibition on a screen which itself became the final exhibit.

Not only is the Exhibition itself the closing chapter in the story of Tambo. Its opening was, for all involved, the final reclamation of Tambo as part of our Australian nation. The Exhibition's story is that of an odyssey of suffering and oppression. The Exhibition itself had become an act of true reconciliation.

Examples such as those which I have given are of themselves important incidents of reconciliation.But their true significance transcends their individual worth. Collectively, all the localised acts of reconciliation have had and will have immeasurable importance in bringing about the environment and attitudes necessary before there could be any realistic hope of a truly national reconciliation with Australia's indigenous peoples. The road ahead is, of course, a long and difficult one. I am, however, sure of two things. The first is that indigenous Australians are not only prepared but anxious to meet us more than half way. In that regard, let me say that, in my visits to Aboriginal and Torres Strait Islander communities and in my contacts with Aboriginal and Torres Strait Islander people, I have been amazed by their generosity of spirit. The second thing of which I am sure is that, however long and difficult the road may be, we will ultimately reach its end – walking together, talking together, striving together, achieving together – as friends and true equals.

3.9 The Delivery of the Deed of Grant to the Urrampinyi Iitjiltjarri Aboriginal Land Trust, Tempe Downs, Northern Territory, 26 July 1999

Less than a month ago I signed, on the recommendation of the Minister for Aboriginal and Torres Strait Islander Affairs, the Deed of Grant which transfers freehold title in the Tempe Downs and

Middleton Ponds land to the Urrampinyi Iitjiltjarri Aboriginal Land Trust on behalf of some 400 traditional owners. Today we are privileged to be here for the completion of that transfer by the handing over of the Deed of Grant.

To the traditional owners I say: these lands have been central to your lives for as long as any of you remember and before that; to your cultures; to your languages; to your songs; to your dances; to your paintings; to your lives. They are the homes of your ancestors. They are the source and the context of your dreaming. You belong to them, as their custodians and their guardians.

And now this Deed of Grant tells you, and enshrines in our law, what you have always known. That is that these lands belong to you. They are your country.

The modern Aboriginal Land Rights movement had its beginnings in 1966, when the great Gurindji elder, Vincent Lingiari, led his people off Wave Hill Station on strike. It was some eight years after in October 1974 – almost 25 years ago – that the Luritja Land Association was formed to seek the return of these traditional lands. It's been a very long struggle. At times it's been a very difficult struggle. But today we celebrate the end of that struggle with the handing over of this Deed of Grant.

In 1974, the then Prime Minister of Australia, Mr Whitlam, went to Daguragu in Gurindji country. There he participated in a ceremony whereby he delivered to the Gurindji people a leasehold title of part of their land. In the course of that ceremony, the Prime Minister took a handful of soil and poured it into the hands of Vincent Lingiari as a symbolic gesture, handing over the land.

Vincent Lingiari spoke a few words in English: 'We are all mates now,' he said. He then turned and addressed the Gurindji people in their language and what he said was, 'Let us live together' that is, with non-indigenous Australians, 'as friends and true equals'. That was of course an eloquent statement of the objectives of the national reconciliation movement of our country … living together, walking together, talking together, striving together, achieving together as friends and true equals.

And so too, this ceremony at which we are all gathered is a moment of true hope and reconciliation as the freehold title to the land is delivered back to you. It is also a significant step for all of us along the road to national reconciliation. The road ahead is a long and difficult one. But it is moments like these that make me feel confident that, however long and difficult it may be, we'll together reach its end. I hope all of you share my confidence that that will be so.

I understand that the traditional owners would like me to repeat the symbolic handing over of the land by the pouring of soil. That I will be happy to do at the time when the formal Deed of Grant is handed over, and these lands become yours under the law of our country in the same way as they have always been in your minds, in your heart and under your traditional laws and lore.

3.10 The Presentation of the Sydney Peace Prize to Archbishop Desmond Tutu, Sydney, 26 November 1999

Archbishop Desmond Tutu was awarded the Nobel Peace Prize fifteen long years ago in 1984. Since then he has made a further immeasurable contribution to peace in South Africa. He played an absolutely crucial role in the lead up to 11 February 1990 – that unforgettable day on which Nelson Mandela at last walked free. He was an inspiration in the period leading to the first democratic election which culminated in the inauguration of Nelson Mandela as President of South Africa on 10 May 1994. And most significantly for this evening's proceedings, through his chairmanship of the Truth and Reconciliation Commission, Desmond Tutu has provided to the world a shining example of peace-making, in the fullest sense of the term, through a process of restorative justice, reconciliation and healing.

The task facing the members of the Truth and Reconciliation

Commission, as they gathered at Bishopscourt in Cape Town for their first meeting on 16 December 1995, a public holiday ... the Day of Reconciliation, was a massive one. By the time the five volume Report was presented in October 1998, some 20,000 submissions had been received, thousands of hearings had been held, and over 7,000 applications for amnesty had been made. And the story and the nature of apartheid had been laid bare. Not only by the spiritually and emotionally shattering accounts of its victims – those bereaved through State sanctioned killings, the tortured, the imprisoned, the betrayed and the broken in spirit. But also by the accounts of the perpetrators, many of them also victims of an evil system, brutalised and dehumanised by what had been required of them.

A chapter heading in Archbishop Tutu's recent book *No Future Without Forgiveness* identifies the essential dilemma which the Commission faced: 'Nuremburg or National Amnesia'. Apartheid's legacy could not simply be ignored and forgotten. But full retributive justice, with the criminal burden of proof, was neither a practical nor a desirable option. The Commission's path to truth and reconciliation was a middle way in which justice was ennobled by charity and forgiveness. And in which justice was restorative ... with the recommendations of the Committee on Reparation and Rehabilitation providing a basis for some affordable recompense and acknowledgment of the immeasurable pain which had been suffered.

Significantly, the Commission took the view that truth, however awful, was a precondition, rather than a barrier, to proper acknowledgment. That there was no truth that could not lead to reconciliation. And that forgiveness was always possible.

The Commission was consistently even-handed in its approach. A gross violation of human rights was just that, regardless of who committed it. The fact that an anti-apartheid act was in a *just cause* did not dispose of the question whether *unjust* – and unjustifiable – *means* had been used in its pursuit.

The essential values underpinning the Commission were personified in its Chairman. They are perhaps best summarised by the African term *ubuntu*. As the Archbishop has written, it is difficult to render the word in English. I quote:

> It speaks of the very essence of being human … generous, hospitable, friendly, caring and compassionate ... It also means my humanity is caught up, is inextricably bound up, in theirs. We belong in a bundle of life. We say 'a person is a person through other people'. It is not 'I think therefore I am'. It says rather: 'I am human because I belong'.

In the Commission's adoption of those values, the influence of two people shine through: Nelson Mandela whose magnanimity after 27 years in captivity provided the basis and the inspiration for the transition to democratic government; and Desmond Tutu, whose courage in the cause of peace, whose achievements, whose generosity of spirit and whose life we are honouring this evening.

Your Grace, in recent times you have shared your experience and your wisdom with other communities striving for reconciliation. I know that, in making the journey to Australia to accept the Sydney Peace Prize, a prize which emphasises peace *with* justice, you have been conscious of the fact that Australia is a country searching for true and lasting reconciliation between our indigenous peoples and the nation of which they form such an important part.

There are obvious difficulties in reading across from the South African experience to our own. But lessons can be learnt. Let me briefly mention three of them.

The first is that there can be no true reconciliation unless and until we acknowledge the facts of our history. And recognise that the past is never fully gone. That it is absorbed into the present and the future. That it stays to shape who and what we are.

Another is that the process of reconciliation in any one place at any one time is a unique hybrid of the personal and institutional, the spiritual and the material. Many things can only be done with the authority of the state through the acts of governments and parliaments. But, just as important, are the grass roots and personal acts of reconciliation. It is there, at the grass roots, that we Australians have, I believe, in the last few years finally begun to make great progress.

And a third lesson is that reconciliation is an ongoing process. Outstanding as its achievements have been, the Truth and Reconciliation Commission is best seen as dealing with the immediate aftermath of apartheid and setting the tone for the future. If we Australians can within the life of *our* Council for Aboriginal Reconciliation, that is to say by the end of next year, achieve the consensus the Council is seeking on a Document of Reconciliation, we will still have far to go. But we will have at least reached a very important stage of the journey.

3.11 The Opening of the Koorie Heritage Trust Inc Flinders Lane Premises, Melbourne, 1 March 2000

Last year the Koorie Heritage Trust was about to open the Koorie Cultural Centre on Lonsdale Street. Just one month before moving in, the Centre was gutted by fire. That fire has delayed the opening of those premises by two years. But courage, resilience, hard work and generous support have ensured that the opening of the Koorie Cultural Centre has not been delayed that long. It is a privilege for us all to be here to share in that opening, albeit in this temporary location.

The Trust itself dates back to 1985. Since then it has been remarkably successful in achieving its stated aims of protecting, preserving and promoting the living culture of the indigenous people of south-east Australia. That culture, of course, extends back over 40,000 years, and lies at the very heart of what it means to be 'Aboriginal'.

Since it was established the Trust has acquired more than

4,000 Koorie artefacts and contemporary works of art, as well as an extensive collection of photographs, historical lithographs and paintings by early Europeans. It has also established the Koorie Oral History Program which, since 1987, has been making and collecting audio and visual recordings of people and cultural activities from the Koorie Community.

In addition to building up its own collection, the Trust has encouraged research into Koorie culture. It has acquired a substantial library, containing some 6,000 items, and has supported the publication of several books and videos.

And, equally important, the trust has endeavoured at all times to share Koorie culture with the wider community. It has developed a range of programs designed to achieve this. Regular visits are made to schools, and teachers have been provided with an invaluable resource, in the 'Koorie Education Kit', to enhance their curricula. Guided tours were offered of the KOORIE exhibition at the Museum of Victoria, and inquiries are fielded from members of the public, interested to learn about particular aspects of indigenous culture. And, through its activities, the Trust teaches the essential lesson that Aboriginal culture and traditions not only lie at the heart of the history of our country … they are a vital – a living part of our present … of who we are, of what we can become, and what we can achieve.

All of these activities of the Koorie Heritage Trust will come together in this Koorie Cultural Centre. Indeed, this Centre will be the centrepiece of the Trust's activities. The premises will house two art galleries, a retail shop and an educational room, as well as the Trust's collections, offices and such like. It will thus represent for Melbourne an unprecedented venue, where the community generally can learn about and enjoy Koorie culture.

Everything about this Centre is therefore calculated to foster the mutual tolerance and respect which is a condition precedent of true reconciliation. By sharing Koorie history and culture with local, interstate and international visitors, the Trust will generate greater awareness and understanding throughout the community. And by understanding better, we will come to value better the contribution that Aboriginal Australians make to Australian culture as a whole

3.12 The Opening of the Queen's Trust Indigenous Future Leaders' Program, Brisbane, 6 April 2000

In so far as reconciliation is concerned, some things are clear as we approach the Centenary of our Federation and the end of the life of the Council for Aboriginal Reconciliation. One of them is that we have not, in recent times, made the progress which many people, including myself, had hoped we would. It is difficult not to sometimes feel depressed and discouraged when one contemplates how much more we have to do … how much further we have to go.

On the other hand, at a time when there seems to be so much emphasis upon the negatives, it is important that we recognise that there *is* a positive side … that much has been achieved … that we *have* made progress along the road. It is upon one aspect of that positive side that I wish to focus this evening … reconciliation at a personal level.

In the more than four years that I have been Governor-General, Helen and I have been constantly conscious of the ever growing numbers of our fellow Australians, both indigenous and non-indigenous and on all sides of mainstream politics, who are working together for true reconciliation. And we have become more and more impressed by the extent to which reconciliation can be advanced by ordinary people acting together. I could give countless instances of such reconciliation in which we have been privileged to participate in all parts of Australia. This evening, let me tell you about but one of them.

In 1884, on a cold winter's day, a 21 year old Aborigine died in Cleveland Ohio in the United States of America. He and his even younger wife had been two of a group of mainly young Aborigines who had, the previous year, been taken from their homeland on Palm Island off North Queensland to the United States where, against their will, they had been exhibited as 'wild' and 'uncivilised savages' – first in Barnum & Bailey's Circus and subsequently in fair grounds in a long list of American towns. Somewhere along the way, the young man had acquired the name 'Tambo'.

When Tambo died, his wife and other companions attempted to accord him the traditional ceremonial rites for the release of his spirit. His body was, however, taken from them and embalmed and sold to the proprietor of a dime museum where it was placed on public display. Within a year or so, a further five of the young captives, including Tambo's wife, were also dead. Within a further two years, the remaining three, who had been taken from America to be exhibited in Europe, were lost to history, presumably also dead.

In October 1993, Tambo's body was discovered in a Cleveland basement. By an extraordinary series of events and coincidences, it was identified and two of Tambo's blood relatives and a senior elder of the Palm Island community arrived in Cleveland to perform the traditional ceremony for the release of his spirit and to take his body back to his ancestral homeland where Tambo was finally laid to rest

Some little time ago, I was privileged to open an exhibition in the National Library in Canberra – the 'Captive Lives' Exhibition – which told the story of Tambo and his companions. The opening was attended by elders of the Palm Island community including collateral descendants of Tambo. The opening itself culminated in a formal gesture of reconciliation involving the painted imprint of hands by the representatives of the indigenous peoples, the organisers of the Exhibition and by me as Governor-General on a screen which itself became the final exhibit. The awful sadness and injustice, though finally acknowledged, remained. Tambo's companions still lay bereft of traditional rites and respect in unknown graves so far away from their ancestral homelands and people. Yet it was among the most moving moments of true reconciliation of my life. It and many other personal experiences have brought home to Helen and me how much can be achieved along the road to true reconciliation by indigenous and non-indigenous people of goodwill acknowledging the past and walking together.

That is not, of course, to deny the plain fact that the road to national reconciliation is a long and extraordinarily difficult one. There are so many challenges to be met and obstacles to be overcome … all the problems of the spirit and all the material disadvantages flowing from past dispossession, oppression and injustice. I have often said that I believe that true and lasting reconciliation at a national level will not be won unless and until it is apparent that we are making real progress towards the position where the future prospects of the ordinary indigenous baby born in this country are at least comparable to those of a non-indigenous one. For, as I said in the inaugural Lingiari Lecture in Darwin some years ago now: 'How can we go forward together as friends and equals if our children's hands cannot touch?'

And that leads me to the subject of indigenous leadership. For without dedicated and effective indigenous leaders – to understand, to represent, to persuade, to act as role models, to strive, to inspire – we would have no immediate hope of reaching that stage. Fortunately, such leaders have emerged. Indeed, some of them are and will be participating in this forum. There is, however, a great need for many more – at all levels. I have been privileged to become close to some of the leading indigenous leaders operating at a national level in recent years. Let me share with you some thoughts resulting from my observations.

Quite apart from the extent of indigenous disadvantage, the role of an indigenous leader in this country is a far from easy one. There is the problem of representation of so many quite distinct peoples with different traditions and cultures. There is the tension between decisive leadership at a national level and customary processes of consultation and consensus. There is the need to observe the traditional respect for tribal elders who may not have had the advantages of formal education or of becoming well informed about wider or national issues. There are the expectations and claims of extended family and even more remote connections to share to an extent and in ways that can sometimes make living away from community in a non-indigenous society extraordinarily difficult.

And indigenous leaders will experience other pressures – often applied by non-indigenous society. To take an obvious example, there is frequently an expectation that an indigenous leader will have detailed knowledge on almost any issue concerning indigenous people generally. There will often be an expectation that, if indigenous leaders are to operate in the modern political arena, they should behave as do non-indigenous leaders. In that context, there may be frustration or irritation with an indigenous leader who requires time to consult with his or her community or to allow the community to talk through an issue to their satisfaction. Conversely, there may be a lack of appreciation on the part of indigenous Australians of the demands and pressures faced by their leaders.

And so the expectations and preconceptions of both indigenous and non-indigenous persons can make the role of an indigenous leader a most difficult one. Indeed, it is a sad fact that indigenous leaders sometimes report feeling alienated from both their own and the non-indigenous communities. I urge you, however, to see these difficulties as challenges to be faced and overcome. For, as I have sought to make clear, I see effective and dedicated indigenous leadership as absolutely essential both to true reconciliation and to the spiritual and material welfare of our nation's indigenous peoples.

And let me also presume to urge you to accept that, our search for reconciliation will be most effective if it is marked by real generosity of spirit – on both sides. And that those of us who are convinced both of the fundamental importance to our nation and of the rightness of the cause of reconciliation should recognise that, difficult though it may sometimes be, we will speak more persuasively to our fellow Australians who are yet to be convinced if we speak reasonably and constructively and avoid personal abuse. If we can do those things, I have no doubt that, however difficult the road may be, we will reach its end.

3.13 Corroboree 2000, Sydney, 27 May 2000

At the outset, I acknowledge the traditional custodians and thank them for the welcome they have given us all to their ancestral lands.

All of us who are pilgrims on the road to Aboriginal reconciliation have reached a crossroads. This is a time to pause and look back to the past, around at the present, and forward to the future.

Looking back, the starting point must be an acknowledgment of facts and truths which are now too well established or obvious to be denied. The dispossession and oppression of the Aboriginal peoples of this country over most of the years of non-indigenous settlement constitute, as Justice Gaudron and I said in a case called *Mabo*, the darkest aspect of the history of our nation.

Looking around at the present, there is the plight of so many of our Aboriginal fellow Australians. In terms of material things such as health, education, employment, housing and living conditions. In terms of things of the spirit, such as hope, belief, self-confidence and self-esteem. And there is the plain fact that that present plight as regards both material and spiritual things – and the problems, including substance and other abuse, which flow from them – are largely the consequence of the injustices of the past.

It's wrong to see those past injustices as belonging, as it were, to *another* country. They have been absorbed into the present and the future of contemporary indigenous Australians and of the nation of which they form such an important part. They reach from the past to shape who and what we are. They – and the land that was taken – are *our* country.

So, as we pause at this crossroads, let us come together in truth, in acknowledgment, in profound sadness and in deep regret. And let us silently mourn for a moment as we reflect upon those past injustices and upon the present disadvantage which flows from them and upon what was taken, what was lost, and what might have been.

But we must also acknowledge the many positives. Particularly on this day towards national reconciliation. Let me remind you of but a few of them.

The first words of our Constitution's preamble – 'Whereas, the people ...' – have always recognised the fundamental truth that it is the people of the Commonwealth who constitute our nation. But the Constitution went on, in s 127, to exclude what it called 'Aboriginal natives' in reckoning the number of those people. On 27 May 1967, the Australian people overwhelmingly rejected that unbearable exclusion. For me, that rejection not only removed an ugly stain from the basic fabric of our society. It constituted the true beginning of the long and difficult road to Aboriginal reconciliation.

Then, in 1975, after the Wave Hill strike, there was the symbolic return of part of the traditional lands of the Gurindji people at Daguragu. That was followed, in 1976, by the Commonwealth's enactment of the first *Aboriginal Land Rights Act*. In 1991, both Houses of our national Parliament unanimously enacted the legislation establishing the Council for Aboriginal Reconciliation. In itself, that was a significant step towards national reconciliation. In 1992, there came the decision of our highest court in the '*Mabo*' case. And there have, in recent years, been the sincere efforts of governments and others to address the health and other material problems of indigenous Australians.

And now today, again on 27 May and 33 years after what I have identified as the beginning of the road, we have gathered for the handing to the Australian nation of the Council's Declaration and Roadmap.

I cannot, of course, as Governor-General, become involved in the differences of opinion about parts of three clauses of the Declaration.Obviously, there is some disappointment on all sides that full and final consensus has not been reached. But not-withstanding any such disappointment, today must surely be seen as a day of celebration. Celebration that the cause of reconciliation has become the focus of our whole nation. Celebration that, notwithstanding some remaining differences, significant consensus has been reached about the contents and wording of the Declaration and that the Council's Roadmap for the future has been publicly unveiled. In that regard, let me pause to pay tribute to all those who have served as members of the Council during its life, first under the leadership of Patrick Dodson with Ron Wilson followed by Ian Viner as his deputy and then of Evelyn Scott with Gus Nossal as her deputy. And I note that our MC, Ray Martin, has been on the Council from the beginning. Our nation is greatly indebted to them all.

Even more important than the specific milestones that I have mentioned has been the ever-increasing grass roots awareness of the importance of both national reconciliation and the battle to overcome entrenched Aboriginal disadvantage. In the years that I have been Governor-General, Helen and I have been privileged to be part of countless unforgettable instances of reconciliation at the personal level in all parts of Australia. They have done much to shape the three thoughts about reconciliation which I wish to share with you as we stand at this crossroads and look to the future.

The first thought is one that I have expressed on many occasions in the past – although I am aware that many disagree with it. It is that all of us who are convinced of the rightness and urgency of the cause of Aboriginal reconciliation will be most effective and persuasive if we have the strength and the wisdom to speak more quietly, more tolerantly and more constructively to our fellow Australians who are yet to be convinced.

The second thought is that reconciliation should be seen both as an end in itself and as a process or journey to a more comprehensive end. It is not a panacea that will miraculously solve all the problems of Aboriginal disadvantage. Reconciliation will, of itself, resolve or help resolve many of the problems of the spirit. But its most important practical effect will be to create an environment of trust and mutual respect and acceptance in which indigenous and non-indigenous Australians can work effectively together to address and overcome the overall legacy of Aboriginal disadvantage.

My final thought is a related one. It goes to the very essence of reconciliation.

I have mentioned the symbolic return of part of their traditional lands to the Gurindji people in 1975. After the soil had been poured into his outstretched hand, the Gurindji leader, Vincent Lingiari, responded: 'We are all mates now'. He then turned and addressed his people in their own tongue. He exhorted them to go forward 'with the whites' as friends and equals.

In that exhortation Vincent Lingiari expressed the essence of my vision of reconciliation in our country. That vision is one of indigenous and non-indigenous Australians together acknowledging the past and walking together, talking together, striving together, working together, and achieving together to build a just and prosperous nation which is, above all else, at peace within itself.

Until that reconciliation and peace are achieved, our nation will remain diminished, unable to fulfil its enormous social, cultural and moral potential. For our search for national reconciliation is not a matter of charity or generosity. It is a matter of basic justice and national decency. It is also a matter of national development in the interests of us all.

The road lies ahead. Today let us celebrate what has been achieved. And let us resolve that together we will continue the journey … with determination, with hope and with confidence in ourselves and one another.

3.14 The Flag Raising Ceremony to Mark the Commencement of NAIDOC Week 2000, Wollongong, 3 July 2000

The theme for NAIDOC Week 2000 reflects an objective that is of critical importance in the quest for true and lasting reconciliation between Australia's indigenous peoples and the nation of which they form such an important part. That theme is 'building pride in our communities'.

Especially as we prepare for the Olympic Games and the Centenary of our Federation, both significant events in the history of our nation, the importance of developing pride in our Aboriginal and Torres Strait Islander cultures and communities cannot be overemphasised. Such pride, both within our indigenous communities and within our broader multicultural society, is essential for the achievement of our full potential as a nation.

In this ceremony, we raise the Australian National Flag, and with it the Aboriginal and Torres Strait Islander Flags, as a mark of our commitment as a community to work together for reconciliation and for a fair, just and inclusive Australian society.

3.15 The Launch of 'Racism. No Way!', An Anti-Racism Project and Website for Australian Schools, Sydney, 27 October 2000

As we approach the Centenary of our Federation, it is absolutely essential to our national health and decency that whatever can be done is done to prevent or eradicate racism in our society in any of its overt or covert forms. There can be no more effective means of combating racism than by ensuring that our young people are not infected by it.

Racism is a global phenomenon which is influenced by a wide range of social, historical, political and economic factors. It takes different forms in different contexts and has been defined in a wide variety of ways. Most of us, however, have little difficulty in recognising overt racism when we encounter it since any form of open denigration; discrimination or prejudice by reference to racism can ordinarily be seen to be tainted. On the other hand covert racism, where prejudice or racial grounds are concealed or even unconscious or sub-liminal, can be all but impossible to identify. In some cases, it can only be effectively prevented or eradicated by education or intellectual persuasion.

Our history is, of course, such that effective prevention and eradication of racism is of critical and vital importance to our national wellbeing. I would mention two related reasons why that is so.

The first concerns relations between Indigenous and non-Indigenous Australians. The dispossession and oppression of indigenous Australians which continued until comparatively recent times provided a context in which entrenched racism was inevitable. Indeed when one recalls that it was only in 1967 that the constitutional prohibition of including Aborigines among the people of the Commonwealth for a number of important purposes was finally removed, there is considerable truth in the assertion that discrimination on racial grounds against indigenous Australians was not only enshrined in many laws and common practices but was even constitutionally required. Those of us who are convinced of the importance to our nation and us all of true and lasting reconciliation between our nation and the Aboriginal people who form such an important part of it must all be conscious of the fact that racism on either side could be an insurmountable barrier on the road.

The second reason why education against racism in all its forms is of such extraordinary importance in this country is the composition of our people. Apart from the Aborigines, we Australians directly or indirectly come from all the races and cultures of the world.

3.16 The Launch Of 'The Sacred Trust Of Memory' – A Mum Shirl Tribute Exhibition , Sydney, 22 November 2000

We Australians are prone to use the words 'great' and 'hero' too lightly and too readily. There are, however, a few people – a mere handful – for whom they really are the only appropriate words. Mum Shirl was one of them. Indeed, I find it remarkable that two of the very few people associated with this city in my lifetime to whom I would unhesitatingly apply those two words, Mum Shirl and Professor Fred Hollows, had so much in common.

Both came to this city from other places. Both could be uncompromisingly outspoken in unforgettable language in fighting sickness and poverty. Both were openly angered by injustice – in Fred Hollows' case to the point of incoherence. Both devoted their lives to selfless service of the most disadvantaged and vulnerable of their fellows – in the case of both with particular emphasis on Aboriginal disadvantage. And appropriately, they worked together to establish the Aboriginal Medical Service and to address the appalling problems of Aboriginal ill health.

One can, of course, find justification for applying those words to Mum Shirl in what she did and what she achieved – for her people and for our country. If anyone doubts that that is so, I suggest that he or she read the staggering list of things in the fifth paragraph of page 6 of this book.[7] The struggle for Aboriginal land rights. The Aboriginal Legal Service. The Aboriginal Medical Service. The Foundation for Aboriginal Affairs. The Aboriginal Children's Service. The Aboriginal Housing Company. Hers was a guiding hand and influence in those and many other pioneering endeavours. And at least as important as all those things were the comfort, help, encouragement and hope she brought and gave to so many individual lives over so many years. If, as I profoundly believe, the ultimate test of our decency and our worth as a democratic community is how we treat the most disadvantaged and vulnerable of our people,

---

[7] The Mum Shirl Tribute Working Group, *Mum Shirl, the Sacred Trust of Memory*, Rozelle, 2000.

Mum Shirl made an absolutely extraordinary contribution towards helping us pass that test.

One can also find obvious justification for seeing Shirley Smith as a great Australian in what she said. Her capacity and ability, as Father Ted Kennedy has written, to comfort the afflicted and to afflict the comfortable. To identify and uncompromisingly speak the unvarnished truth about things that truly matter. Some of those plain truths are reproduced at pages 9 and 10 of this book. Let me paraphrase but two of them

First. 'on the present' at page 9. People are far more comfortable hearing about problems that are too far away for them to be able to do anything about them than hearing about problems in their own backyard.

That leads me to two thoughts. The first is the danger of speaking in abstract terms about 'Aboriginal reconciliation' as if it were a panacea. As we approach the Centenary of our Nation the search for reconciliation is of overwhelming national importance. But reconciliation of itself will not solve the searing problems of Aboriginal education, unemployment, sickness, premature death, imprisonment, lack of opportunity and other disadvantage which Mum Shirl fought to overcome. To the contrary, true and lasting reconciliation will not be achieved unless and until we together make much more effective progress along the road towards resolving those problems.

My second thought is that the time has come when none of us Australians can properly see any of the problems of Aboriginal disadvantage as being too far away to be of immediate concern. All the problems of Aboriginal disadvantage regardless of where they occur are in the backyard of, and of immediate concern to, each one of us. And it is the duty of each of us to face them and help resolve them.

The second of Mum Shirls' plain truths to which I'd refer is the last on page 10: 'on religion'. There's nothing out of plumb with the Catholic religion; it's the way Catholics practise it. I suspect that Mum Shirl was referring to the fact that those of us who are Christians commonly close our minds to how unqualifiedly radical the message of Christianity is. I'm sure, for example, that she would want to remind us of its uncomfortable teaching that to fail to feed the man dying from hunger is to kill him.

In truth, of course, Mum Shirl was a great Australian and one of our few real Australian heroes because of the sum of her all; of what she did; of what she said; but most of all of what she was. I believe that it's primarily because of what she was that her spirit will increasingly walk abroad in this city and in our land to teach, to guide and to inspire.

This Exhibition and its catalogue constitute a wonderful tribute to Mum Shirl. Appropriately, they tell us much of the despair and disadvantage among her people against which she fought. And they tell us much about Mum Shirl herself. About her generosity; her selflessness; her understanding; her outspokenness; her anger; her humanity. And her love. The Exhibition celebrates the relationships between Mum Shirl and all who have contributed to her. But most of all it is a worthy and living celebration of her life.

3.17 The Conferral of The Degree of Doctor of Laws *Honoris Causa* and the Delivery of the Occasional Address, University Of New South Wales, Sydney, 18 May 2001

This year, as we celebrate the Centenary of our Federation, we Australians have much to be grateful for … our land itself; our democracy under the rule of law; our multiculturalism; the cumulative achievements of our fellow Australians; the spirit of our people. At the same time, as we look to the future, we must be conscious of the challenges which lie ahead.

In the forefront of those challenges are the challenge to heal the divisions in our society including the unacceptable gap between the haves and the have nots; the challenge to protect and preserve our environment for future, as well as present, Australians; the challenge to overcome entrenched Aboriginal disadvantage and to achieve true and lasting Aboriginal reconciliation. In that regard, my abiding regret as my term as Governor-General expires is that we Australians failed to achieve more before the life of the Council for Aboriginal Reconciliation ran out at the end of last year.

In the search for Aboriginal reconciliation, our Universities have an absolutely critical direct and indirect role to play. The direct role includes the obvious one of encouraging and effectively teaching those indigenous Australians who are fortunate enough to come within their reach. I say 'fortunate enough' because of the immense gap which continues to exist in many areas of our nation between the educational standards, including literacy and numeracy, of the average indigenous student leaving school and the average non-indigenous one. While the position varies in different areas and while there is room for informed disagreement about some details, a number of plain facts are beyond intelligent dispute. For me the most basic of them is that in many remote indigenous communities, there is, for practical purposes, no chance that an indigenous student will reach matriculation standard. Indeed, in some of those communities, the standard of the average Aboriginal student at the conclusion of formal education is Year Three (3) primary school. Obviously, in the context of the past treatment of our indigenous peoples, our Universities have an immense responsibility to ensure that, consistently with the maintenance of academic standards, every legitimate encouragement and assistance is extended to the indigenous students who succeed in entering their doors.

Education is a key to achieving true and lasting reconciliation in at least three less direct respects. First the education of indigenous Australians, particularly indigenous youth, is the key to overcoming disadvantage in other areas such as health, life expectancy, employment, living conditions and self-esteem. Second, as the Council for Aboriginal Reconciliation pointed out in its final

Report, education of decision makers and people who provide services is the key to their working effectively through partnerships with indigenous people. Third, education of the wider community is the key to the general understanding and acknowledgment of the issues of reconciliation, including the basic facts of past dispossession and oppression and present disadvantage and the extent to which the present entrenched disadvantage of indigenous Australians flows from past injustice.

3.18 The Ceremony of Reconciliation with the Kija People, Mistake Creek, 7 June 2001

Since I first heard the story of the terrible events which occurred at Mistake Creek, I have wanted to come here in the spirit of reconciliation. Just as Helen, my wife, and I have been to so many other parts of Australia. To see this dry creek bed, this old boab tree and this commemorative tablet with its searing words: 'In memory of our ancestors who were shot and burnt here'.

There may be room for disagreement about some of the precise details of the killings at Mistake Creek more than 60 years ago. The essential elements of the story are, however, tragically clear enough. They reflect the terrible approach, implicit in the discredited doctrine of *terra nullius* and the facts of the dispossession, that indigenous Australians were somehow less than human.

The Mistake Creek story is one of great wrongs and injustice. It is also a story of forgiveness which has been explained by an elder of the Kija people: 'if we do not forgive them … the evil spirit will enter us'.

There are three particular matters which I would mention.

The first is that it is essential to the process of reconciliation that we acknowledge, frankly and fully, the facts involved in the past dispossession and oppression of Australia's Aboriginal peoples. To the Kija people I say how profoundly sorry I personally am that events such as those which occurred here at Mistake Creek could ever have been allowed to deface and defile this land.

The second is to say to the representatives of the Kija people who are present this morning: 'Thank you for your generosity of spirit in having us here with you today and being part of this ceremony of reconciliation'. I also express my thanks to the West Australian Minister for the Kimberley, Mr Tom Stephens, for all his help in organising this visit; to Bishop Chris Saunders for conducting this ceremony; and to everyone else who has assisted in making the visit such a memorable one.

Finally, I ask everyone here to join me in a moment of silent prayer … for our country, for all Australians and for true and lasting reconciliation.

4

Multiculturalism and Social Cohesion

4.0 Editor's note

Writing to the Queen on 10 February 1999, Sir William reported on a recent visit to Sir Donald Bradman who was in his 90th year. He advised: 'Sir Donald shares my conviction of the importance of reconciliation between our indigenous peoples and our nation as a whole. He and I also share a belief in the importance of what we call our 'multiculturalism' – I would prefer to say 'multicultural inclusiveness' – which is enabled us to build a pretty harmonious nation notwithstanding that, apart from the Aborigines, we come from all the regions, races, cultures and religions of the world. He has very fond memories of the 1948 tour of England and of his meeting with Your Majesty at that time. I regard him as a truly great Australian.' Deane often espouses the value of multicultural inclusiveness insisting that it promotes national identity and unity 'by building upon and adding cohesion to what we are'.

4.1 The Opening of Law Week 1996 in New South Wales, Sydney, 12 May 1996

As all major political parties are now agreed, the four and two-third years which remain until we celebrate the centenary of our nation on 1 January 2001 are going to be of critical importance in the constitutional history of this country. The Commonwealth government has already announced that a constitutional convention will be held by the end of 1997 to – and I quote – 'give the people a new opportunity to have their say about their Constitution and their system of government'. Obviously, the issues which must be addressed by the Australian people in the coming years can only be intelligently considered and resolved if there is informed debate about them and if there is at least basic understanding of relevant competing considerations and arguments. In that regard, it should always be borne in mind that the ultimate source of all governmental authority in a true democracy such as ours is the people, all the people.

It follows that Law Week 1996 will perform a very important national service if it succeeds, through the promotion of the concept of peoples' constitutional conventions and through the provision of convention kits, in preparing the ground for intelligent, informed and tolerant discussion and decision of the questions involved in determining the Constitution and structure of our nation as it enters its second century. I say tolerant discussion and decision for the reason that it is essential that, when the views and aspirations of the majority, whatever they may be, ultimately prevail, there is respect for, and tolerance and understanding of, the views and aspirations of the minority. Otherwise, the unbearable cost of our development as a nation will be bitterness and disunity.

4.2 The Opening of The Queen's Trust National Forum for Young Adult Australians, Melbourne, 7 July 1996

We Australians are truly one people, one nation. What injures one of us injures us all. To belittle or discount the convictions, the loyalties, the ideals or the aims of some is to demean the whole. It is of the very essence of a great and compassionate democracy such as ours that, when the views and aspirations of the majority, whatever they may prove to be, ultimately prevail, there is respect, tolerance and understanding of the views and aspirations of the minority. Otherwise, the unbearable cost of our development as a nation will be our own disunity.

4.3 The Opening of the New South Wales Government's Constitutional Centenary Convention, Sydney, 10 September 1997

As we approach the centenary of the foundation of our nation, it is particularly important that we Australians should be conscious of our national achievements – of the things we should be proud of and the things we should be thankful for. It is true that, like all nations, there are some things which are a cause of sadness; things which we still have to overcome. We are, for example, all conscious of the plight of our disadvantaged, such as our indigenous peoples, our homeless and our unemployed. Nonetheless, the story of our nation is, on balance, a wonderfully positive one with many things to celebrate. Among the most important of those things is the achievement of our founders who, through the Conventions of the 1890s, were responsible for framing the Constitution under which the people of each of the six Australian Colonies agreed to become a nation.

An important function of this 1997 Centenary Convention in this Parliament of the Mother Colony of New South Wales is to commemorate and celebrate the Second Session of the 1897-1898 Federal Convention which was held here a century ago. That commemoration and that celebration are, in themselves, of great importance. The reason why that is so is not only that the achievements of the founders of our nation are an essential part of our history. They are also of enduring significance to our national unity, our national identity and our national pride. Accordingly, and notwithstanding that your own deliberations at this 1997 Convention will be largely concerned with the future, I shall, in these brief opening comments, seek to help identify the context of the Convention in the past.

By the time the Sydney Session commenced in this place and month in 1897, much progress had been made. A draft Constitution for the new nation had emerged from the 1891 National Australasian

Convention which had also been held here in Sydney. The first Session of the subsequent Federal Convention held in Adelaide in the Autumn of 1897 and attended by representatives of all the Australian Colonies other than Queensland had decided, at the outset, to set about producing a new draft Constitution. The delegates in Adelaide had before them, however, the 1891 draft and the draft Constitution which emerged from their deliberations to be sent forward to the 1897 Sydney Session after discussion in the Colonial legislatures was clearly the 1891 draft subject to amendments, additions and deletions.

A considerable number of things had happened between 23 April, the last real sitting of the Adelaide Session, and the following September when delegates from the five participating Colonies gathered here for the Sydney Session.

The five Premiers who had been present in Adelaide, together with Premier Nelson of Queensland, had travelled to London for the Queen's Diamond Jubilee Celebrations and for a Colonial Conference called by Joseph Chamberlain, the then Secretary of State for the Colonies. The officials of the Colonial Office, had received a copy of the Adelaide draft through the South Australian Governor. They had prepared a variety of amendments. Some of these amendments were seen in London as essential before a draft Constitution Bill could be allowed to proceed to enactment by the Imperial Parliament. Others were seen merely as helpful improvements in content or in drafting. The history of the three printed documents incorporating those proposed amendments is a story in itself. For present purposes, it suffices to say that, instead of being handed to Kingston, the President of the Convention, or to the Premiers generally, they were entrusted by the Colonial Office to Sir George Read who ultimately passed them on to Barton, the leader of the Convention, and to the Drafting Committee at the 1897 Sydney Convention.

In conformity with the various Enabling Acts, the Adelaide draft had, in the intervening months, also been subjected to lengthy debate in both Houses of the Legislatures of the 5 Colonies. In some, the debate had been constructive and the amendments adopted had been intended to help progress along the road to Federation. In others, including the Upper House in this place, the debate had been largely destructive and occasionally even seemed to be aimed at raising obstacles upon that road. Professor La Nauze has summarised the overall effect of all the suggested amendments which emerged from the various Colonial Legislatures in the following passage:

> In fact, between them the parliaments so cut the Adelaide Draft about, freely amending, omitting or inserting clauses, that a coherent document could never have been assembled from the pieces. Since both Houses of each parliament made their own amendments, and since no votes of confidence were involved, there was room for every kind of alteration and for diverse combinations of voting. The results ranged from seriously constructive suggestions through routine reflections of provincial 'interests' to mere frivolity, sometimes malignant. There were, no doubt, personal jealousies and antagonisms involved; some members clearly believed that they could frame a better Constitution than those who had been elected to do so; some, hostile to federation in any form, seized the opportunity to do as much damage as they could.

In the event, the Sydney Session of the Convention did the only sensible thing and firmly adhered to the approach that the basic document was the draft Constitution which had emerged from Adelaide and that the relevant question in relation to each topic that was raised was what, if any, amendment should be made to that basic document. It is not my intention to seek to trace the differences between the 1891 draft, the Adelaide draft of 1897, the draft which emerged from the Sydney Session in the Spring of 1897 and that which was adopted, with cheers, on Wednesday, 16 March 1898, the second last day of the Melbourne Session. Suffice it to say that the Constitution which was finally adopted by the Australian people in the subsequent referenda was in structure and in spirit that which had emerged from the 1891 Sydney Convention.

Certainly, by the time the 1897 Sydney Convention opened, the synthesis of basic features or principles which made our Constitution unique had well and truly evolved. Those basic features or principles can be shortly identified:

(i) a Federation of the participating Colonies to form a new nation, the Commonwealth of Australia, in which the former Colonies continued as States;

(ii) a local Westminster System of representative and responsible Government under the Crown of the United Kingdom;

(iii) a bicameral Parliament consisting of a House of Representatives and a Senate;

(iv) the entrustment of designated exclusive or concurrent (but paramount) legislative powers to the Commonwealth with residual (including subsidiary concurrent) legislative powers remaining with the States; and

(v) the separation of judicial from executive and legislative powers.

The Constitution as ultimately adopted contained approximately 25 essentially original clauses. Otherwise, the different elements both of that synthesis and the actual provisions of the draft and final Constitutions which incorporated it, can be traced to one or more of a number of sources. Those sources were: the unwritten Constitution of the United Kingdom; the written Constitutions of the United States of America and Canada (and in some minor respects Switzerland); the various written Colonial Constitutions; and, the *Federal Council of Australasia Act* which had been enacted by the Imperial Parliament in 1885. The principal draftsman of that Imperial Act and the main guiding mind and the leading draftsman at the actual Convention in Sydney in 1891 had been Samuel Griffith. Undoubtedly, however, the main author of that unique synthesis of basic features and principles – and of some of the completely original clauses – was Andrew Inglis Clark. His preliminary draft, which had been circulated before the 1891 Sydney Convention, was as clearly the basis of the 1891 draft Constitution as that 1891 draft Constitution was, in turn, the basis of all that followed, including the Constitution finally adopted by the people of the federating Colonies who combined to establish our Nation. Thus Mr Justice Frank Neasey, in an important essay on Andrew Inglis Clark, calculated that of the 96 sections in Inglis Clark's draft Constitution 'all but eight found their way into the [1891] Draft Bill in similar or reworked form, and only ten failed to find a recognizable counterpart in the [final] Constitution'.

Clark was not present at any of the Sessions of the 1897-1898 Convention though some of his written comments or notes in relation to matters being discussed were brought to the attention of the delegates. In 1898, he was appointed a Judge of the Supreme Court of Tasmania. He served on that court with great distinction. Initially, it was anticipated, at least by Deakin and Griffith, that the High Court, when established, would consist of five Justices of whom Inglis Clark would be one. When the Court was established, however, it consisted of only three members – Griffith as Chief Justice and Barton, who had apparently changed his mind after firmly declaring that he would not go on the Federal Bench, and O'Connor as the other Justices. When the Court was expanded to five Justices in 1906, it was widely anticipated that Clark would be among the two additional Justices. But others – on this occasion Isaacs and Higgins – were again preferred. The following year, 1907, Andrew Inglis Clark was dead.

Even in the comparatively short period between the establishment of the Commonwealth and his death, Inglis Clark had made a not insignificant further contribution to the law of our *Constitution*. In 1901, he published his *Studies in Australian Constitutional Law*. That book remains a work of profound importance to those who, like myself, believe that our Constitution must, to use Clark's own words, be read and construed 'as a living force' and 'not as containing a declaration of the will and intentions of men long since dead ... who cannot have anticipated the problems that would arise for solution by future generations'. Again, as a judge of the Supreme Court of Tasmania, Inglis Clark wrote the dissenting judgment in the seminal case of *Pedder v D'Emden.* That dissenting judgment was unanimously upheld in the High Court.

Recently, I read a major newspaper article by Les Carlyon on the subject of who are our Australian 'heroes'. The article named a very large number of people from different fields of endeavour who might arguably be seen as Australian heroes. Interestingly enough, the only reference to any of the founders of our nation was a passing statement to the effect that Alfred Deakin is little remembered by contemporary Australians. At the time I read it, it occurred to me how different it would be if such an article were being written in the United States where names such as Washington, Franklin, Hamilton, Jefferson, Adams and Madison would inevitably have jostled each other for inclusion as American heroes.

Nonetheless, it is true to say that a considerable number of those who participated in the Australian Constitutional Conventions stretching from 1891 to 1898 have been rightly accorded prominent places in our history. The names of Parkes, Griffith, Barton, Deakin, Kingston, O'Connor, Isaacs and Higgins come readily to mind. Perhaps because he did not go on to play a prominent role on the national stage after Federation, the importance of the work of Andrew Inglis Clark would, however, seem to have been largely neglected at least outside his native Tasmania until fairly recently. Indeed, his name is not even included in the substitute pantheon of major and not so major Convention participants constituted by the names of Canberra suburbs. Thus, Canberra boasts suburbs named after every one of the other Convention figures whom I have mentioned. There are also, for example, the suburbs of Turner, Holder, Hackett, Braddon, Downer, Fraser, Forrest, Gordon and Fyshwick. Alas, there is neither an Inglis Clark nor a Clark.

There is one other of the framers of our Constitution to whom I would make brief reference in speaking of the Sydney Session of the 1897-1898 Convention. He is Patrick McMahon Glynn, a member of the South Australian Parliament and a South Australian delegate to the Convention. The Convention reports disclose that he made some significant contributions in the course of debate. He went on to be a member of the first Commonwealth House of Representatives and served in different Ministries as Attorney-General, Minister for External Affairs and Minister for Home and Territories. However, it is not to those contributions or subsequent achievements that I wish to refer. Rather I wish to refer to Mr Glynn to illustrate the point that the Sydney Session was not all work and no play. Certainly, Patrick McMahon Glynn was no dull boy.

At this time on 10 September 100 years ago, which was a Friday, Glynn had taken leave from his Convention duties. He had just arrived in Melbourne, having absented himself from the continuing debate in Sydney for a very good reason. On the following Monday, back in Sydney for the Convention, he explained that reason in the following hastily written letter to his mother in Ireland:

> We are again in the thick of the Federal Convention work, the second, or Sydney sitting being now on. It is to consider the amendments suggested by the various Australian Parliaments to the Bill drafted by the first, the Adelaide Convention. I accomplished rather a record last week. On Tuesday, during the sitting, I wrote a proposal of marriage to a girl whom I had only spoken to once; had a telegram accepting on Wednesday; made what the audience considered a Great Speech on Thursday at 5.30 pm; took the 7.15 pm Express to Melbourne same night, got married on Saturday & returned same day, arriving here on Sunday. You will think I am mad. Perhaps a little, but it may have saved me from a reckless step. She is at all events what will please you; a Catholic, a good one, with enough religion for the two of us.

The following night, the newlyweds were the undoubted stars

at a grand Convention Ball held at Government House here in Sydney. Their marriage would seem to have been a very happy one and they had eight children. I regret to say that the name Glynn is likewise absent from the Pantheon of Canberra suburbs.

While it is important to commemorate and celebrate the past, the importance of this Centenary Convention lies at least as much in the opportunity it offers for discussion and deliberation in relation to some of the important constitutional issues which confront the people of our country about the present and the future. I am sure I speak for all Australians when I wish you well in all your discussion and consideration of those issues. I am also confident that you will, by the standard of your contributions and by your tolerance and courtesy in the discussion of different points of view, set an example which can be emulated by all Australians over the period of national debate which lies before us.

4.4 The Presentation of the 1997 Human Rights Awards, Sydney, 10 December 1997

We Australians are both fortunate and privileged in that there is general recognition in our country of the importance of respect for, and observance of, the fundamental human rights and dignity of all our people. Indeed, our whole system of government embodies basic notions of equality and political and social freedoms and rights under the law.

But, on this Anniversary of the United Nations Universal Declaration of Human Rights, we most inevitably recognise that, to a significant extent, the aspirations of that Declaration have not been completely fulfilled even in this country as regards the most vulnerable and disadvantaged. To that extent, the provisions of the Declaration remain objectives towards which we must strive rather than as a catalogue of rights and advantages which are in fact enjoyed by all our citizens.

Let me, for example, remind you of the first sentences of each of Articles 23 and 25 of the Universal Declaration of Human Rights proclaimed by the United Nations General Assembly 49 years ago:

The first sentence of Article 23 reads: 'Everyone has the right to work, to free choice of employment, to just and favourable conditions of work and to protection against unemployment.'

In these days of high unemployment, particularly youth unemployment, it is important to remember that, as long ago as 1948, the Nations of the World recognised the opportunity to work and protection against unemployment as basic human rights ... not as privileges.

The first sentence of Article 25 commences: 'Everyone has the right to a standard of living adequate for the health and well-being of himself and of his family, including food, clothing, housing and medical care and necessary social services ...'.

Internationally, the mere reading of those words makes one conscious of the extent of the denial of the basic essentials of human existence to so many people, including so many children, in so many other parts of our world. But even nationally, no one who is well acquainted with the plight of the homeless and other disadvantaged in our country, with the numbers living in poverty and with the still increasing discrepancy of almost 20 years between the life expectancy of a non-indigenous baby and that of an indigenous one would seriously maintain that those fundamental rights are yet enjoyed by all Australians.

Today, however, at this gathering to honour the recipients of Human Rights Awards, we should rather be looking at the positives – of the things in our human rights record of which we can be justly proud. In that context, I wish to pay tribute to the Human Rights and Equal Opportunity Commission, its officers and its staff and to the many other Australians who work and have worked so tirelessly both in this country and overseas to promote the cause of human rights. They deserve the respect, admiration and gratitude of us all. And that is so regardless of whether their efforts are publicly recognised or left unacknowledged or even unknown. Thus, while we publicly acknowledge those outstanding proponents of human rights, human opportunity and human dignity who have been selected as winners in the various categories of the 1997 Human Rights Awards, we should also be mindful of the countless others of our fellow Australians who work and have worked in so many capacities to advance human rights and dignity, both internationally and nationally. For in this area, as in so many others, it is the *cumulative* effect of the many working in their own ways and in their own particular areas of concern, that ultimately enriches and sustains our society.

Over the years, the Human Rights and Equal Opportunity Commission has been served by three notable Presidents, a number of outstanding and hardworking Commissioners and a loyal and dedicated staff. I hope it will not be thought inappropriate if I single out two of the Presidents for particular mention. Each of the two is playing a special role in today's proceedings and has a very special place in the history of the Commission.

The first is Dame Roma Mitchell. She is, undoubtedly, one of the leading Australians of our time. She was the first Australian woman to become a Queen's Counsel. She was the first Australian woman to become a Supreme Court judge. She was the first Australian woman to become Chancellor of a major University. She was the first woman to become the Governor of an Australian State. And she was also the Foundation President of the Human Rights and Equal Opportunity Commission. Her example, her ability, her dedication and her great humanity were of inestimable importance in establishing the standing and effectiveness of the Commission.

The other person to whom I wish to pay a special tribute is Sir Ronald Wilson. As you know, on 31 July this year, he completed his seven-year term as President of the Human Rights and Equal Opportunity Commission, having followed Justice Marcus Einfeld in that office in 1990.

On this first Human Rights Day after the completion of Sir Ronald's service as President, I want to say a little about his life because I think all Australians can take pride in it. Indeed, it tells us something very good about our country and ourselves.

The impact of Sir Ronald Wilson on our nation and the influence that he has had on our perceptions of national standards and basic decency are all the more remarkable given the difficulties of his early years. When he was only four his mother died. At seven, his father suffered a stroke and spent the next five years in a hospice 300 miles from home. At 14, family financial pressures forced Ron to leave school and take his first job as a messenger with the Geraldton Local Court. During the Second World War he served as a pilot flying spitfires during the Battle of Britain – one of Sir Winston Churchill's famous 'few'. At War's end, he enrolled at the University of Western Australia on a returned serviceman's scholarship, graduating in law in 1949. He took silk in 1963. In 1969, he became Western Australia's Solicitor-General. In that role, he became one of the most effective and persuasive appellate advocates our country has produced.

I might say that the only doubtful thing about his appointment to the High Court in 1979 was his personal doubt about whether he should accept it. Otherwise, the appointment was greeted with universal acclaim. This was particularly so, since he was the first Western Australian to be appointed to the Court. A deeply religious man, Ron was among those Presbyterians who helped found the Uniting Church. While on the High Court, he became President of the Assembly of the Uniting Church in Australia. It was one of a number of positions he has held over the years with the Church.

His retirement from the High Court came as a surprise to us all. He still had so much to offer as a judge. It was not, however, retirement. It turned out that he had as much, or even more, to offer in other capacities. We have all seen that demonstrated, in the aftermath of his retirement in his continuing work with the

Uniting Church, as President of the Australian Chapter of the World Conference on Religion and Peace, as Deputy Chair of the Council for Aboriginal Reconciliation, and, of course, for seven notable years, as President of the Human Rights and Equal Opportunity Commission. In that role, he has become a great national advocate for the disadvantaged and for human rights.

The culmination of Ronald Wilson's work as President of the Commission is, of course, *Bringing Them Home*, the Report of the National Inquiry into the Separation of Aboriginal and Torres Strait Islander Children from their Families. That Report by Sir Ronald and Mr Michael Dodson, assisted by other members of the Commission, is of inestimable national importance. Naturally, as Governor-General, I refrain from any comment on the individual recommendations or the responses to them being developed by government. But I can point to the fact, which everyone of goodwill would acknowledge, that it has served to focus the attention of the community upon the human tragedy of what is now called 'the stolen generation' and, by so doing, has immeasurably helped our understanding and our compassion – those two supports of all of us who journey together towards reconciliation. I take this opportunity to pay my personal tribute to Sir Ronald Wilson in respect of the many capacities in which he has served our nation so loyally and so well.

Ladies and gentlemen, next year will mark the 50th Anniversary of the proclamation of the Universal Declaration of Human Rights by the General Assembly of the United Nations on this day in 1948. This date, 10 December, also marks a decade since the Human Rights Medal and the Human Rights Awards were first initiated and presented by the Commission. They recognise those who are considered by the judges to have made the most outstanding contributions to the cause of human rights in each of the various categories. But as I remarked earlier, it is the commitment of *all* who work to this end that so enlarges our nation. And therefore, in congratulating the winners in advance of the presentations, let me also congratulate everyone who was nominated and considered. Without each of you and your individual commitments to the protection and promotion of human rights, our society as a whole would be markedly the poorer.

4.5 The Opening of the Mission Australia National Conference, Newcastle, 2 February 1998

What is common to so many areas of disadvantage, even in our affluent Australia, is the stark face of poverty: material poverty in the form of homelessness, inadequate clothing, sustenance, care or help which, as we know, can lead to other consequences and other disadvantage such as alcoholism, physical and sexual abuse and family break-down. For so often, the grim companion of material disadvantage is poverty of the spirit – the absence of hope, the deprivation of self-esteem, and the loss of confidence in one's ability to do anything about it.

It is my firm belief that the ultimate test of our worth as a democratic nation is how we treat our most disadvantaged and vulnerable. And by 'we' I refer to all of us, as members of the community. Certainly the collective assistance provided through government is essential. Indispensable. But, inevitably, it is not always of itself sufficient. There are a great many human needs which require the personal compassion and vision and assistance that so often can only be found among committed men and women working individually or, more generally, through agencies such as Mission Australia.

In the course of our past visits to the Newcastle region, we have been privileged to have considerable contact with many of the disadvantaged of this region – the unemployed, the mentally impaired, the physically disabled, the frail aged to name but some. We have also met many of those involved in working for them. Progressively, we have become conscious not only of the strength of spirit of the City but also of the extraordinary goodness – there is no other word – of those who serve its disadvantaged. Among them have been those who work for, and contribute to the work of, the Hunter Mission. Apart from visiting outreach services of the Hunter Mission, I was entrusted, last July, with the launch of the 1997 Winter Sleep Out. I must confess that I feel somewhat guilty that I did not return for the actual event. I did, however, feel that I was part of it in that Helen and I were permitted to sponsor some of the early registrants. I presume, since we heard no complaints, that they did us proud. I might say, even if I don't achieve anything else in this job, I may be gaining a reputation as a launcher of sleep-ins and outs since I note that I recently received an invitation to launch Melbourne City Mission's 1998 Winter Sleep Out. Helen says that she does not mind as long as I don't get a reputation as a supporter of sleeping around.

The cause in which you are engaged – the fight against poverty in all its manifestations – is a noble one. For those of us who are Christians it is also an obligation and a measure of our commitment to the central mission of the modern day Universal Christian Church, namely, the mission of outreach to the disadvantaged and oppressed. For, if I might presume to remind you of the parable of the rich man in Luke, Chapter 16, who among us would deny that Lazarus lies in need at the gate of each of us. But it is also a national cause in which I believe all caring Australians should engage. For, as I have said, the ultimate test of our worth as a democratic nation is how we treat our most vulnerable and disadvantaged.

4.6 The Chinese Australian Forum Dinner, Sydney, 14 October 1998

As Governor-General, I have learnt much that has helped shape my own vision of Australia. Tonight, I wish to refer briefly to three matters of particular importance in that regard. While they are distinct, they at some points merge with one another. The three matters are multiculturalism, reconciliation and disadvantage.

The history of indigenous Australians and their cultures stretches back some 50 or 60 thousand years. From very early times in this ancient continent, there was a real diversity of indigenous cultures. Some of those cultures perished in the wake of European settlement, dominance and oppression which commenced in 1788. Other indigenous cultures survived and developed.

Those who came from other parts of the world brought with them their own cultures. Initially, the introduced cultures were essentially those of the British Isles. Quite apart from the appalling treatment of the Aborigines, the 19th century and the early days of our nation in the present century, were stained by a degree of ignorance and intolerance in relation to other cultures and races which, I believe, most Australians now look back on with profound sorrow.

Today, it can truly be said that we Australians immediately or more distantly come from – and reflect – the regions, races, cultures and religions of the world. Thus, for example, since the Second World War we have received several million migrants from some 140 different countries.

Yet, notwithstanding our cultural diversity, we are united as one nation. The approach and the conviction which have made that possible are what we call our multiculturalism. In my view, that multiculturalism sustains our national unity. In essence, it means that our distinctive Australian culture and our distinctive Australian identity encompass, and are enriched by, all the different racial, ethnic and religious backgrounds and cultures from which we come. It also means that our citizens are entitled to expect and demand that there be mutual respect for, and genuine acceptance of, all those backgrounds and cultures. Conversely, all our citizens owe a duty to honour all their obligations as Australians and to refrain from infecting our nation with hatreds and intolerance flowing from old conflicts in other lands.

My own personal commitment to encouraging that mutual respect and acceptance has never wavered during the period in which I have been Governor-General. Indeed, I have found that the longer I am Governor-General the more convinced I am that to deny or to undermine that mutual respect and acceptance is to defy or to undermine the unifying basis of our nation. Our multiculturalism seems to me to be not only decent, just and right. It is not only our Australian way. It defines what we are.

I have mentioned these things tonight because I know how much the Chinese-Australian Communities throughout Australia have done, over the years, to develop, strengthen and maintain that mutual respect and acceptance which I see as lying at the very heart of our nation and our way of life.

Nor, during the period in which I have been Governor-General, have I made any secret of my belief that the achievement of a just and lasting reconciliation between the Aborigines and Torres Strait Islanders and the Australian nation as a whole is one of the most significant issues we face as we move towards our second century as a nation and the new millennium. To achieve such reconciliation, we must address the problems of the spirit and of lack of self esteem as well as the appalling problems of material disadvantage in health, housing, education and employment where, on virtually every measure, indigenous people are far worse off than other Australians.

Over the past two and one-half years, Helen and I have visited many Aboriginal communities. The impressions formed on our first visit, which was to Maningrida in the far north of the Northern Territory, have been reinforced by all our subsequent visits. Let me summarise some of those impressions for you.

Maningrida is in many respects an outstanding community. The local council works hard. The school is well run. Problems of alcohol and petrol sniffing are under control. Supported by the community's senior elder, I opened a new local museum during a traditional Aboriginal ceremony. It should have been a very happy day.

But the visit was in the company of some medical experts from the Menzies Research School, in Darwin of which I am Patron. It was marred by the haunting reality of the dreadful health statistics of the community. For there, as elsewhere in Australia, the average Aboriginal baby has a life expectancy of some 20 years less than the average life expectancy of the average non-indigenous one. And the incidence of particular diseases makes the point even more forcefully. For example, the incidence of rheumatic heart disease at Maningrida is said to be the highest ever recorded anywhere in the world. Worse than in Soweto. That visit symbolised two things for us. First, that we have made real progress along the road to reconciliation. Second, how far we have to go.

In recent times, it may sometimes have seemed that progress towards true reconciliation had slowed or almost ceased. I am, however, hopeful that, with goodwill on all sides, we can again begin to make significant progress towards the goal of true reconciliation by the time we enter our second century as a nation. But those of us who are joined in a pilgrimage towards that goal must recognise that we will not reach it unless and until it can be seen that we are at least making real progress towards the position where the future prospects of the average Aboriginal baby are comparable to those of the average non-Aboriginal one. For, as I commented in the inaugural Lingiari Lecture in 1996, how can we be truly reconciled while our children's hands cannot touch?

When my appointment as Governor-General was first announced, I indicated that Helen and I hoped to do what we could to draw attention to the problems of the disadvantaged in our country. Since then we have tried to make good that pledge. We have visited an extraordinarily large number of organisations in every State and Territory serving the needs of the unemployed, the sick, the lonely, the homeless, those who have suffered some form of physical or mental abuse … to name but some. I have, on many occasions, sought to draw attention to the fact that the plight of the disadvantaged in our country is a national problem of overwhelming significance. And that it is not a problem which can be – or which should be – simply left to governments to solve. It is a problem which must be faced by us all. It has consistently seemed to us that the gap between the advantaged and the disadvantaged, the haves and the have nots, is actually widening.

What is common to so many areas of disadvantage is the stark face of poverty: material poverty in the form of homelessness, inadequate clothing, sustenance, care or help which of course can lead to other consequences and other disadvantage such as alcoholism, physical and sexual abuse and family break-down. For so often, in these days of high unemployment – particularly youth unemployment – the grim companion of disadvantage is poverty of the spirit: the absence of hope, the deprivation of self-esteem, and the loss of confidence in one's ability to do anything about it.

On the other hand, the more contact that Helen and I have with the most vulnerable and disadvantaged of Australians, the more impressed we are by the extraordinary goodness – and that is the only word for it – of all those who work to help them. And we have met many thousands of them, both volunteers and employees of government and non-government organisations and institutions. I pay tribute to them all but make special mention of the volunteers.

I cannot express too strongly Helen's and my conviction that voluntary work is one of the most important influences in this country in maintaining both our sense of social identity as individuals and the minimum standards of social justice and decency required in any caring society. Whatever form that voluntary work takes, each hour that is freely given to help others is a significant contribution to the community and, through it, to our nation and us all.

My comments this evening have probably already indicated to you my personal touchstone and my main objective in performing the functions of Governor-General. My personal touchstone is a straight-forward one. It is that the ultimate test of our worth as a truly democratic nation is how we treat the most disadvantaged and vulnerable of our fellow Australians. My guiding objective should be apparent from the emphasis I have placed in these comments on multiculturalism, reconciliation and the disadvantaged. It is the objective that we Australians, indigenous and non-indigenous and regardless of our racial or cultural or other backgrounds, will go into the second century of our nation united as a people … walking together, talking together, working together, and achieving together – and with mutual respect, acceptance and care for one another. If, but only if, Helen and I have, at the end of my term of office, contributed just a little towards the satisfaction of that ultimate national test and the attainment of that objective, I will see my time in office as having been worthwhile. If we have not, I will count myself a failure.

4.7 The Presentation of the Inaugural Sydney Peace Prize, Sydney, 27 November 1998

The World Health Organisation has famously, and in my view correctly, defined good health as 'the complete state of physical, social and emotional well-being, not merely absence of disease'. In much the same way, peace is rather more than merely the absence of war.

For true peace, like good health, is a condition that involves physical, social and emotional well being: both of individual men, women and children and of the communities of which they form part. It is a 'complete state' in which people are at liberty and have the means to pursue their essential economic, educational, material and spiritual needs without the fear of violence, oppression and conflict.

Peace is also a matter of justice, as the Sydney Peace Foundation has cogently pointed out. For in a world where the population is approaching six billion – half of whom will soon live in urban areas – and where human suffering and premature death is overwhelmingly related to poverty, a cessation of overt hostilities may be only temporary and illusory if injustice continues to thrive. To quote directly from the Foundation: 'Peace requires initiatives to abolish the injustices of hunger and poverty, homelessness and illiteracy, unemployment, infant mortality and domestic violence'.

And such initiatives must necessarily involve more than short-term aid and assistance from donors to recipients, however well intentioned. If we are to work effectively for peace in the long term, what we really need are programs to build creative and trusting relationships … partnerships, if I may use words from the Code of Conduct developed by the Australian Council for Overseas Aid, that 'encourage self-help and self-reliance among beneficiaries, and thus avoid creating dependency'. And it is essential for the achievement of those objectives that we recognise and encourage such programs and identify and acknowledge, as role models, those who can properly be described as true peacemakers.

The objective of The Sydney Peace Foundation in maintaining and awarding the Sydney Peace Prize is to advance global peace and non-violence by recognising, acclaiming and rewarding outstanding work towards peace with justice, including efforts and achievement towards the abolition of the injustice of hunger and poverty, homelessness and unemployment.

It is difficult to envisage a more distinguished recipient of the inaugural Sydney Peace Prize than Professor Muhammad Yunus an outstanding scholar and academic, an economic adviser to governments and the World Bank, and the founder of the Grameen Bank of Bangladesh which exists to lend money to the poorest of the poor, thereby improving standards of living, combating poverty and giving access to dignified employment. By precept and by example, Professor Yunus has demonstrated the enduring virtues of self-help – of giving, as they say, 'a hand up' as opposed to a 'hand out'. He is one man who, in and through his life, has made an immeasurable contribution to the search for true peace. Truly, he is one of the great peacemakers of our time.

4.8 The Presentation of the 1998 Human Rights Medal, Sydney, 10 December 1998

We Australians are fortunate and privileged in that our very system of government embodies basic notions of equality, freedoms and rights under the law. But no one could seriously maintain that the fundamental rights enunciated in the Universal Declaration are yet *fully* enjoyed by *all* Australians. That point is adequately made simply by referring, in the context of the unemployment and poverty which exists in our affluent Australia, to the declarations, in the first sentences of Articles 23 and 25, of the right of everyone to protection against unemployment and of the right of everyone to a standard of living adequate for the health and well-being of himself and of his family. This 50th Anniversary is an occasion when we should realistically assess and acknowledge how much more needs to be done. And it is also an occasion when we should renew our commitment, as individuals and as a society, to the quest for the practical enjoyment of full human rights by all Australians.

But golden anniversaries should be a time for celebration. And celebration surely is the theme of this anniversary luncheon. I understand that, at each of the tables, there is a copy of this document listing the names and achievements of 50 great Australian men and women – one for each golden year. Each in his or her own way has made a significant contribution to the human rights movement in this country. Some of those names are well known … my friend and former chair of the Human Rights Commission, Dame Roma Mitchell; surgeon, humanitarian and internationalist, 'Weary' Dunlop;' Faith Bandler, to whom it was my privilege to present the Australian Human Rights Medal last year. Some of the names are not so well known, at least not to the general public. They are, however, shining examples to all who know of their work and their achievements in the cause of human rights.

There are 50 names here. But, of course, we could collectively add another 50 times 50 names, and we would still be merely describing the tip of the iceberg in each of a variety of fields of endeavour: in the women's movement, in the promotion of multicultural Australia, in reconciliation between Aboriginal and non-Aboriginal Australians, in overseas aid, refugee assistance and international peace; in religious ecumenism; in health and education; in the fight against poverty here in affluent Australia; and in promoting the well-being of Australians and non-Australians everywhere. There are names of people who are still with us, and some of whom are sharing this occasion. Others have died: Jessie Street, who accompanied Doctor Evatt to the United Nations founding conference in 1945; Bishop Burgmann, who dreamed of a time when the enduring truths of human faith and spirituality would be expressed in a manner, if I may borrow his words, 'thoroughly baptised into the Australian scene, blown through by Australian winds, bathed in Australian sunshine, and even coated now and then with Australian dust'.

Some of those mentioned have only recently died, and we still mourn their loss: Fred Hollows, the Human Rights medallist of 1990; Shirley Smith – 'Mum Shirl' – whose special place among Aboriginal Australians in this city and beyond was evident to all of us who attended her funeral last May; 'Nugget' Coombs whose breadth of vision, interests and activities was such that, as I observed at his memorial service, there is not one of us whose life has not been in some way touched and shaped by him, and almost invariably for the better.

Ladies and gentlemen, constraints of time preclude me from mentioning more than a few individual names. We each have our own special memories of those listed here and of those whom we each would add. What characterises them all is a dedication to the cause of human rights which transcends mere words and is evidenced by their lives and in their deeds. As the Human Rights and Equal Opportunity Commission quite rightly points out, universal declarations of any kind lack meaning without a commitment by individuals, no less than by governments and organisations, to give them life and application.

In that regard, it is well to remember that when, on this day in 1948, the General Assembly proclaimed the Universal Declaration of Human Rights as a common standard of achievement for all peoples and all nations, it also urged every individual and every organ of society to strive by teaching and education to promote respect for those rights and freedoms and by progressive means, nationally and internationally, to secure their universal and effective recognition and observance. There can be no doubt that each of those 50 people singled out for mention and all those others whom we remember have striven by word and deed to teach, to promote, to secure respect and observance of human rights. So that even as we look around the world on this 50th Anniversary and recognise how far we have to go before the Declaration is a universal reality, we are entitled to celebrate what has been achieved over the past half century. And to acknowledge how much is owed to the commitment, the compassion and the concerted efforts of individuals everywhere. Their achievements, and the achievements of bodies and organisations such as the Human Rights and Equal Opportunity Commission, provide the starting point for the work that lies ahead.

4.9 The Irish Government Lunch, Dublin, 30 April 1999

Over the past fifty years we have seen a remarkable transformation in Australia. During that half-century, more than five and a half million people have migrated to our shores from 140 different countries, representing all the regions, races, religions and cultures of the world.

That influx of new Australians from all parts of the world has not, however, undermined nor weakened Australia's Irish heritage which dates back to the first European settlement in 1788. To the contrary, the emphasis upon mutual acceptance of, and respect for, racial, religious and other differences which it has necessarily involved has served to heighten awareness of the Irish ancestry which so many Australians, including Helen and myself, share with you who live on this island. It has also helped to obliterate bitterness and antagonisms growing from differences of religious or regional backgrounds or from old antagonisms or injustices. In the result, the Irish influence in Australia is as vibrant, dynamic and as far-reaching as it ever was. Currently, more than one-third of Australians are Irish born or descended from Irish immigrants. That proportion is higher than in any other country outside Ireland itself. In total there are well over six million Australians who can claim some Irish ancestry. Considerably more than the total population of this island!

That being so, it is not surprising that the largest Parliamentary Friendship Group in the Australian Parliament is the Australia-Ireland one. It includes more than half the members of our national Parliament. When it became known that I was making this visit to Ireland, I was asked by the Executive of the Group to bring a message to the President of Ireland, and through her, to the Irish people. That message emphasizes the ideals of freedom, equality and a fair go for all which it recognises as coming to us from Ireland through the Irish who settled in Australia. It ends, with the expression of the hope and the prayer that those involved in the Northern Ireland peace process will succeed in bringing about a just and lasting peace and equal dignity for all. I should add that both the Australian Prime Minister, Mr Howard, and the Leader of the Opposition, Mr Beazley, have specifically asked me to tell you how fervently they support that message and that hope and prayer for true and lasting peace.

Before I came to Ireland for this visit, I thought carefully about the message I should bring to the Irish people from Australians, including those more than six million Australians of Irish descent … the Irish Diaspora under the Southern Cross. Ultimately, I had no doubt about what the character and the content of that message should be. In its character, it is a message of friendship and fellowship. In so far as Australians of Irish descent are concerned, it is a message of family … of true kinship. And from all Australians it is a message of real affection. In so far as content is concerned, it is the message of hope which our Australia-Irish Parliamentary Group asked me to convey … the hope of all Australians, that those involved in the present Northern Ireland peace process will succeed in achieving true and lasting peace and justice. We look to you the Government and all the people of Ireland, south and north, with real affection, with heartfelt support and with confidence that you will ensure that, in a world where there is so much present suffering by reason of past conflicts, hatreds and wrongs, the peace process is not allowed to falter or to fail.

4.10 The Turkish State Luncheon, Ankara, 3 May 1999

Eight days ago I had the privilege of making a visit to the Gallipoli Peninsula on Anzac Day – April 25 – the 84th Anniversary of the first landings there in 1915. I attended a number of services, including the joint Australia-New Zealand Dawn Service, the Turkish International Service, the Australian Service at Lone Pine and the Turkish 57th Regiment's service. These services brought home to me the central place that Gallipoli continues to have in the sense of nationhood of both our countries. We Australians are honoured that the name 'Anzac Cove', where the Australian and New Zealand soldiers first landed, was officially recognised by the Turkish authorities some years ago. Today it is within the Peace Park project on the Gallipoli Peninsula, which you, Mr President, have initiated. I express my own enthusiastic support of that project and my gratitude for your efforts.

Australians have taken part in many other battles since Gallipoli. But nothing in our subsequent war experience comes near what military historians have called the 'respect approaching affection' that the Australian and Turkish soldiers came to feel for each other. Indeed, the only memorial to a former wartime opponent on Anzac Parade in Canberra, outside our Australian War Memorial, is the Kemal Ataturk Memorial Garden, honouring the great man who commanded the Turkish troops on Gallipoli and who went on to become the founder of modern Turkey.

The visit to Turkey for Anzac Day and this official visit have given me an opportunity to gain a direct impression of Turkey's long history and culture and the issues and concerns which now confront it.

We in Australia recognise Turkey as a major power which plays an important role in an important – but volatile – region, and more widely. We welcome the constructive role which Turkey can play, as demonstrated most recently with respect to the situation in Kosovo, including the considerable humanitarian assistance which Turkey has provided. As you know, Mr President, my country is also assisting to relieve the tragic plight of the Kosovo refugees. The first of them is expected to arrive in Australia this week.

One cannot help but be impressed by the transformation of Turkey into a modern and dynamic state – initially under President Kemal Ataturk and now, Mr President, under your guidance and that of your Government. We recognise the strength of Turkey's rapid economic development of recent years. I congratulate you on all your achievements. We also recognise the importance to both our countries of the trade relations between us. We sincerely hope that they continue to grow.

And this visit has confirmed for me the great strength and the truly unique quality of the relationships between our countries .... between the Turkish and Australian people.

That close and friendly relationship between our two countries has many dimensions in addition to the growing trade and investment and the frequent cultural exchanges between our countries. The most important are the enduring bonds of human attachment and sentiment that have steadily strengthened since the first Turkish families arrived in Australia under the bilateral migration program 30 years ago.

Since late 1968, more than 40,000 Turkish people have made that journey. With the second and third generations, there are today some 100,000 people of Turkish heritage living in Australia. All those Australians of Turkish background are making an enormously important and much-valued contribution to the prosperity, stability and diversity of Australian society. It is not at all surprising that the bonds of friendship between our two countries should be so strong.

Indeed, Mr President, how could it be otherwise? For, as Kemal Ataturk pointed out in his compassionate words immortalised in the wonderful monument at Anzac Cove, our Australian young men who died at Gallipoli and remain buried in Turkish soil have also become your sons and part of your nation. Just as the Turkish men and women who have travelled, in later years, across the world to Australia – and their sons and their daughters – have become part of ours.

4.11 The Conferral of Degree of Doctor of Letters *Honoris Causa*, The University of Western Sydney, Bankstown, 24 September 1999

As we all know, Australia's indigenous peoples are immeasurably disadvantaged, as compared with non-indigenous Australians, on almost every measure of material well being – health, welfare, housing, employment to name but some. In all those areas of disadvantage, education provides an essential ingredient of successful resolution.

I wish to pay special tribute to the University for the extent to which its teaching and research are devoted to the areas of cultural studies and multiculturalism. In part, that reflects the fact that a large proportion of the students are from non-English speaking backgrounds. But it also indicates an appreciation of the importance, and the richness, of the multiculturalism which sustains our nation.

That 'multiculturalism' must, of course, be understood in our Australian context in a special way, that is, as referring to multicultural inclusiveness. So understood, it does not merely refer to the fact of the existence of many cultures. Rather, it refers to a policy of national inclusiveness. Its essence lies in a proper balance between respect for, and genuine tolerance of, the different national, racial, ethnic and religious backgrounds and cultures from which we come and the fundamental requirements of national identity, national unity and national standards.

So understood, multiculturalism does not detract from or threaten our national identity or national unity. To the contrary, while recognising and protecting our diversity of backgrounds, cultures and beliefs, it promotes that identity and unity by building upon and adding cohesion to what we are. It follows that our multiculturalism is not only decent, just and right in that it reflects mutual understanding, acceptance and respect. It is in our own interests as a nation.

Of course, many of today's graduates have come from abroad to study at the University of Western Sydney. The University has more than 3,000 foreign students … mainly from our region, but from more than 50 countries in all. Their presence reminds us of the undeniable fact that education is so much more rewarding when we are exposed to the often very different experiences of those from other countries. I hope that all the graduates today from overseas have enjoyed their time in Australia and return home with not just happy memories, but an understanding of and warmth towards our country thanks to their experience as students here at UWS.

4.12 The Presentation of the 44th Walkley Awards for Excellence in Journalism, Brisbane, 2 December 1999

Much has been written and spoken in recent weeks about the alleged waning influence of the media in this country. In these times of what amounts to a revolution in the popular means of communication, there is, of course, some truth in the suggestion that conventional written journalism, and *a fortiori* editorial writing, are under challenge. I claim no expertise whatsoever but I do know, from personal experience, that looking at a newspaper on the Internet is for me a much more hurried and cursory experience than when a newspaper is in one's hand. And that, if I am looking at a newspaper on the Internet, I am most unlikely to click onto the Editorial page.

The other side of the equation is, however, that the revolution in the electronic media, particularly with digitalisation and globalisation with all their aspects and possibilities, is exponentially increasing the overall actual and potential influence of the media as a whole. Those developments, and the so-called 'CNN factor', bring with them an increase in advantages and potential disadvantages. Advantages … in the way that knowledge can promote effective democracy, encourage international friendship, draw attention to disadvantage and deprivation and expose abuses of power and human rights … to name but one. Potential disadvantages … in the increased ability to arouse international ill-feeling, to distort and to mislead and to undermine the national and cultural integrity and identity of smaller vulnerable societies … again to name but one. As those advantages and potential disadvantages increase, the responsibilities of the media and those who work in it progressively become more onerous.

And, of course, at its most basic, the power of the media to affect the reputation and the lives of the individual, often ordinary, people who are the subject of its attention remains, and will remain, immense.

In combination, those and other considerations leave no room for doubting that it is essential that the fundamental principles that underlie your Code of Ethics be respected and upheld. Honesty, accuracy, fairness and a respect for the rights of others are perhaps the most important of them.

4.13 The Presentation of the 45th Walkley Awards for Excellence in Journalism, Sydney, 7 December 2000

In less than a month, we Australians will celebrate the Centenary of the Federation which brought our nation into being. In the forefront of the things to celebrate will be the fact that we are one of a comparatively few countries which can look back on a century of democratic rule uninterrupted by foreign occupation or by dictatorship of the left or right.

A well-informed public is an essential prerequisite of the effective working of such a democracy. In the circumstances of our community, much of the responsibility for providing essential information about public affairs necessarily falls upon the media. That responsibility can only be adequately discharged by a reasonably strong and efficient media which generally recognises and observes acceptable minimum standards of fairness and conduct.

And it is not just the wellbeing of our democracy that is heavily dependent upon high standards in our media. The continuing revolution in the electronic media is exponentially increasing the overall positive and negative potential influence of the media as a whole. Positive in the increased ability to encourage international friendship, draw attention to disadvantage and deprivation and expose abuses of power and human rights. Negative in the increased ability to arouse international ill feeling, to distort and mislead and to undermine the integrity and identity of smaller vulnerable societies or communities.

And, of course, at its most basic, the power of the media to affect the lives of those – often ordinary – people who are the subject of its attention remains immense.

These considerations all remind us how essential are the qualities of honesty, accuracy, fairness and respect for others prescribed by the Media Code of Ethics.

4.14 The Opening of the 2001 Sydney Royal Easter Show, Sydney, 11 April 2001

This is our Centenary of Federation Year Show. But the Royal Agricultural Society existed long before 1901. It was established in 1822, that is, within 34 years of the arrival of the First Fleet. Its first Show was held at Parramatta in 1823, some 78 years before Federation. Over the following 178 years, the Royal Easter Show has become firmly established as a central part of the life of this, our nation's oldest and largest city.

As a showcase of rural industry, the Sydney Show is absolutely pre-eminent. It is 'The Great Australian Muster' of the best of everything Australian, particularly rural Australian. It is also the flagship of our national Show movement which contributes so much to the economic, cultural, agricultural and sporting development of rural Australia.

At the same time, the Show helps remind city people of the abilities and achievements of rural Australians and of the difficulties which many of them face. Even within recent weeks, we have seen the devastating floods in northern New South Wales. I hope the Show will help to reassure those country people who are facing difficult times that they have the understanding and support of their fellow Australians everywhere.

As I approach the end of my time as Governor-General, I am particularly concerned about some of the continuing divisions within our Australian society: between the haves and the have-nots; between indigenous and non-indigenous Australians; between the city and the country. By bringing the country to the city and by bringing so many Australians together, the Easter Show is a powerful influence in resisting and overcoming those divisions.

4.15 The Opening of the Australian Education Assembly 2001, Melbourne, 18 April 2001

The Australian Education Assembly's 2001 theme – *Celebrating the Past, Shaping the Future* – is a most appropriate one. Primarily, that theme would seem to be directed to the past and future of *education* in Australia. So understood, it reflects the objective of affirming the centrality of education in the past and future shaping of our nation. That objective can, however, be equally well served by understanding the theme's references as being not merely to education in Australia but to the past and future of our nation as a whole.

Looking back, there is, as the theme suggests, much to celebrate as we recall the coming together, one hundred years ago, of the people of the six Australian colonies to 'be one nation'. There is our land itself – this matchless continent, its islands and surrounding seas. There is a century of democratic rule, unbroken by dictatorship, military coup, civil war or conquest. There are our Australian people, reflecting as they do our greatest achievement as a nation, namely, the way we have, at least in recent decades, made our diversity of origins, race and culture a source of national strength and unity rather than a cause of weakness and division. And there are so many other things.

At the same time, and notwithstanding that this is a time for national celebration, there is little real point in looking back unless we are prepared also to acknowledge the flaws which detract from or mar the achievements of the past. Similarly, any acceptable blueprint for the future should not only celebrate and seek to build upon past and present achievements. It should also address and seek to overcome past and present flaws and their effects. For the past is never fully gone. It is absorbed into the present and the future. It stays to shape what we are and what we do.

What then is the message that should be drawn from this Education Assembly's theme if it be understood as referring to celebrating the past and shaping the future of our nation generally? It seems to me that the answer to that question can be expressed in a four-word phrase: 'Education is the Key'.

For one thing, education is the key to claiming and understanding our past. Take, for example, our history of democratic rule. Obviously, education is the key to understanding the worth and the extent of that past achievement. And equally obviously, education is the key to maintaining and building upon it by safeguarding the effective working of our democracy in the future.

And, probably even more important, education is the key to identifying and acknowledging past flaws and to understanding and facing the resulting challenges which we Australians must meet if we are successfully to shape and own our future. Let me illustrate that point by reference to the great challenge of justice and basic decency which reaches from the past to confront all Australians as we enter our second century as a nation.

As the Council for Aboriginal Reconciliation recognised in its Final Report last December, education must play a key direct and indirect role in the search for true and lasting Aboriginal reconciliation.

The direct role is in addressing the immense gap which continues to exist between the educational standards, including literacy and numeracy, of the average indigenous student finishing school and the average non-indigenous one. While the position varies in different areas and while there is some room for genuine disagreement about some details, a number of basic facts are beyond intelligent dispute. For me, the most basic of them all is that, in many remote communities, the standard of the average Aboriginal student at the conclusion of formal education is far far below the literacy and numeracy level required for effective functioning in mainstream Australia.

Education must also play an indirect role in achieving reconciliation in at least three respects. First, the education of indigenous Australians, particularly the young, as the key to overcoming disadvantage in other areas such as health, life expectancy, employment, living conditions and self esteem. Second, to quote the Reconciliation Council's Final Report, the 'education of decision makers and people who provide services' as the key to their working 'effectively through respectful partnerships' with indigenous people. Third, the education of the wider community as the key to the general understanding and acknowledgment of the issues of reconciliation. Those issues include the shameful facts of past dispossession and oppression and present disadvantage and the extent to which the present entrenched problems, both spiritual and practical, of indigenous Australians flow from those past injustices.

To see education as the key to celebrating the past and to shaping the future of our nation is necessarily to draw attention to the critical importance – and also the extent – of the task of our educators, particularly those entrusted with the education of the nation's young.

There has, over recent years, been a rather depressing tendency in some places to measure the success of our secondary schools and their students almost exclusively by reference to the narrow yardstick of results in the final year certificate. That is not surprising in circumstances where the combined effects of the distressing rates of youth unemployment and the very high marks required for entry to the most sought-after tertiary courses are such that, once the transitional Years 11 and 12 are reached, the pressures upon schools, teachers, students and parents to concentrate on achieving high examination marks to the exclusion of just about everything else are, at times, almost overwhelming. In that context, academic results are, of course, very important. But they are not all-important. To the contrary, it is essential that our schools, teachers, students and parents keep a proper sense of proportion and pay due regard to the legitimate claims of other things which are important to the personal development of the individual student and the fulfilment of his or her complete potential.

Moreover, as the Draft of An Australian Declaration for Education 2001 which will be put before your Assembly points out, our schools must be concerned with discharging the public purposes of education. Those public purpose include – and I quote some of the words of para 7 of section 3 of the Draft – 'induction into citizenship, so that people can act as responsible citizens and participate effectively in community and national affairs; the inculcation of common understandings about what it means to be Australian and what are the core values of Australian society; and the promotion of strongly espoused national issues like equity, social justice and equality of opportunity.'

The challenges and issues which you face are as diverse as the backgrounds, personalities, vulnerabilities and capacities of your students; as exacting as the values and legitimate hopes and expectations of our community; and as dynamic and complex as our twenty-first century Australian society and its relationship with the world.

5

Religion and Respect

5.0 Editor's note

The cover of this book includes a photo of a mosaic on the mural wall at the Australian Centre for Christianity and Culture in Canberra. The mosaic is an accurate reproduction of a painting by Hector Jandany from the Gija/Kija people in Warmun in the East Kimberley. The painting is entitled 'The Holy Spirit in our Land' and it depicts the white owl of the Kimberley. The painting was commissioned by Sir William Deane and Lady Helen Deane in 2005. They gave it to the National Gallery of Australia in 2008. William Deane first became familiar with the art of Hector Jandany when Hector came to Canberra during the World Council of Churches Assembly in 1991. Artists from the Warmun community featured in the 'Aboriginal Art and Spirituality' exhibition which was put on display in the foyer of the High Court when Deane was a Justice of the court. During his term as Governor-General, Deane was a great supporter of the Australian Centre for Christianity and Culture. As patron, he had mentioned to the Queen his 'hope that a ceremony related to the commencement of construction of the new National Centre for Christianity and Culture in Canberra should be one of the major activities of the (Queen's 2000) visit'. That was not to be. He acknowledged earlier advice that Her Majesty 'should not be involved in the laying of a foundation stone in case the project was not completed'. He provided great support and drew much inspiration from the Anglican Bishop George Browning and the Uniting Church minister and scholar James Hehir. Deane, a Catholic, was always ecumenical in his outreach as Governor-General and took every opportunity he could to foster inter-faith dialogue.

When sworn in as a High Court judge, Deane had spoken of 'the God in whom I profoundly believe'. As Governor-General, when commemorating the dead at national events he would often conclude his remarks saying: 'May they rest with God'. As Governor-General, he constantly encountered 'an unspoken perception of a common bond which exists between all Christians regardless of denominational boundaries'.

After his retirement as Governor-General, Deane agreed to be interviewed about his faith on the ABC *Encounter* program. He told the interviewer Bill Bunbury: 'More and more the whole of Christianity ... for me comes down to Chapter 25 of St Matthew's Gospel: I was hungry and he gave me food; I was thirsty, he gave me drink; I was without a home and he took me in ... I was in prison and you came to me. That, if you think about the context of St Matthew's Gospel, is the whole touchstone by which according to Christian belief, one's life ultimately tends to be assessed, or stands to be assessed.' Deane's respect for people of all faiths and none was always exemplary. A week after this interview, Deane spoke at the opening of the Chapel for the Australian Centre for Christianity and Culture. He commenced his remarks: 'Forever there was God: the spirit and the source of life. Then there was creation and time began: with its story of matter, of our universe and of human beings inhabiting our world, including, throughout all the millennia of the Dreamtime, this ancient Continent.' He then traced his vision of a Universal Christian Church:

> When Christianity finally came here, it was accompanied – and betrayed – by the dispossession and oppression of the indigenous peoples based upon the doctrine of *terra nullius's* cruel untruth that their ancestral lands had been uninhabited. It was also weakened by divisive interdenominational rivalries and intolerance. While countless good – and sometimes great – men and women of vision and action achieved extraordinary things for the various Christian churches, it is only in very recent times that the yearning among Christians everywhere for the fellowship of common witness has found concrete expression and that the heightened perception of a Universal Christian

> Church has largely stilled the divisiveness of past internal bitterness and intolerance.

He proclaimed that the fundamental truth of Matthew Chapter 25 'is shared by other great religions of the world'. He footnoted 'Judaism's recognition that I *am* my brother's keeper and Islam's 'Golden Rule' and prescription of 'true charity' to all in need.' He said this fundamental truth 'should guide our nation. For, surely, it is the measure of the worth of any true democracy such as ours'. He concluded: 'Finally, to all our fellow Australians, Christian and non-Christian, we say: join us in our pilgrimage towards reconciliation, tolerance and justice and towards overcoming the divisions within our land. Let us talk together, walk together, strive together and achieve together. That way, we will also walk with God. Come with us.'

5.1 The Cardinal's Dinner, Sydney, 2 August 1996

It is now a little over five months since I was 'sworn in' as the twenty-second Governor-General of Australia. In that short period, Helen and I have travelled throughout the country, visiting every state and territory, in most cases on a number of occasions. Part of those visits have been taken up with official things such as official dinners, receptions and military occasions. Much of our activities have, however, been of our own choosing. The things which we have chosen to do have included accepting many invitations to visit, and to be associated with, the activities of organisations helping the sick, the needy and the disadvantaged. Those visits and that association have done much to heighten our awareness of the problems which are being faced by the many disadvantaged in our country.

Underlying a large proportion of those problems is, of course, the terrible blight of unemployment, particularly youth unemployment which the prime minister last week identified as the major social problem facing our nation. Real social justice for the disadvantaged must remain a myth unless and until current levels of unemployment are drastically reduced. Our visits to a large number of centres giving aid to the disadvantaged, including unemployed young people, have made us much more conscious than we ever were in the past of the devastation, including loss of dignity and self-respect, which too often flows from inability to obtain work. Where the young are concerned, it is so often all to difficult to persuade them that unemployment is more likely to result from community deficiencies rather than personal inadequacy.

Another overwhelming problem of which we have become increasingly aware is the plight of Indigenous Australians. The modern view is that one must – in the current jargon – adopt a holistic approach. While that is no doubt correct, it would now seem to be accepted by both governments and professionals that the problem of Aboriginal health must be urgently acknowledged and faced.

The publication 'Australia's Health 1996' which was launched by the Minister for Health and Family Services, Dr Wooldridge, within the last few weeks documents a widening gap between the health levels of Aboriginal and Torres Strait Islander peoples and other Australians.

However one views those figures, the problem which they represent is one which, I suggest, must be more effectively addressed in the short period of four and one-half years leading up to the centenary of our nation than it has been in the ninety-five and one-half years that have passed since Federation. And that notwithstanding the dedicated efforts of many political leaders and government and private professionals. Unless it is more effectively addressed, true reconciliation with the Aboriginal peoples will be unlikely and Australia will remain a diminished nation as it enters its second century.

Those are depressing things which we have learnt or of which we have become increasingly aware. There are, in contrast, many uplifting things. Our many visits to organisations serving the disadvantaged throughout the country have made us conscious of the extraordinary goodness – and that is the only word – of those who serve in them. Most of those organisations have been conducting outreach programs of the various denominations of the Christian Church. Our visits to them have brought home to us with considerable force the fact that the Christian Church's mission of service and compassion for the sick, the needy and the disadvantaged is being jointly discharged throughout this country by Christians of all denominations. Those involved in them demonstrate a Christian spirit which transcends the divisions between individual churches. That leads me to a related topic.

As you all know, the last few months have been marked by two national tragedies: one in the south at Port Arthur; the other in the north near Townsville. The effect of each was to focus public attention upon religious matters. After each, I was privileged to visit privately with the families of those who had been killed and to participate in a series of ecumenical memorial services. It seems to be widely known that I am a practising Catholic – apparently the first to be appointed Governor-General – and I have received a very large number of letters from practising Christians and Christian organisations about the tragedies and their aftermath and the fact that the national reaction to them was expressed through the Christian Church.

The thing that has struck me most about all those communications, whether through personal contact or written correspondence, is that they have reflected an unspoken perception of a common bond which exists between all Christians regardless of denominational boundaries. That and Helen's and my involvement in the activities of the members of other churches has led me to pause and think about how far we Christians have come in recent years and how much further there is to go.

Those of you who are of my generation will recall the environment in which our faith was instilled. That environment was one of great intolerance between Christians of the Catholic Church and Christians of other denominations. On the Catholic side, we can recall sad and hurtful incidents of anti-Catholic prejudice and bigotry even from close non-Catholic friends. If we are honest, however, we can also recall incidents and actions on the part of Catholics which were equally insulting and hurtful to Christians of other denominations and which any informed mind would today regard as lacking in charity. Our attitude seems to have been that we Catholics were completely and exclusively right and that our fellow Christians of other denominations were completely and infectiously wrong.

Thus we were taught that to attend the christening of a friend's child in a Presbyterian church, to attend a friend's marriage in a Methodist church or even to attend a friend's funeral in an Anglican church was, in the absence of permission which was often refused, grievously sinful. Unconscious of the bitter irony, we were actually instructed that our attendance at such a service would give scandal to others attending it: scandal to the parents who had asked us to share their child's induction into Christianity; scandal to the friends who had wanted us to share their Christian wedding; scandal to the relatives who wanted us to share their grief at a Christian burial. The memories of those past times may now seem bizarre and irrelevant. But the past is never fully gone. It stays to help shape the present and the future. I fear that its unconscious aftermath may be a reluctance on the part of some Catholics to acknowledge and proclaim the importance, in a largely secular world, of the principles and beliefs which are shared by all true Christians.

For me, one abiding effect of my first five months as Governor-General is a heightened appreciation of the bond of belief and principle which unites sincere Christians of all denominations: what Bishop Heather has recently called 'the areas of common understanding'. That is not, of course, to deny, again to quote

Bishop Heather, the 'important differences of interpretation and practice' between different denominations. It is, however, to assert that those differences must not be allowed to conceal or diminish the deep fellowship which should exist between all who, in their different ways, seek to follow the teachings of Christ.

Our Catholic Church is, as Bishop Geoffrey Robinson has recently pointed out with his customary insight, now a pluralist church. With pluralism has come an acceptance by most Catholics of our diversity and an environment in which it is much easier to look beyond the boundaries which mark our own identity and appreciate and admire the splendour of the lives and faith of Christians of other denominations. It is in that environment that we approach the momentous coming events of the years 2000 and 2001. Olympic Games in this very city. The centenary of the establishment of our nation. Hopefully, reconciliation with Indigenous Australians. Surely, to borrow the words of *Ut Unum Sint,* as we approach the 2000th jubilee of the incarnation, we should be looking at least as hopefully for full reconciliation, if not full unity, between the Christian people of all denominations. For true reconciliation, there must, of course, be acknowledgment of past shortcomings.

It was, with the benefit of hindsight, absurd and wrong that mainstream Christian denominations in this country focused upon things which divided Catholics and non-Catholics rather than the basic tenets of Christianity which united them. It is true that, in this country, we at least did not organise to kill one another purportedly in the name of God. Nonetheless, it seems to me to be of critical importance that we recognise that it is only by acknowledging past shortcomings and appreciating the essential community of all Christians that we will adequately discharge our obligations of charity within the universal Christian church of the future.

Finally, a few words about Helen's and my aspirations for the period I am Governor-General.

A former Governor-General once said that the main function of the office, as he saw it, was to interpret the Australian nation to itself. There is wisdom in that. We hope, to the best of our ability, to represent all the Australian people and to interpret and identify, as best we can, the things that are important to our national spirit, including the things that make us one people and one nation. That is not, of course, an easy task.

On a more personal note, we hope to focus our personal efforts on the disadvantaged. That sounds like words and it may end up like words. Nonetheless, we are going to do the best we can. Hopefully, at the end of the road, we will have done a little bit of good. If we have, it will only be because we enjoy the goodwill and support of people such as yourselves.

5.2 Executive Council Of Australian Jewry, 10 September 1996

First of all let me say how extremely welcome you, the members of the Executive Council of Australian Jewry, are to Yarralumla. Helen and I are very conscious of the great work done by the various constituent bodies and affiliated organisations of the Executive Council and of the important role played by the Council itself for both the Jewish Community and Australia.

It is a particular joy to have Sir Zelman Cowen and Lady Cowen here with us this evening. As you are aware, Sir Zelman was the first Honorary Secretary of the Executive Council of Australian Jewry when it was established in 1944. That, of course, was while the holocaust was continuing. How extraordinary it is to think that that is now more than half a century ago. We all have a duty, as much to the future as to those who were slaughtered, to ensure that its awful lessons are remembered for so long as our world exists. I would add the comment that it is not surprising to me that the Executive Council has recently been speaking out in support of the Aboriginal peoples who were also dispossessed and devastated or that, through Mr Jeremy Jones, the Executive Council is in the forefront of the search for reconciliation between them and our nation as a whole.

Yarralumla is Aboriginal for the place where the cry comes back from the mountain. The mountain, out there, was known as the Blacks' Mountain. It is now Black Mountain. The central structure of the house, which is built on the ancestral lands of the Ngunnawal people, already existed in 1901 when our nation came into being. It was purchased by the Commonwealth in 1913 and became the official residence of the Governor-General in 1927. In it, successive Australian Prime Ministers have been sworn in and have resigned. Here, the first Australian born Governor-General, Sir Isaac Isaacs, took up residence in February 1931. His appointment had been bitterly opposed by the then King, George V, on the ground that Isaacs was by birth and allegiance an Australian. In the study, across the hall, there occurred the critical act of November 11, 1975 when a subsequent Australian born Governor-General dismissed a Prime Minister who clearly retained the support of a majority of the House of Representatives but who was, in the Governor-General's view, unable to obtain the passage in the Senate of the legislation necessary to supply the funds of government. Here, that great healer, Sir Zelman Cowen, with Lady Cowen, came in 1977 as the nineteenth Australian Governor-General.

5.3 The Opening of the Seaford Ecumenical Centre, Adelaide, 24 November 1996

There are many depressing things which we have learnt or of which we have become increasingly aware. Such as the terrible plight of many of the Aboriginal peoples. And the overwhelming problem of unemployment, particularly youth unemployment. There have, in contrast, been some uplifting things, including something which is of particular relevance today's gathering. That is that our many visits to organisations serving the disadvantaged throughout the country have made us conscious of the extraordinary goodness – and that is the only word – of those who serve in them. Most of those organisations have been conducting outreach programs of the various denominations of the Christian Church. Our visits to them have brought home to us with considerable force the fact that the Christian Church's mission of service and compassion for the sick, the needy and other disadvantaged is being jointly discharged throughout Australia by Christians of all denominations. Those involved in them demonstrate a Christian spirit which transcends the divisions between individual churches.

It is that Christian spirit of goodness and charity which has inspired the coming together of five mainstream Christian Churches – the Anglican, the Catholic, the Churches of Christ, the Lutheran and the Uniting – not only to establish this Centre of Christian worship and Christian outreach to the community, particularly the disadvantaged, but also to be associated with the South Australian Health Commission, through Noarlunga Health Services, in the establishment of a community health and welfare Centre.

For Helen and me, an abiding effect of my first nine months as Governor-General is a heightened appreciation of the bond of belief and principle which unites sincere Christians of all denominations. That is not, of course, to deny the importance of the differences of interpretation and practice between different denominations. It is, however, to assert that those differences must not be allowed to conceal or diminish the deep fellowship which should exist between all of us who, in our different ways, seek to follow the teachings of Christ.

With the mutual tolerance, understanding and respect that lie at the heart of the modern ecumenical movement, there has fortunately come an environment in which it is much easier for a Christian of one particular denomination to look beyond the boundaries of that denomination and to appreciate and admire the splendour of the lives and faith of Christians of other denominations. It is in that environment that we approach the momentous coming events of the years 2000 and 2001. The end of a millennium. The centenary of the establishment of our nation. Hopefully, reconciliation with indigenous Australians. Surely, as we approach the 2000th jubilee of the incarnation, we should be looking at least as hopefully for mutual support and respect and full reconciliation, as distinct from full unity, between Christians of all denominations.

It is in that context that one must view this coming together of five great Christian churches to establish this ecumenical Centre of Christian worship and outreach services. The Centre of Christian worship represents a wonderful example to all Australian Christians of ecumenism in practice while the discharge of the Christian mission of outreach in co-operation with State funded health and welfare agencies and services reminds us all of something which our modern materialistic society often makes it to easy to forget, namely, that the Christian mission of outreach to the sick, the needy and other disadvantaged is the central thesis of our Christian faith.

The theme of togetherness which permeates this new Centre of Christian welfare and community service will, I sincerely hope, also be an inspiration to the Seaford area generally, to the State of South Australia and to the country as a whole. Apart from the Aborigines, we Australians are all immigrants or descended from immigrants. Out strength lies in the mutual tolerance which has allowed and fostered the combination of our diversity of cultures, races and backgrounds to form a single nation. While we immediately or more distantly come from all the regions and all the races of the world, we are united as one people. The approach, the ethos and the conviction which underlie that strength and that unity from diversity, and which have enjoyed bipartisan support in national and State Parliaments, is that of multiculturalism.

Multiculturalism does not mean that those habits, customs, cultures or traditions are immune from examination or reasoned criticism within Australia. It does, however, mean that, within the limits that are consistent with the overriding obligations and loyalties of Australian citizenship and with the duties imposed by valid Australian laws, all our citizens are entitled to expect and demand that the mutual respect and tolerance which are of its essence should be encouraged and, in some circumstances, protected. The reason why that is so is that to undermine that mutual respect or to defy or deny that tolerance within our land is to defy or to deny the very basis of our Australian nation. Once it is recognised that we are, with all our cultural, ethnic and religious backgrounds, truly one nation one people, it necessarily follows that to hurt or diminish any of us is to hurt or diminish us all. It is essential that we Australians be vigilant to defend the mutual respect, support and tolerance upon which our multicultural nation was built and which still underpin it. And that is not so much because we are concerned about what other nations or other people might think or expect of us. It is because our multiculturalism is decent, just and right. It is not only our Australian way. It is what we are.

In that wider context, this Centre sends a message of mutual tolerance, respect and support which reaches far beyond this community. May its message be heard throughout the land.

5.4 The Graduation Ceremony at Notre Dame Australia University, Perth, 3 March 1997

A University and a Law School established and conducted with the traditions and standards of a tolerant and compassionate Christian institution has much to offer the Australian Christian Churches and the general Australian community. I also venture to think that a specifically Catholic University and Law School which, to paraphrase some words of Bishop Ernest Burgmann, transposes the things of abiding value in the Catholic tradition so that they are 'thoroughly baptised into the Australian scene, blown through by

Australian winds [and] bathed in Australian sunshine' has much to offer the universal Christian Church.

I have, on a number of occasions, expressed the conviction that the achievement of a true and lasting reconciliation between the Aboriginal peoples of Australia and the nation of which they form such a significant part is one of the most important challenges facing Australia as we approach the new millennium and the centenary of our Federation. There are many complex issues involved – health, housing, employment, land, social and economic injustices. But as regards each of them, an essential ingredient of successful resolution is education ... access to full educational opportunities for Aboriginal people themselves; education for the broader community about Aboriginal perspectives and approaches and disadvantage that will, in time to come, lead to new understandings and respect and to general recognition of past injustices.

The University of Notre Dame has established a Campus at Broome specialising in Aboriginal education, and largely composed of Aboriginal students. All students at the College of Law will be given the opportunity to study indigenous law and culture at Broome, to help them understand and value Aboriginal perspectives and approaches. Through the contribution it is making to Aboriginal education on its Broome Campus and through the contribution it is making to non-Aboriginal appreciation and understanding of Aboriginal perspectives and approaches, the University is making, and the new College of Law will make, a significant contribution to the whole process of reconciliation. I might add that that contribution accords well with the traditions and ethical standards to which the University subscribes.

5.5 Rotary District No 9600's Annual Conference, Caloundra, Queensland, 22 March 1997

During the period of more than 13 months that I have been in this job, Helen and I have visited and become associated with a very large number of organisations helping the sick, the needy and other disadvantaged throughout all the States and Territories of the Commonwealth. Those visits have brought home to us a number of things. One of them is the plain fact that the collective plight of the disadvantaged in this country is an overwhelming national problem. The gap between the haves and the have nots, the advantaged and the disadvantaged, seems to us to be widening rather than narrowing. In particular, unemployment, especially among the young and the indigenous peoples, is having devastating consequences across the whole spectrum of our society. In the case of youth unemployment, it is undermining and even destroying the self-esteem and self-confidence of a significant proportion of a whole generation of Australians.Another thing these visits and direct association have brought home to us is that, again and again, we have found either in the forefront, or somewhere in the background of some other organisation, helping the disadvantaged there is a Rotary Club or a Rotarian providing financial or practical support or guidance.

The Rotarians of today in this country face increasing difficulties and discouragements in discharging Rotary's mission of service to the community. Working hours are often longer. The pressures of family life are often greater. Sponsorship and access to the corporate dollar are often more difficult to obtain. Those whom it is sought to assist are often more unresponsive. In the case of the entrenched disadvantaged, particularly the young unemployed who have reached the stage where self-respect and self-esteem are diminished or even lost they may be defensive, abrasive and sometimes even resentful of those who seek to help. I sincerely hope that those increasing difficulties and discouragements will not be allowed to discourage or diminish the work of Rotary and Rotarians in this country at this time when that work is so greatly needed.

The theme of this conference is Rotary's famous four-way test. That four-way test flows naturally from the qualities that lie at the heart of Rotary International. This morning, I propose to seek to place the four-way test in context by identifying those qualities which underlie it.

In one sense, the story of Rotary International corresponds with the history of tolerance and freedom throughout the world. Thus, Rotary, like tolerance and freedom, were suppressed and lost under fascism and restored in the enemy countries only after the Second World War had been fought and won. In another sense, Rotary International has represented almost a counter-point to the history of outside events and attitudes. It has stood steadfast and true to principles and virtues that the world has seemed to be questioning and discarding. Where mere pragmatism and selfish materialism have seemed the norm, it has proclaimed its unqualified message of honesty and selfless service.

Rotary International insistence on principle has not given rise to self-righteous self-importance or undue seriousness. The starting point of Rotary lay in a search for companionship. That search was rewarded by the fellowship of Rotary throughout the world. With that companionship has come a shared sense of fun which has precluded self-importance or self-righteousness. Vision and selfless service may be the hallmarks of Rotary International but humour and light-hearted companionship has been the adhesive that has held together the individual Clubs which, in their totality, constitute world Rotary.

Rotary's visionary central thesis of service above self has consistently been marked by its determination and practical commonsense. In all the countries in all the corners of the world where it exists, it has been translated by Rotarians into the hard fact of achievement.

No one could satisfactorily discharge the task of listing the achievements of Rotary throughout the world in the 50 years that have passed since Paul Harris died. Even if one could catalogue all the individual works of all the more than 27,500 Rotary Clubs, one would have but part of the complete picture. On the larger perspective, there is the global work of Rotary International itself. For example, there are the educational scholarships and exchange programs which have a total yearly budget that, on the most recent figures I have seen, was approaching $100,000,000. There are other vast projects such as the current plan to eliminate polio by the year 2005. One also has Rotary International's role in the establishment of important world economic and social entities, including a number of the United Nation's agencies. And always, from the local to the world stage, there has been the contribution which has probably been the most important, albeit the least tangible of all, the influence of the example of dedicated service to others, particularly the disadvantaged, by the members of Rotary International, individually and collectively.

And, of course, we finally come back to the noun which Paul Harris himself identified as the single most important attribute of Rotary, namely, toleration or tolerance. The existence of that quality in a movement dedicated to a denial of discriminatory distinctions based on racial, cultural or religious persuasion or background is surely inevitable. Its importance cannot be over-estimated. Nor can the importance of the practical and symbolic role which Rotary plays in promoting tolerance in every major community of our multicultural nation. That tolerance and the mutual respect which flows from it are the very essence of the multiculturalism which sustains our nation.

In what I have said, I have endeavoured to illustrate how the qualities of Paul Harris persist to inspire the great world movement which exists as his monument 50 years after his death. In truth, of course, the essence of Rotary International is to be found not so much at the world level as at the level of the individual Clubs. As I have indicated, for me it lies in a unique mixture of vision, selfless service, companionship, humour, commonsense, tolerance and plain goodness.

5.6 The Launch of the Mary Mackillop Foundation, Sydney, 22 July 1997

In the context of the status of women in the Australian colonies of the 19th century, the story of Mary Mackillop is one of the great epics of our land. She was born in Melbourne in 1842. By the time she turned 25 she had founded the Congregation of the Sisters of St Joseph. Through the closing three decades and more of the 19th century and throughout the whole of the 96 year history of our nation, the Sisters of the Order have directly and indirectly served countless Australians in the course of discharging the Mission which Mother Mary of the Cross prescribed for herself and for those who followed and follow in her footsteps. That Mission was from the outset essentially one of outreach to those who were in need of education or otherwise deprived of basic ingredients of social well-being or self-respect.

Necessarily, that mission of service of the disadvantaged has been adjusted – and expanded – over the years to meet contemporary needs. Its essence of courage, sacrifice and sheer goodness has however remained constant. It has encompassed teaching, nursing, sustaining, encouraging, befriending or otherwise helping those in need in all parts of our country – especially in rural areas – and beyond.

Today, as we approach the centenary of our nation and the commencement of the third millennium of our time, we are gathered to launch a Foundation which will help the Josephite Order, which that great Australian woman founded, continue that mission of service.

Some of you may recall that, when I took on the job of Governor-General, I indicated that Helen and I hoped to help focus community attention upon the disadvantaged and, in particular, to contribute in a small way to the process of reconciliation between Australia's indigenous people and the nation of which they form such an important part. In seeking to make good that undertaking, we have, in the past 17 months, visited or become associated with an extraordinarily large number of government and non-government agencies and institutions serving the many categories of disadvantage in every part of the country: the Aboriginal peoples, the unemployed, the direct and indirect victims of physical and sexual abuse, drugs and gambling, the homeless, the frail aged, the mentally disturbed, those seeking rehabilitation after imprisonment and those who, even in multicultural Australia, are subjected to racial discrimination and intolerance ... to identify but some of the categories of need. Those visits and that association have confirmed what we already instinctively knew, namely, that the collective plight of the disadvantaged in our country is overwhelming. Indeed, the gap between the haves and the have nots, the advantaged and the disadvantaged, seems to us to be widening rather than narrowing. And, in many critical areas, that impression of a widening gap is supported by cold hard statistical facts. Thus, for example, recent research has established that the gap – already almost 20 years – between the average life expectancy of indigenous Australians and that of other Australians is, despite all the efforts of governments and private agencies, actually increasing. Again, the statistics of youth unemployment, which seem to me to understate the problem, show that approximately 30 percent of young people who wish to exercise their basic right to work are unable to do so. In many areas, and particularly among Aboriginal communities, youth unemployment is over 50 and 60 percent and, in many cases, is second and, in some cases, even third generation.

Behind those cold statistics there lie the human facts. Behind the statistics of youth unemployment, there lie the disillusionment and the awful loss of self-respect and self-esteem of a significant part of a whole generation of young Australians. Behind the statistics of indigenous mortality and morbidity, there lies the terrible story of the suffering and premature deaths of fellow countrymen.

Not surprisingly, in that context, the message which I bring you today is that in our wealthy contemporary Australia there is as great a need for the discharge of the Josephite mission of outreach to those in need as at any time since the Second World War.

Two of the three major projects which the Foundation is addressing at the outset lie at the heart of contemporary Australian need. The first is the furtherance of the work of the Sisters for Australia's indigenous people. In Helen's and my travels and in our contacts with Aboriginal communities and people, we have heard nothing but praise for the work of the Sisters of St Joseph for Australia's indigenous people ... particularly in the East Kimberley region of Western Australia. Recently, at the Reconciliation Convention in Melbourne, Helen gently pointed out that the place of women in the crusade for true reconciliation is absolutely vital and that non-indigenous and indigenous women, through communication, co-operation and joint work and influence, must show the way if we are to achieve the objective of true reconciliation by the time we enter our second century as a nation. With adequate funding, I have no doubt that the Sisters of St Joseph will continue in the forefront of that crusade and that the Mary Mackillop Foundation, which those of us who are gathered here today are establishing, will make a most significant contribution to the achievement of that objective. If it does that, it will make an invaluable contribution to our national identity, decency, self-respect and well-being.

The second of the initial projects is the important grief education program for young people in crisis – a program called 'Seasons for Growth' – which was launched last year for both primary and secondary students. We are all aware of the terrible youth suicide statistics in Australia. We have one of the highest rates in the industrialised world, particularly among young men in rural areas – a constituency that has always been of special concern for the Sisters. The Seasons program is directed towards helping vulnerable young Australian as they seek to cope with grief, loss and perceived failure and inadequacy in all its forms. The need for the program and its worth seem to me to be beyond question.

The third initial project involves support for the Mary Mackillop Institute of East Timorese Studies. That Institute was founded in 1994, after a visit to Sydney by the recent Nobel Laureate, consultation with Bishop Carlos Belo. Since then, the Sisters have committed themselves to developing educational programs in East Timor. Through the medium of the Tetum language, the Institute aims to support the well-being of all East Timorese people, to promote human dignity and to preserve their cultural and religious traditions. The program is non-political and in no way calculated to damage relationships between Australia and Indonesia.

In combination, those three initial projects – two to aid Australians in need and one to advance the welfare of the neighbouring people of East Timor who so gallantly helped our countrymen in time of war – are as well chosen, well targeted and truly worthy as one could hope. And let me stress that we who support the Foundation are not giving to the Sisters. Rather, we are entrusting them with the means of sustaining the dedication of their lives to the service not of themselves but of others. May our support and their labour combine to continue the mighty work of the great Australian woman whose name the Foundation bears.

5.7 The Opening of the 1997 Religion & Cultural Diversity Conference, Melbourne, 28 July 1997

'Religion And Cultural Diversity: Global Challenges And Local Responsibilities'

The cultures and traditions of the original inhabitants of our continent stretch back into the Dreamtime of 60,000 years ago. When the first Europeans arrived in 1788 to establish a militarily-run penal settlement, they made little sustained effort to understand the nature or the content of those cultures and traditions or the strength of the bonds between the indigenous peoples and their land or territory. Nor was there any real understanding of the extent to which indigenous belief in the supernatural enriched the lives of the Aborigines, provided continuity with the past while explaining the present, identified and regulated relationships, provided the context and content of aspirations and regulated almost all aspects of life and conduct.

This afternoon is not an occasion for me to become involved in a debate about what can and cannot properly be characterised as 'a religion'. I would, however, venture the view that, if one accepts - as Theravada Buddhism demonstrates and the highest court in this country has held – that one can have a religion which is not based on the relationship with a particular personalised deity, it would seem clear enough that not only the first cultures but also the first religions of our land were those of the indigenous peoples. I say cultures and religions, the plural rather than the singular, for the reason that there were great variations, in spiritual beliefs and cultural traditions and practices, between the many distinct clans and local territories of pre-European times. For example, it has been conservatively estimated that more than 200 distinct and mutually unintelligible languages were spoken in different localities and by different clans.

It follows that, from earliest times, our continent was the home of a diversity of cultures and religions. Over the years following European settlement and dominance, some of those indigenous cultures and religions perished in the immolation of dispossession and the killings and deaths by violence and introduced disease. Others survived.

The Europeans themselves brought with them their own cultures and religions. Up until the 1830s and subject to some numerically minor exceptions, the introduced cultures were those of the British Isles and the introduced religions were various Christian denominations. Thereafter, and even prior to the discovery of gold during the 1850s, there were considerable numbers of immigrants from other places, particularly from Germany to South

Australia. With the discovery of gold, the gold rushes brought a large influx of migrants from many countries and all the settled continents of the world. From then on, through the 19th and 20th centuries, there was a constant increase in the numbers of countries to which non-indigenous Australians traced their origins.

Today, it can truly be said not only that, apart from the Aborigines and Torres Strait Islanders, we Australians are all immigrants or descended from immigrants but also that we immediately or more distantly come from, and through our different origins reflect, almost all the regions, races, cultures and religions of the world. Particularly over the last 150 years, the Australian continent has been a crucible of the world's different races, cultures and religions.

Both at the international and national level, diversity of cultures and of religions can be a source of knowledge and understanding, an impetus and challenge to development and improvement, a broadening of human horizons and an enrichment of human life. On the other hand, cultural and religious diversity can, as history abundantly demonstrates, be a source of national disharmony and disunity and international distrust, ill-will and dispute and a cause of, or excuse for, national or international conflict and even war.

The theme and sub-themes of this Conference focus on the challenge and responsibility of best exploiting the advantages, while avoiding the pitfalls, of religious and cultural diversity at both national and international levels. The specific topics to be discussed are, to a significant extent, concerned with particular aspects of that challenge and responsibility. Their importance cannot be overstated. Indeed, the challenge and the responsibility to ensure that religious and cultural diversity is a source of advantage, benefit and good rather than a cause of disharmony, conflict and evil lie close to the heart of the quest for happiness, fulfilment and survival of our kind.

Clearly enough, both at the international level and on the domestic scene, the key to real success in relation to that challenge and responsibility lies in mutual and genuine understanding, tolerance and respect of and for different cultural and religious traditions, practices and beliefs. The real difficulty lies in the identification and effective implementation of the best means of fostering and maintaining such understanding, respect and tolerance particularly in circumstances of actual or perceived competition, inconsistency or antipathy. The challenge to identify and implement those means is unlikely to be met at the international level unless the responsibility to foster and maintain such understanding, respect and tolerance is discharged on the domestic scene. That responsibility on the domestic scene is a responsibility not only of governments but of us all as individuals. And the starting point is, as with so many things, with ourselves.

It may be of some interest in the context of this Conference if I seek to identify some of the lessons we in Australia have learnt as we have built a nation and forged national unity notwithstanding our extraordinary diversity of racial, cultural and religious backgrounds. In that regard, I hope it will be not be seen as presumptuous for me to recall that President Clinton, in a public speech in Sydney in the course of his visit to Australia last year, expressed the opinion that, notwithstanding our great diversity of cultural, religious and racial backgrounds, he could not – and I quote – 'think of a better place in the entire world, a more shining example of how people can come together as one nation and one community'.

Over the years, we have, of course, made our mistakes. There is, I venture to think, no country – certainly no country in which indigenous inhabitants were over-run by foreign settlers – which has not. We have been guilty of intolerance and, on occasion, we have acted oppressively. At times, shameful acts, such as the dispossession of the Aborigines and the forcible removal of their children, have been done with the authority of government or even, on occasion, through the mistakenly well-meaning agency of Christian Churches. Those are things which must be profoundly regretted by us all as a nation. At other times, particularly when we have been concerned about the effects of immigration upon jobs, living standards and what we have seen as our traditional values, we have acted wrongly and intolerantly towards particular racial or national groups, such as the Chinese in gold rush days and Island labourers in the Queensland canefields. Nonetheless, there are many things of which we are entitled to be extremely proud. One of them is that, throughout its short history, our nation has provided refuge for extraordinary numbers of immigrants seeking a new home, new opportunities and new loyalties. Another is the ultimate achievement of the multiculturalism which enriches and sustains our nation.

The Australian nation came into being on 1 January 1901 as a Federation of the six States which formerly had been British Colonies. Our basic law is a written Constitution which confers designated legislative powers on the central or Commonwealth Parliament and preserves the residual legislative powers of the State Parliaments. That basic law contains no formal Bill of Rights. It does however contain a number of important express guarantees, including s 116 which, reflecting the United States Constitution's First Amendment, precludes the Commonwealth Parliament from making any laws 'establishing any religion, ... imposing any religious observance, or ... prohibiting the free exercise of any religion'. Section 116 also provides that 'no religious test shall be required as a qualification for any office or public trust under the Commonwealth'. In so far as laws of the Commonwealth Parliament are concerned, s 116 would seem to represent as effective a guarantee as one could wish against laws interfering with religious freedom.

Section 116 is, however, confined to limiting the content of Commonwealth laws and requirements. It does not impose any positive obligation of mutual tolerance or respect between adherents to different religions (or of none). It does not apply to State laws. Nor does the Constitution contain any provision guaranteeing freedom from racial or cultural discrimination or oppression. In those circumstances, protection from racial cultural or religious discrimination or oppression in this country has been largely dependent on the conscious framing of a general policy of multiculturalism which has been developed and promoted, with bilateral support, by governments and which now enjoys the support of all our major political parties and of the overwhelming majority of Australians.

The word 'multiculturalism' must be understood in an Australian context in a special way. It does not mean the mere fact of the existence of many cultures. It refers to a national policy of acceptance and protection of the diverse cultural, racial and religious backgrounds and origins of Australians. It is a policy whose essence lies in a proper balance between respect for, and genuine tolerance of, the different national, racial, ethnic and religious backgrounds and cultures from which we come and the fundamental requirements of national identity, national unity and national standards. Thus, our multiculturalism recognises the entitlement of all Australians to preserve and cherish with affection, with respect and with pride, the customs, cultures and religions which they or their forbears have brought from the lands or regions of their birth but subjects that entitlement to the limitation that all Australians are bound by the overriding loyalties and obligations of their Australian citizenship and their duties under valid Australian laws.

It follows that multiculturalism does not mean that indigenous or introduced cultural or religious practices are immune from examination or reasoned criticism within Australia. It does not, for example, protect practices which damage the person or property of other citizens – such as, to take an extreme case, the suggested religious duty of the Thugs to rob or to kill – or which are simply unacceptable according to the standards of our society – such as polygamy or the practice of suttee. Nor does multiculturalism require that we impose no limitations or controls with respect to potential immigrants. There is no country in the world which imposes no such limitations or controls.

What multiculturalism means is that, within the limits that are consistent with the overriding obligations and loyalties of Australian citizenship and with the duties and standards imposed by valid Australian laws, all our citizens are entitled to expect and demand that the mutual respect and tolerance which are of its essence should be observed and encouraged. In that regard, multiculturalism does not detract from or threaten our national identity or national unity. To the contrary, while recognising and protecting our diversity of backgrounds, cultures and beliefs, it promotes that identity and unity by building upon and adding cohesion to what we are.

It follows that our multiculturalism, is not only decent, just and right in that it reflects mutual understanding, tolerance and respect. It is in our own interests as a nation. It is our responsibility as Australians to protect and maintain it and to observe its standards and its dictates.

5.8 The Launch of the Australian National Islamic Library Complex, Canberra, 23 August 1997

The Australian National Islamic Library project is a significant one not only for Muslims but for all of us who care about the need to reaffirm and strengthen the genuine mutual understanding, respect and tolerance which are the essence of the multiculturalism that is such an important feature of our nation. The Library will eventually include some 100,000 volumes and other works. That will make it the largest repository in the Southern Hemisphere of material in the English language on Islam and the Muslim people.

The heart of any Islamic Library is, of course, the Holy Koran, Indeed, an Islamic Library is both a repository of the Holy Book and a monument and a means to its fulfilment. As you know, the word Qur'an (*Koran*) itself derives from an Arabic verb 'to read' or 'to recite'. The first words directly revealed to the Holy Prophet were: 'Read! (or proclaim!) in the name of thy Lord and Cherisher ...'.

As the commentary in my copy of the Qur'an puts it, in worldly letters the Prophet 'was un-versed, but with spiritual knowledge his mind and soul were filled, and now had come the time when he must stand forth to the world and declare his mission.'

From those first words we can trace the rich tradition of Islamic literature as it has developed over the centuries throughout the Muslim world ... a tradition so vast that, to quote the *Encyclopedia Britannica*, 'even a very large team of scholars could scarcely master a single branch of the subject.' Works of religious importance; of history; of poetry; of story; of scholarship in the many branches of the arts and sciences ... geometry, mathematics, medicine, music, architecture, language, ethics and philosophy, the domestic arts ... that have had such a global influence on thought and expression for well over one thousand years.

With *reading*, of course, comes a necessary commitment to *writing*: and it is not surprising that the art of calligraphy came to assume such importance in the Muslim tradition deriving, in large part, from the work of the historic school at Basra in codifying the structure of the Arabic language. As I am sure most of you will be aware, there are still hundreds of thousands of books that even today are available only in manuscript form. Those Australians who were fortunate enough to have seen the exhibition in Sydney a few years ago of treasures from the palaces of Suleymann the Magnificent, saw some splendid examples of the very finest Muslim calligraphy.

My reference to the ancient art of calligraphy should not be seen as suggesting that the Library will not be up-to-date. To the contrary, it will be equipped with the most contemporary of electronic communications. The cataloguing will be in a format acceptable to the Australian National Library. When the infrastructure is in place, the collection will be available through the Australian Bibliographic network, not only within Australia but of course through the Internet to the world at large. Hence the Library's significance to the region, particularly to scholars interested in material in the English language.

Indeed, in the shorter term, one important ancillary aim of the Library is to establish a translation service to help readers and researchers with material that is at present not available in English. In the longer term, and in collaboration with other academic institutions, the organisation hopes to translate those works at present unavailable in English but which are of interest to all Australians interested in Islam and the Muslim people. Certainly the community here has within it the broad range of expertise and language skills to be able to provide a valuable service and to make available this great resource to Australian business, governments, academic institutions and the public generally. In this respect, I was interested to note that the Library has already received approximately 20,000 books and journals and there are pledges for another 15,000 works. It is already well on the way towards the target of 100,000 volumes.

Apart from books and manuscripts, a collection is being made of items of cultural and historical interest that will be incorporated within the Museum of Islamic History in Australia – another very important element of this project.

Contact between Islam and Australia goes back a very long way. Indeed, it significantly *pre*-dates the arrival of the First Fleet. From at least the middle of the 18th century, and possibly much earlier, seaman from Macassar, on the Indonesian Island of Sulawesi, were spending up to four months a year collecting trepang (a form of edible sea-slug) along the northern Australian coastline. There was considerable contact between the Macassans and the Aboriginal peoples of that part of our country ... 'Marege' as the Macassans called it ... although it appears no permanent settlements were established.

The trepang trade ended in the early years of this century, but by then Muslim divers from Indonesia and Malaya were an important part of the pearling industry of the North-West. And, of course, there were the camel drivers from Afghanistan, the first of whom arrived in Australia around 1860. They played such an important part in the history of exploration and transport in the great inland deserts of Australia, that they have become a legendary part of the story of our country. Their settlements, known as 'Ghans', were the first real Muslim communities in Australia. Today, the train between Adelaide and Alice Springs is known as 'The Ghan'; and the descendants of many of these men continue to play an important role in the life of our nation.

In more recent years, of course, there has been significant immigration by Muslims to Australia from many parts of the world – most notably the Middle-East (Turkey and the Lebanon), and the countries of former Yugoslavia, the Indian Sub-Continent and South-East Asia. Currently, Islam is probably the fastest growing of the non-Christian religions in Australia. The last census recorded some 200,000 people who indicated they were of the Islamic Faith – a 36 percent increase on the number five years earlier.

Hence the importance to our local community of the Canberra Islamic Centre which we are also launching tonight and of which the Australian National Islamic Library and Museum are outstanding components. The Centre itself began in 1993. Operating out of the Tuggeranong Community Centre, it has offered a valuable range of cultural, educational, religious, charitable and social services not only to members of the Muslim community but to the broader community as well.

I am told that one aim of the Centre is to provide some employment and work experience opportunities for young people and vulnerable groups such as recently-arrived refugees. At a time when unemployment is such a dreadful social problem, that will be a particularly valuable service. There is the work the Centre does by helping migrants make the transition to Australian society through language classes and a broad understanding of our social mores within a supportive, familiar environment.

The intent is, I am told, 'to produce a socially cohesive multicultural group which would retain their own cultural identity and yet contribute positively and affirmatively to Australian society as a whole'.

That objective has my wholehearted support. As I said earlier, the essence of multiculturalism is genuine mutual understanding, respect and tolerance. That mutual understanding, respect and tolerance has sustained our nation over the years. Within the limits that are consistent with the overriding obligations and loyalties of Australian citizenship and with the duties and standards imposed by valid Australian laws, multiculturalism means that all our citizens are entitled to expect and demand that the mutual respect, tolerance and understanding which are of its essence should be observed and encouraged. In that regard, multiculturalism does not detract from or threaten our national identity or national unity. To the contrary, while recognising and protecting our diversity of backgrounds, cultures and beliefs, it promotes that identity and unity by building upon and adding cohesion to what we are.

It follows that our multiculturalism, is not only decent, just and right in that it reflects mutual understanding, tolerance and respect. It is in our own interests as a nation. It is our responsibility as Australians to protect and maintain it and to observe its standards and its dictates. In saying that Helen and I are delighted to be with you tonight, I express the firm belief that the Library and Centre which we are launching will continue to flourish and to assist in promoting the mutual respect, understanding and tolerance that lies so close to the hearts of all of us who profess the virtues of multicultural Australia.

5.9 The Launch of the National Project Compassion for Caritas Australia, Sydney, 24 February 1998

1998 has been designated the 'International Year of the Ocean'. For the people of the islands of the Pacific and Indian oceans, and for those who live on the shores of the countries that border them, fishing is a source of both food and of income. And yet, as we know, issues such as rising sea levels, pollution, competition and fears of depleting fish stocks are causing problems in some areas. The assistance given many of these people through Project Compassion is of great importance to them, and in many cases quite literally helps, as the theme this year has it, in 'Keeping Hope Alive'.

Then again, from the earliest days of the Christian era, the fish has been an important symbol of the Christian Church. And fish have traditionally been associated with the season of Lent. Each year Caritas Australia encourages people to have a simple meal of rice just once during Lent, to remind us of those who each day involuntarily go without adequate food. This year, as part of the general theme, that has become a 'fish and rice day'.

It's good to have with us this morning a number of children from St James' Catholic School at Glebe. Their presence reminds us of the importance of ensuring that, from an early age, our Christian young people are encouraged to adopt the practice of going without something during Lent to help the poor and the disadvantaged. That practice goes back a very long way. I personally can remember that, when I was a child, a small box would appear at this time each year on the table in the kitchen at home, just like the Project Compassion boxes or envelopes. We would place in it the pennies and threepences – the few cents – we saved by giving up things for Lent.

I can't say that our savings ever amounted to a great deal. Money was never plentiful and we used to put something aside to equip ourselves for the break in the Lenten fast on the feast of St Patrick. But the point was, and still is, that every little bit one gives helps somebody in real need, somewhere in the world. And surely no-one can deny that the needs of the disadvantaged today are at least as great as they have ever been. One dollar given will pay for a patient to visit a medical clinic in a Cambodian village. Three dollars fifty will buy a white hen to help start a poultry project in Fiji. Ten dollars will buy four bush knives for farmers in Kenya. Thirty five dollars – less than the cost of a tank of petrol – will buy a sack of grain to feed a displaced family in southern Sudan for a month.

At home, Caritas Australia is in the process of redefining its assistance programs to our indigenous peoples, after extensive consultation, under the broad theme 'Fostering Indigenous Identity'. I am quite certain that those programs will continue to make a valuable contribution to both the physical and spiritual well-being of Aboriginal and Torres Strait Islander peoples, and thereby help to establish an essential condition for the process of reconciliation. The achievement of a just and lasting reconciliation between indigenous and non-indigenous Australians is one of the most important challenges facing our country as we head towards a new millennium and a new century – our second century – as a nation.

As regards overseas, Caritas Australia is, in turn, part of Caritas Internationalis, one of the world's largest non-government aid and development networks, with some 146 autonomous agencies in 194 countries. Major community infrastructure programs … health, welfare, education projects … often cost more than any one individual or family can contribute, even in affluent Australia. In such cases we have to combine our aid resources to make them as efficient and useful as possible. On the other hand, there are many extraordinarily important things which are quite beyond the reach of people living close to poverty in other countries but which are wholly within the reach of ordinary Australians – or a small group even of Australian schoolchildren – who wish to help.

This year's Project Compassion poster shows the smiling

face of a young Vietnamese boy, Dinh Van Cong, sitting with his family's new cow. Cong's family is one of the poorest in the Yen Dong commune, and for them the new cow is vitally important. His parents bought it with money borrowed from a revolving loan fund run by the community and supported by Caritas Australia. Already one calf has been sold, and the profit has been put towards building a new house – with a reed door and bamboo rafters, as the Project Compassion people remind us. The cost of the cow? About $250: a vast sum for a family as poor as Cong's, yet for us in Australia it amounts to the price of perhaps ten compact discs (CDs).

This is but one of the many thousands of examples where Caritas Australia is helping those living in poverty around the world. There are clean water, electricity and sewerage programs in South America; literacy, nutrition and farming projects in the Pacific island countries; basic health clinics in remote villages in Cambodia; programs to help reunite families and rebuild shattered lives in places like Rwanda. Every little bit given to Project Compassion can indeed make a big difference to someone, somewhere, every day of the year.

As I said a little earlier, the needs of the disadvantaged, especially those living in poverty and who need our help, are at least as great today as they have ever been. As the Holy Father recently reminded us in his reference to the parable of Dives, the rich man, as told in the Gospel of Luke, Chapter 16, who of us can deny that the poor man, Lazarus, still lies starving at our gate?

'Caritas' is a Latin word that means love, compassion and charity. These are words that should be constantly in the hearts of those of us who believe that outreach to the poor and marginalised of the world remains the central mission of the Christian Church, or who are convinced as I am, that the ultimate test of a true democracy such as Australia is how we treat our most disadvantaged and vulnerable.

5.10 The Launch of Publications for the Australian Theological Forum, Canberra, 7 June 1998

Today, of course, is a doubly auspicious one for the launch of these two publications. In the Western Christian tradition, it is Trinity Sunday with its commitment to God as One and as a community of Persons. In the Orthodox tradition it is Pentecost Sunday, commemorating the descent of the Holy Spirit on the disciples and regarded as the birthday of the Christian Church.

These two publications call upon and are deeply relevant to both traditions. The first is the book edited by Reverend Dr Victor Pfitzner and Mr Hilary Regan, *The Task of Theology Today:Doctrines and Dogmas*.[8] The second is the inaugural ATF Journal, *Interface: a Forum for Theology in the World*[9] which, in this opening edition, edited by Sister Veronica Brady and Mr Regan, is devoted to a topic of great significance for all Australians, 'Reconciliation and Responsibility'.

The book, *The Task of Theology Today: Doctrines and Dogmas*, brings together papers from the colloquium of the same name held in Brisbane last July. The participating systemic and philosophical theologians, some of whom are with us today, come from a variety of Christian traditions and from different parts of the world: from within this country, from New Zealand, Britain and the United States. As you know, the task the Forum has set itself is to facilitate the engagement of Christian theology with other disciplines in addressing areas of social and cultural concern in the modern world. In doing so, it seeks to bring together not only theologians but also other members of the church, scientists and a variety of professional men and women – whether Christian or not – to explore the connections between faith and life.

And yet, as the editors of the book point out in their introduction,

---

[8] Victor Pfitzner and Hilary Regan (eds), *The Task of Theology Today: doctrines and dogmas* (Australian Theological Forum, 1998).

[9] *Interface: a forum for theology in the world*, Journal, Australian Theological Forum 1998-2013.

if theologians are to engage meaningfully and profitably with people in other disciplines, they must be clear on what they seek to contribute to the dialogue. The papers in this book, without exception, satisfy that requirement. They are sincere, scholarly and readily understandable contributions to it. It gives me great pleasure to launch the Book.

The first edition of the Journal *Interface* which we are also launching this afternoon deals with an issue of concrete concern to all Australians – namely, reconciliation between the indigenous peoples of Australia and our nation as a whole. The authors of the various articles bring a variety of perspectives to the matter. Raimond Gaita, for example, approaches the issue as a philosopher. Father Frank Brennan is a theologian and lawyer who has been very closely involved in the process of negotiation. The theologians come from different traditions and, as the editors note, 'take different positions on the vexed issue of the proper relations between the church and social and political issues'.

In this respect, I was interested to read the review by Veronica Brady of *Rainbow Spirit Theology*, and in particular the statement by Norman Habel in the introduction to that book.

> Behind the tragedy of many Aboriginal communities (poor health, high infant mortality, low life-expectancy, high unemployment, poor housing, alcoholism, malnutrition, deaths in custody – the list goes on) lies a deep spiritual crisis.

This is a view that I have shared and spoken about for some time. It is certainly true that those of us – both indigenous and non-indigenous – who are now joined together in a pilgrimage for true reconciliation all know that we will not reach our journey's end until our nation has made significant progress towards resolving the current plight of the Aboriginal peoples in relation to practical things such as health, education, employment and living conditions. And how could it be otherwise in a context where the gap between the average life expectancy of an Aborigine and that of a non-Aborigine is almost 20 years and actually widening and where Aborigines are dying from particular diseases at rates up to 12 times or more those of non-Aborigines? Clearly, we will not achieve reconciliation until we reach the stage where it can be seen that we are at least *approaching* the position where the life expectancy and future prospects of an Aboriginal baby are in the same realm of discourse as those of a non-Aboriginal one.

But, equally clearly, we have no real prospect of reaching that stage until we also effectively address the terrible problems of the spirit as well as those of the body – the present effects on the spirit and on the self-esteem of Australia's indigenous peoples of all that has happened, all that has been lost and all that has been destroyed during the two centuries and more that have passed since the arrival of the First Fleet in 1788. Since taking up this office, I've been privileged to officially open a number of exhibitions at which these matters of the spirit have been seriously and movingly addressed. One was the wonderful exhibition of Aboriginal art telling the story of the Wagilag Sisters at the National Gallery of Australia here in Canberra last year. Another was the exhibition at the National Library – 'Captive Lives' – which told the tragic story of Tambo and the other Aborigines – men, women and children – taken from Palm Island and exhibited as freaks at circuses in America and later Europe at the end of the last century. On a less sad note, there was the opening in Adelaide of a permanent Gateway and Dreaming Trail recounting the legend of the Tjirbruki, the ancestral hero of the Kaurna people.

This launch is another such occasion. Through it, we help to promote and foster mutual respect and understanding between indigenous and non-indigenous Australians generally. As Father Brennan writes, 'Dialogue and discernment are essential to the process. Reconciliation is neither a matter of sitting on the fence nor of taking sides to the exclusion of all other viewpoints. Above all, it requires trust.'

5.11 The Liturgy for Ecumenical Pilgrims to Celebrate the 50th Anniversary of the World Council of Churches, Canberra, 20 September 1998

Today is a day of Thanksgiving, one that is being acknowledged by the churches around the globe which belong to the great Christian family of the World Council of Churches.

It is a day of particular significance for us in Canberra. The 50th Anniversary – the Golden Jubilee – is being especially celebrated in each of the seven cities where previous Assemblies of the World Council have been held. The first of those cities was Amsterdam where, in 1948, in the words of the first General Secretary, 'The creation of a World Council of Churches, which had seemed such an impossibly difficult task in the 1930s and which had seemed a hopeless affair in the dark moments of the World War, proved now to be such a simple and undramatic operation'.

Perhaps. But in its response to the yearnings among Christians everywhere for the fellowship of common witness – of what, in modern parlance, we call the spirit of ecumenism – the work of the Council has been profound in its impact upon the life of the Universal Christian Church as a whole and on the spiritual and material lives of men and women everywhere. As witness the fruits of the subsequent Assemblies: in Evanston, New Delhi, Uppsala, Nairobi, Vancouver and – unforgettably for us – in Canberra in 1991.

Now, of course, we are approaching the 8th Assembly, to be held in Harare this coming December under the theme *Turn to God – Rejoice in Hope*. Helen and I express our wishes for the successful outcome of that Conference, and in particular our fervent prayer that it will advance us further towards fulfilment of the vision of Christian ecumenism.

In saying that, I am conscious of the fact that today's Liturgy for Ecumenical Pilgrims is being held at the Tent of Meeting, here on the site in the National Capital once reserved for an Anglican

Cathedral. Today, that concept has been displaced by a broader vision for a new millennium and the second century of our nation, namely, a National Centre for Christianity and Australian Culture. It will be a Centre where the enduring truths of the faith and of human spirituality will be expressed and celebrated in a manner – if I may use the words of the late Bishop Burgmann – 'thoroughly baptised into the Australian scene, blown through by Australian winds, bathed in Australian sunshine, and even coated now and then with Australian dust'. That Australianness is central to the vision which inspires the planning of the new Centre and also, if I may be so bold to suggest, the individual experience that we Australians bring to the life of the Church in this country. Also central to it is our shared longing for true and lasting reconciliation between indigenous Australians and the nation of which they form such an important part.

And surely, as we approach the 2000th jubilee of the birth of Christ, we Christians should be looking at least as hopefully for full reconciliation, if not full unity, between us all at all levels of our respective Churches. For, in our hearts we surely all know that it is only by acknowledging past shortcomings and appreciating the essential community of all Christians and the pervading splendour of our Christian inspiration and of our shared mission of outreach to the disadvantaged that we will adequately discharge our obligations of charity – to use that word in its fullest sense – within the Universal Christian Church of the future.

5.12 The Launch of 'Dreaming of the Resurrection – A Reconciliation Story', Sydney, 12 November 1998

This book provides an extraordinarily enlightening insight as it compares and contrasts indigenous and non-indigenous art focused upon the resurrection. Different people will discern different messages and learn different lessons from the comparison and contrast. At first glance, one might gain the impression of an almost childlike simplicity in the spiritual perceptions underlying the Aboriginal art. But then one is struck by the deep complexity of a painting such as 'Jesus Risen' by Teddy Jabangayi Dixon on page 18 of the book or Patricia Marrfurra's 'Easter' on page 27. The plain fact is that the more one examines and thinks about the paintings, the more obvious it becomes that the perceptions underlying the indigenous art are not so much to be characterised in terms of childlike simplicity but in terms of being unerringly concerned with what is essential.

And that leads me to what is for me perhaps the main lesson of this book. It is the identification of what truly are the essentials. As I examined the indigenous paintings and compared them with the non-indigenous ones, my constant thought was that the essentials are those of a universal Christian faith which is largely unconscious of the differences of dogma and practice which constitute the divisions within the universal Christian church. Indeed, it is difficult to escape the impression that, putting to one side the transcending importance of the real presence for those of us who believe in it, those differences of dogma and practice should sound somewhat bizarre in the ears of the deeply religious indigenous artists whose works are produced in this book.

Another thing that struck me as I examined the indigenous paintings and drawings was the importance of the role of the Holy Spirit in indigenous Christianity. That had struck me before on each occasion when I have been privileged to participate in indigenous Christian services. It is not surprising when one thinks of the role played by the dreaming in indigenous thought, culture and belief. Up until recent times, the Holy Spirit has played only a largely incidental role in my own religion. Personal contact with indigenous Christianity is educating me about the fundamental importance of the 'Holy Spirit in – or sometimes 'of' – our Land'. And, when one understands the critical importance of fire and water in the Aboriginal dreamings and in indigenous life, how could it be otherwise? In that regard, let me simply direct attention to the painting of Pentecost by the late Peter Jabangayi Tchooga on page 70 of this wonderful book.

There are many other comments I would like to make about '*Dreaming of the Resurrection*'.[10] I will confine myself to some brief remarks on the subject of reconciliation. For the book is correctly described as '*A Reconciliation Story*' on its cover and I have no doubt that it is because it is an instrument of true reconciliation that it is a project of the Mary MacKillop Foundation.,

I have, since I became Governor-General, constantly sought to stress the importance of reconciliation between the indigenous peoples and the nation of which they form such an important part. Indeed, my views in that regard appear in an extract from my Australia Day message this year which is reproduced on page 5 of '*Dreaming of the Resurrection*'. We will, of course, not achieve true reconciliation until we are further advanced towards addressing the appalling problems of material disadvantage which oppress Australia's indigenous peoples. But it is also of critical importance that we address the problems of the spirit as well. In particular, the problems of coping with what has been lost and, of course, the problems of lack of self-esteem. And we will only achieve true reconciliation if we learn how to communicate – not loudly, abrasively and divisively but quietly, convincingly and inclusively.

In its own way, '*Dreaming of the Resurrection*' in itself and of itself makes a significant contribution towards addressing one aspect of the problems of the spirit and of self-esteem. It brings home, through a comparison with outstanding non-indigenous religious art, the depth and splendour of indigenous artistic abilities and spiritual perceptions. It does it in a way which is quiet in its expression but spectacular in its result. To at least this non-Aboriginal reader, the book is a cause of soaring pride in the scope, the skill and the worth of our indigenous art.

---

[10] David Burke, *Dreaming of the Resurrection: a reconciliation story* (Mary MacKillop Foundation, 1998).

'*Dreaming of the Resurrection*' also demonstrates the correctness of my wife, Helen's, message to the Reconciliation Convention in May 1997 about how important to reconciliation it is that indigenous and non-indigenous women and men learn to communicate by exchanging stories and experiences. Indeed, '*Dreaming of the Resurrection*' is reconciliation in practice as it compares, contrasts and reconciles indigenous and non-indigenous material and spiritual experience as depicted through art.

And, finally, '*Dreaming of the Resurrection*' teaches reconciliation in the overall story it narrates. In that regard, let me refer specifically to the story of the 'Women at Mistake Creek' which is told at pages 33 and 35 of the book. It matters not whether the particular story is accurate in its details. Its elements have undoubtedly occurred in many different parts of our nation during the comparatively short time since we Europeans first came here. It is a story of the slaughter of Aborigines. And of a perceived reason for the slaughter that was as mistaken in fact as it was utterly unjustifiable in principle. And it is a story of forgiveness which is explained by an Elder of the Kija people: 'if we do not forgive then ... the evil spirit will enter us'.

There is a monument, pictured on page 33 of the book, at the foot of an old boab tree beside the ordinarily dry bed of Mistake Creek. It bears the inscription: 'In memory of our ancestors who were shot and burnt here'. On All Souls Day each year the Kija people gather there to pray to their and our Christian God. One day, Helen and I hope to have the privilege of joining with them.

5.13 The Inauguration of the Jesuit Lenten Seminars to Celebrate the Sesquicentenary of the Jesuits in Australia, Melbourne, 17 February 1999

It is now 150 years since the first Jesuits came to Australia. They were Austrian Priests under the leadership of Father Aloysius Kranewitter. Their primary mission was to care for the German speaking migrants, many of them refugees, arriving in South Australia. Two or three years after their arrival, they established Sevenhill in the Clare Valley which has fulfilled so many purposes over the years: mission, school, seminary, Jesuit house of studies and, continuously, parish and winery. During the years to 1900, almost 60 Austrian Jesuits – 59 to be precise – served in South Australia, Victoria ... and the Northern Territory.

It was in 1886 that the Jesuits established their first Aboriginal mission site at Daly River. In 1899, a century ago this year, they departed the last mission site there. Its name was Uniya – 'bend in the river'. More than 90 years later, that name was, as you know, adopted by the Jesuit Social Justice Centre in Kings Cross in Sydney which has become such a powerful influence for reconciliation and for human rights within our country and region.

Meanwhile, the combination of the preponderance of Irish among the Catholics of the Colonies and the gift by Father Therry of his estate to the Irish Jesuits combined to encourage the arrival of Jesuits from Ireland. They came first to Melbourne in 1865. In 1877 they accepted an invitation to extend to Sydney. They established schools and parishes which served and continue to serve the Catholic community. At the tertiary level, they staffed University Colleges and Chaplaincies and, in addition to their own training houses, the diocesan seminary for Victoria and Tasmania.

It is, of course, impossible to accurately assess the full extent of the contribution which the Jesuits have made to our Australian Catholic Church and our Australian nation. Possibly the most important contribution to the nation has been the indirect one through the lives of the countless students whom the Jesuits have educated at schools such as this College – Xavier – in Melbourne, St Ignatius in Adelaide, Riverview, St Aloysius and much more recently, Loyola in Sydney. That indirect contribution to the nation has, of course, also been through the priests and University graduates whom the Jesuits have trained or helped educate in the

Seminary or at the University. It has also been through the many other Australians, both Catholic and non-Catholic, whose thinking, whose morality or whose approach to life has been influenced by the Jesuits.

The *direct* influence of the Jesuits for good on our nation has also been formidable. As has been mentioned, the Jesuits' mission of outreach to the disadvantaged goes back all the way to their arrival in South Australia 150 years ago. The intensity and effectiveness of the discharge of that mission seems to me to have increased in recent years notwithstanding that, in conformity with the general trend in this and most other countries, numbers have declined.

In so far as the Jesuit influence on the Australian Catholic Church is concerned, the critical impact has, I suggest, been on the intellectual life, the spiritual quality and the essential morality of the Church itself. That influence has, particularly in recent years, been an influence for tolerance and for recognition of the essential equality and the claim to a 'fair go' of all Australians – indigenous and non-indigenous; immigrant or refugee and native born; the privileged and the disadvantaged; those who have and those in need.

The series of Seminars which are commencing here this evening – *The Jesuits Lenten Seminar Series* – constitutes an outstanding means of celebrating 150 years of Jesuit achievement in Australia. It invites a discerning assessment of our country as we approach the third millennium of the Christian era and the second century of our nation. It provides the opportunity for a hard look at the widening gap between rich and poor; at the need for all Australians to be reconciled with one another and with the facts of our history; at the need for all persons with a social conscience to accept that there **is** time to speak and to contribute fully to our national life; at the challenge for those of us who are Christians to recognise that the heart of our Universal Christian Church lies in its mission of outreach to the disadvantaged; at the need for all

Australians to address the fact that the ultimate test of our worth as a truly democratic nation is how we treat our most vulnerable and disadvantaged.

And the starting point must surely be a frank identification and appraisal of our standards and qualities as a people – of our 'Australian values'.

5.14 The Opening of the Jewish Holocaust Museum's Hadasa & Szymon Rosenbaum Research Centre, 24 October 1999

May I say at the outset how pleased Helen and I are to be with you this afternoon for the Official Opening of the Jewish Holocaust Museum's new Hadasa & Szymon Rosenbaum Research Centre. I should, however, mention that our pleasure at being here again with Melbourne's Jewish Community is tinged with sadness over the death last Thursday of Ron Castan AM, QC. Ron was, of course, not only a leading member of your Community. He was truly a leading Australian who worked tirelessly for a number of important national causes, including Aboriginal reconciliation and the welfare of Australia's indigenous peoples in areas such as Native Title and health. His death is a great loss to the whole nation. He will be sadly missed by all of us who were his companions on the long road towards reconciliation and who share his ideals and dreams.

Though, as I say, tinged with sadness, this is a very special occasion.

For one thing, it is an opportunity to acknowledge and thank all those who have directly or indirectly been involved in the planning, the design or the actual construction of the new Centre, including the many hundreds of people, including children, whose voluntary work and financial contributions have made this important project possible. The result of their skills, their dedication and their generosity is that the Jewish Holocaust Museum and Research Centre will be very well equipped to continue its vital teaching and research roles into the next millennium.

Particular mention must, of course, be made of the couple after whom the new Research Centre is named. As most of you know, it was a substantial donation from Mrs Hadasa Rosenbaum and her husband, Mr Szymon Rosenbaum, which enabled the new building to proceed. Sadly, Mr Rosenbaum did not live to see the building completed. As Mrs Rosenbaum has said, the couple's gift to the Holocaust Centre constitutes a memorial both to her husband and to all those who died in the Holocaust or Shoah, including the members of Mr and Mrs Rosenbaum's own families. Many others, including pensioners, have made large and small donations towards the cost of the new building.

We all have a duty, as much to the future as to the approximately six million people, including the approximately one and a half million children, who were killed simply for being Jewish, to ensure that the awful facts of the Holocaust are remembered for as long as our world exists. That is the Centre's central reason for being. We also all have a duty to be conscious of the lessons to be learnt from those terrible years and of their contemporary relevance and importance even in a true democracy such as Australia. Thus, for example, the Centre serves as a dramatic reminder of how essential to our decency is the mutual respect and acceptance which should be implicit in our shared humanity and which lie at the heart of the multiculturalism which both inspires our nation and sustains our national unity. We must be vigilant to safeguard that mutual respect and acceptance – and that multiculturalism – against those who would deny or undermine them.

Today is also a special occasion in that it gives us an opportunity to acknowledge the wonderful dedication and service of the Holocaust survivors who are currently working as volunteers at the Holocaust Centre, and all those earlier volunteers who have now retired or died. Their responsibility has been – and is – not only to explain to visitors the horror of what happened more than half a century ago but also to stress the need for mutual acceptance and understanding … the present need to combat racial, religious and cultural hatred, prejudice and intolerance wherever they exist in society. In the 15 years since the Centre opened, those Holocaust survivors have guided more than 210,000 Victorian school students around the Centre. I have read some of the letters and comments that students have written after a visit and it is clear that they are profoundly affected by the experience. For example, one student wrote: 'I learned a lot from a short visit. I learned to fight for freedom and to speak out against issues that I feel are wrong'. So it is that, through the unquenchable courage and spirit of truly noble people, good and wisdom can flow from unutterable injustice and suffering. 'Through', to quote Jacob Rosenberg's words written for this occasion, 'survivors out of a nightmare's darkest night, reaching out for a world of human light.'

This is also a special occasion in that it gives us the opportunity to admire and acknowledge the quality and the design of the new Centre, which doubles the space of the Holocaust Museum. The building includes a new Library for the Centre's extensive collection of books, an Auditorium/Exhibition Hall and temperature-controlled storage space for fragile archival material. Indeed, the Centre has a rich collection of archives, not least of which are the 1,000 taped testimonies of Holocaust survivors. The new building will enable researchers, including students – from Melbourne, the rest of Australia and overseas – to further their studies of the Holocaust and Nazism.

One of the truly unique aspects of the new building is the six-and-a-half-metre high bronze sculptured columns at the entrance created by Andrew Rogers. The six columns, called 'Pillars of Witness', are designed to explain the Holocaust, and related emotions and attitudes, to future generations when direct living memory of the horrors of that time no longer persists. Mr Rogers' images are powerful, moving and accessible. In their vicinity at the entrance of the new building is Peter Schipperheyn's beautiful sculpture of the vessel for the Eternal Flame. Together, the works of the two sculptors will, I believe, become synonymous with the Centre.

5.15 The Millenium Dinner for the Southern Queensland Theology Library, Toowoomba, 5 November 1999

Viewed from a human perspective, the scope of theology obviously includes the relationship between God and man. For a Christian, as St Matthew makes clear – '*as you do it to one of the least of these my brethren*', that relationship encompasses the relationship between man and man. That being so, I see the relationship between Australia's indigenous peoples and the nation as a whole as not only raising basic issues of justice and decency. I also see it as one of the most important theological issues confronting us as we approach the new millennium. For it lies at the very heart of my vision of the relationship between Australian Christians and God. In that context, the subject on which I wish to speak this evening – '*A Few Instances of Reconciliation*' – seems to me to be a particularly appropriate one for this Millennium Dinner of the Southern Queensland Theology Library.

Some of you may recall that, at the time my appointment as Governor-General was announced more than four years ago, I indicated that Helen and I hoped that we would be able to do a little to further the process of Aboriginal reconciliation. In the four years since then, we have tried to make good that undertaking. Inevitably we have sometimes felt discouraged by the slow pace of reconciliation. Similarly, we have often been depressed by the appalling facts and statistics relating to indigenous health and mortality and by the extent of the material disadvantage suffered by most Aboriginal and Torres Strait Islander peoples. For example, the undeniable fact that the statistics indicate that, unless things change, an Aboriginal baby girl born in our country this night can expect to live some 20 years less than a non-Aboriginal one. And the further fact that the statistics give no basis for believing that the discrepancy is narrowing. Quite the contrary.

But we have constantly been encouraged and uplifted by the fact that in countless ways – very often far removed from the public eye – Australians, black and white, are working to address and, one hopes, to reverse the material disadvantage of which I have spoken. Every bit as importantly, we are convinced that there has, of recent years, been a slow but perceptible development of the mutual respect, tolerance and forgiveness – the spiritual dimension, if I may so put it – without which reconciliation is simply impossible. There have been many occasions when Helen and I have been directly involved in instances of true reconciliation. On many other occasions we have had indirect contact – through a meeting, through sharing thoughts and experiences or in other ways – with such instances. This evening I want to share but a few of those occasions with you.

One such occasion, with a distinctly theological touch, took place last November when I launched a book by David Burke, *Dreaming of the Resurrection – a Reconciliation Story*, for the Sisters of St Joseph. It is a book which examines aspects of the Christian story as interpreted both by non-indigenous and indigenous artists – particularly Aborigines from Northern Australia. From the theological point of view, an outstanding feature of the Book is the way it illustrates the importance in indigenous Christianity of the Holy Spirit of our land. But its importance for present purposes is that, both in its entirety and its individual parts, it teaches reconciliation.

On page 33 the book tells the story of the 'Women at Mistake Creek'. It matters not whether the particular story is accurate in all its details, for the elements undoubtedly occurred in many parts of our nation in the 211 years since European settlement. It is a story of the slaughter of a large number of Aboriginal women and children of the Kija people who were shot and burnt in or near a dry creek bed in the Kimberley at the foot of an old boab tree. And of the perceived cause for the slaughter – the assumed theft of a milking cow which had merely strayed – a reason as mistaken in fact as it was barbarous in principle. Yet the story is one of forgiveness and reconciliation.

The Kija have placed a small monument at the foot of the old boab. It bears the words: '*In memory of our ancestors who were shot and burnt here. R.I.P. Mistake Creek*'. On All Souls Day every year Kija and non-indigenous people gather at the monument to pray, in remembrance, in sorrow, and in forgiveness. I understand that they prayed there last Tuesday.

In July of last year we attended a major reconciliation event for young people, the Croc Eisteddfod, at Weipa. There, a vast mixed audience of indigenous and non-indigenous Australians was overwhelmed by a performance by the children of the school at Mapoon here in Queensland of the Midnight Oil song – 'How can we sleep when our beds are burning?' The song tells of the events at Mapoon in 1963 when, after the discovery of bauxite in the area, the Queensland authorities forcibly transported the remaining Aborigines to other places and torched their old Mission homes. Some of the children in the performance were indigenous descendants of those who had been forcibly removed. Others were non-indigenous. We met them and their indigenous and non-indigenous teachers. And felt renewed.

In June of this year, as the guests of Galarrwuy Yunupingu and Gatjil Djerrkura, Helen and I were privileged to attend a ceremony at Yirrkala involving the return to the local indigenous people of two traditional Message Sticks. One had been sent from Fannie Bay Jail in Darwin in 1934 to Wonga, the local indigenous leader, by his three sons who had been unjustly imprisoned after being involved in resistance to unlawful and aggressive intrusion on traditional lands and unprovoked abuse, including rape, of indigenous women. The other Message Stick had been sent by Wonga to a Commonwealth Government representative as a gesture of peace.

The ceremony was attended by indigenous and non-indigenous people from all parts of the Gove Peninsula. With typical generosity, the present elders invited me to accept the Message Sticks on behalf of the Australian people and, as a gesture of reconciliation, to return them to Wonga's last living son, who has since died, as representative of his people. All of the people present were greatly moved. Indeed, some were in tears.

Again, last July, I was privileged to take part in a ceremony at Central Mount Wedge and to hand over on behalf of the Government a Deed of Grant to the traditional owners of part of their country. It is land which, during the present century, has been marked by tragedy and oppression; for it was only 70 years ago that what has become known as the Coniston Massacre took place at Coniston Station near the claim area. At least one of the claimants, with whom I spoke, had childhood memories of those terrible events. It was a moment of profound humility for me when the traditional owners asked that the conclusion of the ceremony take the form of a symbolic act of reconciliation, namely, the pouring of earth by me into their outstretched hands – a gesture recalling that of 1975, when part of the traditional lands of the Gurindji people were returned to Vincent Lingiari after the Wave Hill strike.

Hands – and the coming together of hands, both black and white – played a very significant part in another experience of reconciliation in action. In November 1997, I opened an Exhibition at the National Library of Australia called *Captive Lives: Looking for Tambo and his Companions*. If measured merely by reference to size or cost, the Exhibition is scarcely a major one. But the story which it tells and the manner of the telling combined to make it a profoundly moving experience of national, indeed universal, significance and importance.

It is the story of nine essentially gentle and trusting Aboriginal people who were enticed from their homes on Palm Island in North Queensland in 1883 by an American entrepreneur and exhibited as 'uncivilised savages' in Barnum and Bailey's Circus and in fair grounds and dime museums across the United States. Within a year one of the nine – a young man of about 21 who had acquired the name of 'Tambo' – was dead. His even younger wife and other companions were prevented from according him the ceremonial rites traditionally seen by their people as essential for the release of the spirit. His body was in fact sold to the owner of a dime museum, mummified and put on display.

Within a year of Tambo's death, a further five of the human exhibits, including his young widow, were dead. Within another two years the remaining three were lost to history, presumably also dead. Remarkably, just six years ago in October 1993, Tambo's mummified body was found in the basement of a Cleveland funeral parlour. His identity was ascertained by an Australian, Mrs Roslyn Poignant, who was at the time fortuitously in the United States researching the story of the group. In February 1994, on the 100th Anniversary of his death, the young man called Tambo was laid to rest in his native soil.

Thereafter, Mrs Poignant devoted herself to collecting materials for what was to become the 'Captive Lives' Exhibition.The opening was attended by Elders of the Palm Island community and the young man's collateral descendants. It culminated in a formal joint imprint of hands, as a gesture of reconciliation, by the representatives of the indigenous peoples, by me as Governor-General and by others associated with the Exhibition on a screen which itself became the final exhibit. Not only was the Exhibition itself the closing chapter in the story of Tambo. Its opening was, for all involved, the final reclamation of Tambo as part of our Australian nation. The Exhibition's story is that of an odyssey of suffering and oppression. The Exhibition itself had become an act of true reconciliation. It is currently at the Australian Museum in

Sydney. For a period from 8 January next year it will be at the Hervey Bay Regional Gallery in this State.

This somewhat haphazard journey to some instances of reconciliation could have taken us to at least a hundred other instances which Helen and I have experienced. I will conclude by letting it take us back to May 1997 … to the Reconciliation Convention in Melbourne. Many instances of reconciliation occurred in its course. One, in particular, remains fresh in my mind. It was when many of the leaders – black and white – in the fight for the 1967 Referendum came on to the stage and stood there, hand in hand, united not so much by the memory of far-off battles, but by their common humanity and their continuing desire to share the reconciliation which they had personally reached with one another thirty years before with our nation as a whole.

I have mentioned Vincent Lingiari and the ceremony at which part of the traditional lands of the Gurindji people were returned to them in 1975 at the end of the prolonged strike at Wave Hill Station. After the Gurindji soil had been poured into his hand and a formal leasehold document had been given to him, Vincent Lingiari's response was: 'We are all mates now'. He then turned and addressed his people in their own tongue, exhorting them to go forward 'with the whites' as friends and equals.

In that exhortation Vincent Lingiari encapsulated the essence of the ultimate vision of true Aboriginal reconciliation in our country: indigenous and non-indigenous people walking together, talking together, striving together, working together, and achieving together. Needless to say, we cannot achieve that vision until we have much more successfully addressed the material and the spiritual problems of indigenous Australia flowing from dispossession and the introduction of foreign disease and their consequences.

The anthropologist, Dr Deborah Bird Rose, has recounted a saga known over much of the Northern Territory, telling of how Captain Cook personally entered the Territory, killing and dispossessing

Aboriginal people and making them work for little or no pay. I leave you tonight with the hope with which I concluded the inaugural Lingiari Lecture, which I delivered in August 1996, namely, that one hundred years from now, when we are approaching the conclusion of the second century of our nation, the dreamings of the Aboriginal peoples will record whether we Australians had the determination, tolerance and goodwill to convert short term possibility into a reality that is timeless. Hopefully, when that time comes, the allegorical saga of dispossession by Captain Cook and those who came after him will have been supplemented by a sequel: one in which an Aborigine and a non-Aborigine went forth together throughout the country as friends and equals to overcome injustice and disadvantage and, thereby, understood the true meaning of reconciliation not only between Man and Man but also between Man and God.

5.16 The Opening of the National Catholic Family Gathering: 'Family – Dare to Dream', Melbourne, 28 April 2000

This National Catholic Family Gathering – 'Family – Dare to Dream' is a national celebration for the Jubilee Year. Through it, Australian Catholics are responding to the Holy Father's call 'to strengthen [our] faith and witness as Christians, so that there may be a true conversion and personal renewal in all the world's families'. It is a great pleasure for me to be here, with you this evening, to formally open the Gathering.

Having said that, I must confess I could be tempted to declare proceedings open and promptly sit down. For I can claim no special expertise either in theology or on the family. However, on balance, it seems preferable that I resist any such temptation and comply with the request that I offer some brief opening comments or thoughts.

The first of those thoughts is that, in a Gathering such as this, there is a need for at least some consensus about terminology. In that regard, it may prove helpful to make a few comments about the phrase 'the family'.

That phrase is an embracing or inclusive one. In the widest sense, it can be used to encompass all humankind – 'the family of man' where 'man' is used as a term which includes not only all adults, but also all infants, male and female. Alternatively, the family can be used in a religious sense – to embrace the membership of our Catholic Church. It seems to me that, for most of the Church's history, this was the predominant sense in which the term was used, at least by theologians. More relevant for present purposes, the phrase can be used to refer to a group of individuals in particular personal relationships.

Even in that narrow sense, however, there are variations of meaning. Commonly, we Catholics use the term to refer to our traditional image of family, – sometimes supported by reference to the Holy Family – namely, a man and a woman living in a married state and any children of their marriage, natural or adopted. In some contexts, the reference to children of the marriage may be limited to infant or dependent children.

The obverse of the family being an inclusive term is that it is also an exclusive one. Used in the widest sense I have mentioned – 'the family of man' – the exclusions, for example of other living creatures, are likely to be largely uncontroversial. As the connotation of the phrase narrows, however, the exclusions become of increasing importance until they may challenge or even exclude the significance of the inclusions. If, for example, one speaks in a modern context, of the 'family of the Church' is one referring to the Catholic Church or to the universal Christian Church which, in this age of Christian ecumenism and inter-denominational charity, many see as a living and overwhelmingly important embodiment of the mission of Christ. If one uses the phrase 'the family' in the narrow sense of the traditional family of male and female joined in a formally binding marriage and any children, what of the corresponding group where the parents, while genuinely and indefinitely committed to one another, are not formally married? Or where the parents, while living together with child or children, are unmarried and essentially uncommitted? And what of the single parent and her or his child or children? And, of course, one can go on and raise other circumstances of considerable social, and even moral, difficulty.

I raise these questions of terminology not for the purpose of engaging in an exercise of mere verbalism. I raise them for the reason they provide the context for some related thoughts, focussing on fundamental and over-riding obligations of charity, which I wish to share with you.

The first is in no way original. Indeed, it is the central message of the document,'The Truth and Meaning of Human Sexuality', published in 1995 by the Pontifical Council for the Family. It is that the true worth of any individual family, however one precisely defines the term, must ultimately rest on the extent to which it is inspired by, and reflects, what the document calls 'the fundamental and innate' human vocation of love. So inspired, the family is the ideal environment for human companionship and for the raising and education of children.

However, where such love is negated or abused, the family, again however defined, can become not only a nightmare for one or both of the adult partners but a completely unacceptable environment for the raising of children. Indeed, anyone who has had close contact with organisations seeking to help street children or other victims of violence and abuse, knows that a family or a household can, in some circumstances, represent not a safe haven towards which a child or wife who has fled should be redirected but a source of sexual, physical and emotional danger from which he or she is entitled to be protected. In other cases, where the child or spouse has not fled, it may be quite wrong to exert moral or other pressure to prevent flight or separation or to discourage the victim or the State from invoking the protection or sanction of the law.

Accordingly, I suggest we should not dare to dream in a way which, by over-emphasis upon the encouragement or protection of the particular formalised relationships which we ourselves accept as constituting a family, neglects the importance of, and the Church's and the State's legitimate concerns and responsibilities in relation to, the internal circumstances of particular families, including the well-being and fundamental rights of individual members in their familial environment. Put differently, we should not allow concern with form, however legitimate, to lead to uncharitable neglect of, or even indifference to, the plight of the individual or the true substance of human relationships and human fulfilment in the particular case.

My final thought is, as I have indicated, a related one. It is that when we dare to dream about the family and to seek to protect it from external threats or provide it with external assistance, we should also be conscious of the possibility of lack of charity or of unfair discrimination against those who do not conform with our own preferred image of what constitutes a family. Thus, for example, as the Pontifical Council for the Family points out, the position of the single parent, commonly unmarried, is deserving of special support rather than exclusion from the dream and ideals of the family.

We human beings are sociable. We are born for love – to love and to be loved. As individuals, we are at liberty to constitute relationships, to join groups, to become members of faith communities and to contribute as citizens of the state. In contemporary Australia, the family remains a constitutive ideal for the majority of people – providing the primary locus for intimate relationship and for the procreation, education and development of children. Such an ideal requires and deserves support and encouragement from church, society and State. But the ideal may lawfully be differently incarnated depending on culture, social supports and community expectations. That means that, in a free, pluralistic and multicultural society such as ours, the public espousal of the ideal as *we* see it and the public airing of *our* dream as at this Gathering, should not be allowed to inadvertently assume a predominantly negative aspect by seeming to be focussed upon adverse judgments of those who lawfully seek other means of personal fulfilment. In that regard, we also do well to remember that the example of Christ simply leaves no room even for argument that our obligations of spiritual and material charity are confined to those who conform to our own religious convictions or standards.

Rather, I suggest, the emphasis should be on the universal positives of the vision or dream of family of those of us who are both inspired and challenged by the teaching and pastoral support of the Catholic Church. That way we will really dare to dream about better ways for family not only for ourselves but also for others who may be very different from ourselves. That way our dream will be of an Australian society which is truly supportive of family, respectful of the diverse religious and other lawful views about family and encouraging – especially of those who find commitment of love difficult and sustained nurturing of children beyond their unaided means or ability.

That way, we will also help our society avoid evils and mistakes of the past such as earlier policies of separating Aboriginal children from their families – or their unstructured familial relationships – which have wreaked such awful and ongoing damage to so many of our indigenous fellow Australians. In that regard, I express the prayer that the deliberations of this Gathering will help us all to avoid justified criticism on the grounds of lack of charity or understanding by future generations which may have cause to scrutinise *our* policies, ideals and dreams for families.

5.17 The Opening of the '*Treasures of Faith*' Exhibition, St Patrick's Cathedral, Melbourne, 27 July 2000

There is something about St Patrick's Cathedral which evokes in me a mixture of pride – in the good sense, admiration and affection whenever I enter it. In that regard, I should mention that, while my life has been largely spent in other parts of Australia, I have never regarded myself as a stranger to Melbourne or to this Cathedral. My great grandfather arrived in this city almost 150 years ago – in 1851 to be precise. That was some 12 years after the first Melbourne Mass had been celebrated – on Pentecost Sunday, 1839. Family legend has it that my great grandfather, had intended to disembark in Sydney from the small vessel, the '*Harry Lorrequer*', on which he, his wife and young family had endured the harsh journey from Plymouth. When he went ashore in Sydney to seek work, however, the first sign that he saw was unambiguously discouraging. It was: 'No Irish'. With what some of you may think was extraordinary good judgment, he immediately got back on the boat and came on to Melbourne. I was born here, in St Kilda, 80 years afterwards.

A second reason why it is a great delight for Helen and me to be here is that this is the first occasion on which we have been able to visit St Patrick's since the completion, in September 1997, of the wonderful work of restoration. I belatedly congratulate Archbishop Sir Frank Little, who is present this evening, Archbishop Pell and all associated with the planning and the implementation of that work. It does you all enormous credit.

The third reason why it is a delight for Helen and me to be here is, of course, the obvious one. The official opening of '*Treasures of Faith*' – an Exhibition of the art and history of the Churches in Australia.

There are many subjects about which it would be possible to talk – and to talk for a very long time – in officially opening this wonderful Exhibition. One could, for example, talk about faith, about hope and about charity. For different exhibits invariably lead one to think of one or more of those virtues. Alternatively, some of the exhibits remind us of the journey of Australian Christians, including Australian Catholics, from times of intolerance and lack of charity towards one another to a greater awareness and appreciation of the worth and goodness of the lives of Christians of other denominations and of the splendour of the Universal Christian Church of which the various Christian denominations form part.

Yet again, other exhibits will remind most, if not all, of the fundamental importance of Aboriginal Reconciliation and of the plain fact that what was seen by the new comers as settlement in a newly discovered country was for others invasion and dispossession of ancestral lands. Other exhibits remind us of the nobility of the human spirit even in the face of awful oppression such as the horror of a World War II Japanese concentration camp.

And, of course, as the Exhibition's sub-title indicates, the exhibits collectively instruct and remind us of the history of the Churches in Australia, and, by extension, the history and nature of our nation itself. It is in that context that I wish to make specific reference to a few of the exhibits.

One is the altar stone carried on board La Perouse's voyage of discovery to the Pacific which was designed to rival the English expedition of Captain Cook. There are persuasive grounds for believing that it was on this altar stone that the very first Catholic service – the funeral of Father Receveur – on Australian land was held in February, 1788.

There is also the pyx in which the Blessed Sacrament was reserved for the first time in Australia. When Father O'Flynn was deported from the Colony in 1818, he left behind the Sacrament. It became the object of devotion of a small confraternity which met on Sundays – as tradition would have it in a house which was to become St Patrick's Convent, Church Hill in Sydney.

Other items which are particularly meaningful to us as Australians include those devotional items which were carried by Vietnamese refugees seeking out new homes in Australia and elsewhere. They remind us of the importance to modern Australia of our multicultural inclusiveness. We Australians directly or indirectly come from all the regions, races and cultures of the world. It is the mutual acceptance of, and respect for, those different backgrounds, characteristics and beliefs which characterises and sustains us as a nation.

The final item I would mention is a lectern, made from native timber, and constructed by convicts at the Port Arthur Penitentiary in the 1830s. I see this lectern as one of a number of exhibits symbolising the process of 'Australianising' that the Church has undergone here. That process seems to me to have been eloquently described by a great Anglican Bishop who said he wanted the great things of abiding value in the Church's traditions 'thoroughly baptised into the Australian scene, blown through by Australian winds, bathed in Australian sunshine, and even coated now and then with Australian dust'.

Let me conclude these short comments by indicating what I think we should, in this Great Jubilee Year, learn from this Exhibition. In so far as the past is concerned, we should carry from it a greater appreciation of the importance of the history of the Churches as an integral – an essential – part of the history of our nation. In so far as the future is concerned, we should, I suggest, carry from the Exhibition a heightened awareness of our custodianship of the Universal Christian Church's message of inclusion, tolerance and reconciliation and of its mission of outreach to the disadvantaged and its commitment to a truly just society. And of the importance of that message, mission and commitment to our nation as a whole.

5.18 The Opening Of Fischl House For Jewishcare, Sydney, 3 December 2000

For me, the noblest affirmation of Judaism will always lie in the profound and extraordinarily difficult challenge and belief: 'I *am* my brother's keeper'. And lest you think I am trespassing in areas where I have no claim to tread, I would mention that I can quote high Rabbinical authority to support the proposition that the essence of Judaism lies in that challenge.

Today is a celebration of the enduring values reflected in that challenge. And that is not surprising. For the Australian Jewish community has long been notable for its concern for social justice and support for humanitarian efforts.

In this city, Jewishcare has, under that and earlier names, embodied and discharged that great tradition for almost 70 years. Its work of compassion in assisting families, refugees, migrants, people with disabilities, survivors of the Holocaust, the aged, the frail and many others is an active expression of an abiding belief in each person's intrinsic worth and dignity. In that regard, it is notable that while the programs offered by Jewishcare are designed to meet the particular needs of the Jewish community, they are made available to all.

Fischl House is a worthy new home for that dedicated mission. It is a monument and symbol of people, of community and of faith. Through the ongoing efforts of staff, volunteers and the people who use the services offered here, it will be a place of commitment and opportunity. It will provide a meeting place to share life's experiences and to gain support in difficult times. And it will be an enduring testament to the cohesion, the religious conviction and the sense of social obligation of the Jewish community and of the fact that, in times of hardship and sorrow, you truly are your brother's and sister's keeper.

Let me conclude these remarks with a comment that I have made on many occasions in the past. It is that the longer I am Governor-General of Australia the more convinced I become that the ultimate test of our worth as a truly democratic nation is how we treat the most disadvantaged and vulnerable of our fellow Australians. Clearly Fischl House and the work to be done here by Jewishcare will makes a significant and continuing contribution towards enabling us to pass that test.

6

Mourning and Hope

6.0 Editor's note

When paying tribute to William Deane on his last day in office as Governor-General, Kim Beazley, the Leader of the Opposition observed: Sir William 'has presided over the memorial services and commemorations of some of the saddest events that we have witnessed in recent times as Australians, as well as the commemorations of past events which require memorialisation. Particularly in the early years of his watch, he had a number of services to attend, which were services related to events in which a large number of Australians had died. He was there as a sympathetic figure, a shoulder to cry on in some circumstances, for a number of Australians who were seeking comfort and an understanding that the Australian community identified with them in their period of distress.'[11]

Deane was punctilious in briefing the Queen about national tragedies. He would often suggest that she send a message of condolence and he would even offer a suggested formula of words which was inevitably adopted. When distinguished Australians like Sir Zelman Cowen and Dame Roma Mitchell were about to celebrate significant milestones, Deane would inform the Queen and arrange for a suitable message to be delivered. He would follow up with an account of how appreciatively the regal greetings were received.

In the midst of tragedy and death, he always brought hope. At such moments he would be accompanied by Lady Helen Deane. He always had the right word to say and the ideal symbol to share, none more so, than when he brought the 14 sprigs of wattle from Canberra to Interlaken to commemorate the 14 young Australians who died in the 1999 canyoning accident. He reminded this

---

[11] Commonwealth Parliamentary Debates, House of Representatives, 28 June 2001, 28869 (Kim Beazley, Leader of the Opposition).

audience that the golden wattles were coming into bloom back home. He offered this message of hopeful remembrance: 'Just as these young men and women were in the flower of their youth. And when we are back in Australia we will remember how the flowers and the perfume and the pollen of their and our homeland were carried down the river where they died to Lake Brienz in this beautiful country on the far side of the world.'

6.1 An Investiture Ceremony for the Presentation of Australian Bravery Decorations and Service Commendations in Respect of Actions at the Site of the Black Hawk Helicopter Accident on 12 June 1996, Government House, Canberra, 23 May 1997

On the evening of Wednesday, 12 June 1996, at the High Range training area near Townsville a mid-air collision occurred between two Black Hawk helicopters from 5th Aviation Regiment during a training exercise with the Special Air Service Regiment. The exercise was a live fire counter-terrorism approach exercise being conducted under black-out conditions. The pilots were using night-vision equipment. The exercise had been rehearsed that afternoon by everyone involved.

As the aircraft approached Fire Support Base Barbara – on a 2000 foot high sparsely timbered plateau – four of the aircraft were in line abreast. Two other helicopters, being used as sniper aircraft, were slightly to the front and to either side of the other four helicopters. About 30 seconds from the Landing Zone with SAS men already preparing to fast rope from the helicopters from a height of about 30 metres, the two aircraft on the lefthand side of the line abreast formation collided. Both aircraft caught fire.

With its main rotor damaged, the far lefthand aircraft crashed straight into the ground landing upside down. Of the 15 people on this aircraft, 14 died and one was critically injured. The tail rotor on the other aircraft was destroyed but the pilot, Captain David

Burke, managed to land it on its wheels despite the fuselage with no tailplane rotating on its axis. Four SASR soldiers aboard that aircraft were killed.

Safety personnel on the ground to monitor the exercise coordinated the rescue effort. The four other Black Hawk helicopters were used to shuttle some of the dying men and the injured to Townsville General Hospital.

That bare summary masks a national tragedy of great dimensions. Eighteen members of the two Regiments were killed. Another 12 were injured. Some of those injured will suffer grave disabilities for the rest of their lives.

The tragedy came only six weeks after that at Port Arthur. Our nation was again plunged into mourning. We all have our own particular memories. For me, those memories include ecumenical services in Townsville, Canberra and Perth and meetings with the injured and the families of those who had died. There is, however, one moment which will always stand out above all others. It was the moment in the ecumenical service under grey skies and in drizzling rain at Lavarack Barracks when the Black Hawk helicopters came flying overhead shortly after the last post had been sounded. It brought home to everyone there, both soldiers and civilians, the enormity of the loss and the plain fact that the victims had died and been injured in the service of Australia. It was a moment of profound sadness. It was also one of great pride in our country and in the members of its Defence Force.

Today, we are all still conscious of the tragic loss of life and injuries sustained on that fateful evening. The loss, and the pain which we as a nation share, will again be evident within two weeks' time when we gather to observe the first anniversary of that dreadful accident. This afternoon is, however, more an occasion for pride than for sorrow as we honour those who responded to the alarming situation in which they found themselves with incredible courage, with selfless concern for the welfare of others, and with a ready appreciation of what needed to be done and risked to save the lives of their mates.

Many contributed towards the amelioration of the injuries and suffering. Their actions were exhaustively examined in connection with a formal inquiry into the accident. After that inquiry, some were nominated by the Chief of Army to the Australian Decorations Advisory Committee for consideration for bravery awards. The inquiry had drawn upon the testimony of those whose lives were spared. No-one can ever know the thoughts of those who died, or what actions they may have performed had they been among the survivors. While recognising the actions of those who have been singled out for special honour today, we are all conscious of the dedication and courage of all the brave men who took part in the exercise that night. And we are also conscious of an overall picture in which extraordinary bravery by soldiers, air crew and ground safety personnel to rescue their comrades from the burning wrecks, despite the flames and exploding ammunition, together with the on-the-scene medical aid and rapid transport to hospital, prevented much higher casualties.

It is a distinctive feature of the Australian honours system that decorations for gallantry *in the face of the enemy* are matched at every level by awards for bravery under all other circumstances.

Today's Investiture of awards for bravery will see the award of three Stars of Courage. When I tell you that the Star of Courage is awarded only for acts of conspicuous courage in circumstances of great peril and that its twin – the Star of Gallantry – is surpassed only by the Victoria Cross, you will appreciate its great national significance.

Similar comments can be made about the bravery medal – awarded only for acts of bravery in hazardous circumstances – and the Commendation for Brave Conduct – awarded for other acts of bravery which are considered worthy of recognition.

In retrospect, the Black Hawk tragedy reminds us all of how

much Australia demands of the members of its armed forces. The Australian Defence Force must be able to react to widely varying circumstances and tasks in maintaining its ability to defend our nation. To achieve that ability, training has to be uncompromising and as realistic as possible. That means that there will inevitably be occasions when the men and women of our armed services are called upon to face danger, including risk of physical injury and death.

While the Black Hawk tragedy reminds us of how much we ask of our service men and women, it also reminds us of how much they give in response. In particular, by today's ceremony, we honour not only the 14 men whose bravery has been singled out. The honour done to them is also an honour to those with whom they served. And, of course, their bravery, their actions and their awards bring great honour to their Regiments.

6.2 The Unveiling of the Black Hawk Memorial, Townsville, 17 August 1997

At the time of the Black Hawk tragedy, Her Majesty The Queen sent a message of condolence which was read at ecumenical services in Canberra and in Perth. Her Majesty has expressly requested that, at this ceremony to unveil this monument, I renew her condolences to the families and friends of those killed in the tragedy. Her Majesty has also specially asked me to convey her thanks and her congratulations to the people of the City of Townsville for their efforts in erecting this memorial to those who died.

On the evening of Wednesday, 12 June 1996, at the High Range training area near this city, a mid-air collision occurred between two Black Hawk helicopters from 5 Aviation Regiment during a training exercise with the Special Air Service Regiment. The exercise was a live-fire counter-terrorism approach exercise being conducted under black-out conditions.

As the aircraft approached Fire Support Base Barbara – on a 2000 foot high sparsely timbered plateau – four of the aircraft were abreast. About 30 seconds from the Landing Zone, the two aircraft on the lefthand side collided. Both aircraft caught fire.

With its main rotor damaged, the far lefthand aircraft crashed straight into the ground landing upside down. Of the 15 soldiers on this aircraft, 14 died and one was critically injured. The tail rotor on the other aircraft was destroyed but the pilot, Captain David Burke, managed to land it on its wheels despite the fuselage with no tailplane rotating on its axis. Four SAS men aboard that aircraft were killed.

That bare summary masks a national tragedy of terrible dimensions. Eighteen young members of our Army were dead ... the lives that stretched before them left unlived and unfulfilled. In their different ways, each had outstanding qualifications and qualities. Each had loved ones who were left to mourn their loss and to try to pick up the pieces of a life bereft of a husband, a father, a son, a brother or a comrade.

We all have our own particular memories of the time of the tragedy. For me, those memories include ecumenical services in Townsville, Canberra and Perth and meetings with the injured and the families of those who had died. There is, however, one moment which will always remain with me. It was in the ecumenical service under grey skies and in drizzling rain at Lavarack Barracks here in Townsville when the Black Hawk helicopters came flying overhead shortly after the last post had sounded. That moment brought home to everyone there, both soldiers and civilians, the enormity of the loss and the plain fact that those who had died had been killed in the service of Australia. It was a moment of profound sadness. It was also one of great pride in our country and in the members of its Defence Force.

Since then, more than a year has passed. But the nation has not forgotten. On the 23rd of May of this year, at a ceremony at

Government House in Canberra, 14 members of the Army who were either survivors of the accident or involved in rescue work were honoured by awards for extraordinary heroism during the events following the collision. On 12 June, many of us gathered in the Army Chapel of St Paul at Duntroon for an ecumenical service to mark the anniversary of the tragedy. Others gathered at services here in Townsville and in Perth. And here today, at the instigation of the people of Townsville, we are gathered for the unveiling of this permanent memorial to the patriotism, the sacrifice and the service of those 18 young men who died.

In retrospect, the Black Hawk tragedy reminds us all how much Australia demands of the members of its Armed Forces. And it also reminds us of how much they give in response. The 18 young soldiers whom we remember today gave everything. They died for our country and for all Australians every bit as much as if they had died in their country's defence in time of war. We mourn them. We honour them. And we will remember them.

I sincerely thank the people of Townsville for this memorial which, with the support of their Council and the State and Commonwealth Governments, they have erected to commemorate the lives and the sacrifice of those 18 soldiers.

6.3 The First Anniversary of the Thredbo Disaster, Thredbo, 31 July 1998

The Snowy, its mountains and its people, have always held a very special place in the folklore and in the affection of our nation. I am sure that my comments here this afternoon have the support of all Australians.

Today is a time both to look back and to look forward. To look back and remember the tragic events of last July: the terrible loss of those whose lives were cruelly cut short by the landslide; the profound grief of their families and close friends; the sacrifice, the determination and, in many cases, the heroism of those who worked tirelessly in the rescue operation; the dedication of the counsellors and all those who provided support; the strength of Stuart Diver. And to look forward to the future of these mountains and of this wonderful alpine village of Thredbo and all its residents.

This Community Centre helps us to do those things. To look back and to look forward. The Centre had long been an ambition of the residents of Thredbo. It became a reality after the landslide. It was completed last summer with funds provided by Federal and State Governments to supplement the funds which had been raised by the residents over many years. It constitutes a memorial to the 18 victims who lost their lives last July and whose names are inscribed on this stone which I am about to unveil. The Centre also, as the victims of the tragedy would wish, looks to the future of the alpine Village which they loved and whose people the Centre will serve through the years to come.

And now it is my privilege, on behalf of all Australians, to unveil this memorial stone to the eighteen victims of the landslide. Let us pause for a moment and silently read their names and say a personal prayer or otherwise remember them. May they rest with God.

6.4 The Memorial Service to Honour the Geelong West Country Fire Authority Volunteers who Died Fighting Bushfires at Linton, Kardinia Park, Geelong, Victoria, 19 December 1998

This is an occasion of profound sadness. We gather to mourn the loss of five brave men – Matthew Armstrong, Stuart Davidson, Christopher Evans, Jason Thomas and Garry Vredeveldt. They died, while life was still young or in its prime, fighting to protect and safeguard the lives and property of others.

But it is also an occasion of great pride as we honour them. The memory of their voluntary service, their courage and their sacrifice will long endure. For they have truly become part of the Australian story.

Fire has a special place in the lives of Australians. It is commonly our friend and companion. It has provided light and protection against the dark and warmth against the cold. But too often it is our most frightening foe. For thousands of years across our ancient land, summer lightning has ignited the tinder dry fuel. And in more recent years, the negligence and sometimes the malice of man has created or intensified the risk of destruction by fire.

Bush fires are with us every summer. The worst of them are burnt into our national memory. South Eastern Tasmania in 1967 … Ash Wednesday in Victoria and South Australia in 1983 … New South Wales in 1994. Closer to here in Geelong, we recall the fires which devastated Lara 30 years ago this summer.

And it is not surprising that fighting fire has helped forge, and has become part of, our national character. From early times we learnt that fire cannot be fought on any scale by people acting separately. Our Bush Fire Brigades and bodies such as the CFA here in Victoria were formed to provide the necessary organisation and teamwork. And since those early times, the ethos of the Bush Fire Brigades has exemplified all that is best in our nation: mateship – particularly the extraordinary mateship between members of a Brigade – courage, strength, selflessness and dedication. And sacrifice, sometimes the ultimate sacrifice, when the inevitable danger becomes reality.

And so it was on Wednesday 2 December. The call came. Matthew, Stuart, Christopher, Jason and Garry dropped everything. They piled into the Geelong West tanker and headed off to save Linton from a serious fire. The stage was reached where their work was more or less done. The town was out of danger. And then disaster struck, as unpredictable as the wind. Their selfless and voluntary service in the protection of the lives and property of others against the menace of fire cost them their own lives.

Here in the heart of the community and the City which they loved, we extend to their families our profound sympathy on their immeasurable loss. Our nation mourns with them as they grieve. The names of those whom they have lost and whom we mourn are numbered among those who have made our country great through sacrifice in the service of others.

To the members of the Bush Fire Brigades across our land, and especially to the members of the Geelong West Brigade, I say this. The tragic deaths of your five colleagues lead us as a nation, at the beginning of this summer, to pause and to take stock of the importance and the danger of your work. We thank you for the selfless service you perform and for the courage with which you perform it. And we assure you of our support.

Finally, on behalf of Australians everywhere, I acknowledge the dedication, the unselfishness, the courage and the sacrifice of Matthew, Stuart, Christopher, Jason and Garry in the cause of protecting our country and its people from the destruction and devastation of fire. We honour their memory.

May they rest with God.

6.5 An Ecumenical Service for the Victims of the Canyoning Tragedy, Interlaken, Switzerland, 5 August 1999

We are gathered in great sadness to mourn the deaths of the 21 young people who were killed in the canyoning accident near here, last week. They came from five nations – Switzerland, the United Kingdom, South Africa, New Zealand and Australia. Their loss is a profound tragedy for their families and friends who are in the thoughts and the prayers of all of us at this service today. We pray with them for their loved ones who have died. And we also pray that, in the words of our Lord (Matthew Ch.5, v.4), they will truly be comforted.

Fourteen of the victims of the tragedy came from Australia.

Collectively, their deaths represent probably the greatest single peacetime loss of young Australians outside our own country. That loss affects not only their families and friends, dreadful though that is. It also deeply affects our nation as a whole and all of its people.

I have, as Governor-General of Australia, with Senator John Herron of our Government, come here on behalf of Australia and of all Australians, to mourn them, to be with and to sympathise with their family members and friends who are here, and to demonstrate how important they were to their homeland. For us, the tragedy is somehow made worse by the fact that they died so far away from the homes, the families, the friends and the land they loved so well.

Australia and Switzerland are on opposite sides of the globe. Yet, in this age of modern telecommunications, one effect of the disaster has been to bring our two countries closer together. On every night since the accident, Switzerland has been in every Australian home that has been tuned into the television news, as well as on the radio, in all our newspapers and other media outlets. Conversely, the fact that two-thirds of those who died came from Australia has given rise to an increased awareness here in Switzerland of my country and its people.

Switzerland has, of course, itself experienced the shock and sorrow of overseas tragedy in the past. Perhaps that has heightened the sympathy and understanding which it has shown in recent days. I have already had the privilege of meeting with you, Madam President, and with Vice-President Ogi and exchanging condolences. I would, on this solemn occasion, like to express to the Swiss authorities and to the people of Switzerland, particularly the people of the Wilderswil and Interlaken regions, our abiding gratitude for all the help and assistance they have provided in the aftermath of the tragedy. In particular, I pay tribute to the bravery of all those who worked in the rescue efforts. We thank them for their skill and dedication. I also particularly mention the competence, the compassion and the kindness of all who have helped to look after the survivors and the relatives who have come here.

The young people – certainly the young Australians – who have been killed all shared the spirit of adventure, the joy of living, the exuberance and the delight of youth. That spirit inspired their lives, and lit the lives of all who knew them, until the end. We remember that and so many other wonderful things about them as we mourn them and grieve for young lives cut so tragically short. And all of us feel and share in their collective loss. For these 21 young men and women were part – a shining part – of our humanity. As John Donne wrote, 'No man is an island'. Anyone's 'death diminishes' us all because we are all 'involved in mankind'.

Yesterday, my wife and I, together with family members and friends of the Australian victims, visited the canyon where the accident occurred. There, in memory of each of the 14 young people who came from our homeland, we cast into the Saxetenbach 14 sprigs of wattle, our national floral emblem, which we had brought with us from Government House in Canberra. Somehow, we felt that was bringing a little of Australia to them.

It was also, in a symbolic way, helping to bring them home to our country. That is not to suggest that their spirit and their memory will not linger forever, here in Switzerland, at the place where they died. Rather, it is to suggest that a little part of Switzerland has become, and will always be, to some extent, part of Australia. As it will also be part of the other countries outside Switzerland – New Zealand, South Africa and the United Kingdom – from whence they came.

It is still winter at home. But the golden wattles are coming into bloom. Just as these young men and women were in the flower of their youth. And when we are back in Australia we will remember how the flowers and the perfume and the pollen of their and our homeland were carried down the river where they died to Lake Brienz in this beautiful country on the far side of the world.

May they all rest with God.

6.6 An Investiture in Respect of the Fire on Board HMAS *Westralia*, Canberra, 13 October 1999

At nine o'clock on the morning of 5 May 1998, the underway replenishment ship HMAS *Westralia* sailed from Fleet Base West. At half past ten, a fuel leak was reported to the Machinery Control Room and the port main engine was shut down for repairs. Approximately five minutes later, a fireball erupted. There followed an absolute nightmare of fire, toxic gas, black smoke and noise.

Under those conditions, there were many acts of bravery and selflessness undertaken by members of the ship's crew. Indeed, it is clear that some personnel chose to remain in the area, fully aware of the danger to themselves, in order to help save the lives of others and to prevent further damage to the ship. It is also clear that it is all but inevitable that acts of heroism and self-sacrifice on the part of those involved, particularly on the part of those who died, remain unknown and unacknowledged.

Four crew members lost their lives: Able Seaman Phillip Carroll; Leading Seaman Bradley Meek; Midshipman Megan Pelly; and Petty Officer Shaun Smith. They were with others in the Main Machinery Space when the fire began. They were among those who immediately began action to fight the fire and helped to locate and assist fellow shipmates to climb escape ladders to safety. We mourn them, and pay tribute to them, at this ceremony today, as we honour the courage and loyalty of those involved in the incident. At the time of the tragedy, I sought to convey to their families my own sorrow and profound sympathy for their loss. Today, I again express that sorrow and sympathy and add how proud we are of them. May they all rest with God.

The efforts of the ship's crew were outstanding. There can be no doubt that their actions reflected their personal bravery and dedication. They are a reminder to us all, yet again, of how much we expect from the members of our Australian Defence

Force. And of the selfless nature of their response in the service of our country.

Conscious as we are of the bravery shown by the *Westralia* crew generally, today we are gathered here at Government House in Canberra to present insignia to those members of the crew – or their next-of-kin – who have been recommended for particular awards. Some of those awards are under the Australian system of honours and awards. They include two Conspicuous Service Crosses, on the recommendation of the Minister for Defence; three Bravery Medals – two of them for deceased members of the crew – and four Group Citations for Bravery, on the recommendation of the Australian Bravery Decorations Council. The Group Citations are to three Hose Teams and to crew members who were in the Main Machinery Space, including the four deceased personnel. There are, in addition, a number of Defence Awards. Five Chief of Defence Force Commendations are to be presented, including for one of the deceased, and three Chief of Navy Commendations.

Ladies and gentlemen, as Governor-General of our country, I congratulate and thank each of the recipients or those who represent them and their families. By these awards we honour the designated servicemen and women. And we also honour those with whom they served. The crew of *Westralia*, on that fateful day in May last year, behaved with exemplary courage and duty, and in the finest traditions of the Service to which they belong.

6.7 The Dedication of the Port Arthur Memorial Garden, Port Arthur, Tasmania, 28 April 2000

For all of all our lives, Port Arthur has been a place of extraordinary national importance. Partly because of its haunting beauty here in the far south of our nation. And partly because of the things that had happened here long before any of us was born. Harsh imprisonments and punishments which, though remote in time, reached across the years to speak to us of the importance to our nation of justice, of human decency and of freedom. And to remind us of the worth of human life and of the fundamental truth that even through the darkest tragedy and the most profound sorrow beauty can persist and good can come.

And then, four years ago today, unbelievably, brutal evil again visited this place. Its outcome was a tragedy which united our nation in grief to an extent that no previous peacetime event, at least in my memory, had done. It was not simply the fact that many of the victims came from different parts of Australia. It was that the tragedy touched us all. Australia itself was a victim in that what had happened was an affront to our people as a whole – seemingly undermining things about our country and ourselves that we took for granted but yet held most precious. Indeed, part of the difficulty in dealing with the events of that day lay in their sheer incomprehensibility.

Now, four years on, as we are gathered to dedicate this memorial garden, it is a time to look back to that day. And forward to the future.

Looking back, we remember the awful events themselves … the evil that was done. And, more than anything else, we remember the lives – many of them young lives – that were so cruelly lost. We are reminded of hopes unfulfilled, dreams unrealised, lives unlived … of what might … what should ... have been.

And we remember all those others whose lives were shattered. The families and the close friends of those who died. The other victims who were physically injured but survived. And those others who were personally involved in the events of that day.

In the immediate aftermath and in the four years since, Helen and I have had personal contact with many of those most directly affected – here at Port Arthur, at the Service Provider Centre at Nubeena, in Hobart and other parts of Tasmania, in Canberra and elsewhere on the mainland. We have seen how the tragedy remains fresh in minds and continues to haunt and devastate lives which will never be the same.

But, even looking back, we must also remember the good. On the day itself, the innumerable displays of bravery and utter selflessness … some acknowledged, others not. The compassion and skill of the members of the emergency services. The outpouring of sympathy and support from fellow Australians. The national revulsion over the violence and the killing manifesting itself in the passage of Australia's uniform gun control laws, which would probably never have otherwise been enacted. The willing public acceptance of the special taxation levy necessary to sustain them. Ultimately, the way that our nation faced the tragedy served to confirm the quality of our national character and soul.

This beautiful memorial garden, here at the place where those things happened four years ago, seems to me to capture the sentiments which I have endeavoured to express. The loss. The search for good transcending evil. The need to remember … and to achieve peace.

And through this memorial garden, set among ruins whose stones and iron remind us of much earlier days, we look forward to the future. For this will be a permanent shrine to which all Australians, especially those affected by the tragedy, may in the future come to reflect upon that day in our national life. Being built using many plants and materials from this area, it reminds us of the wonderful beauty of the Tasman Peninsula and of the fact that there is so much to value in this place and in our nation. And it provides a fitting memorial to those who died.

For those who come to this garden in the years to come – to mourn, to pay their respects, to reflect, to pray or simply to observe – will take from it not only an awareness of continuing beauty but also a sense of shared humanity and peace. And, through this memorial, those who died here on will be not merely remembered because of the tragedy that befell them but honoured for what they were. That way their special qualities and their spirit will gently linger here to infuse this place with goodness and with hope.

And now, let us join together in tribute, in sadness and in love, to dedicate this wonderful garden to the memory and honour of those who died here on the Peninsula on this day four years ago.

6.8 The Memorial Service for the Childers Palace Backpackers Hostel Fire Tragedy, Childers, Queensland, 25 June 2000

This is an occasion of profound sadness. I know that I speak for all Australians when I say that our hearts go out to all affected by the terrible tragedy that occurred in this beautiful small Queensland town of Childers last Thursday night.

To the families and loved ones of those who died. We pray that they may be comforted in their grief and loss. To the survivors who are still emerging from a nightmare experience. They have our deepest sympathy and our support. And to the people of this region who identify so closely with the young people who come at this time each year to work with them and become part of their community. And the gratitude of us all goes to those who have been involved in the difficult and harrowing rescue and support work.

But most of all we are gathered to mourn – and to join in prayer for – the young men and women who have died. They came from different parts of the world – from the United Kingdom, from the Netherlands, from Australia, from Japan, from Korea, from Spain. Yet they shared so much … youth, energy, enthusiasm, the spirit of adventure, the joy of life and of living. And, as we mourn them, we are conscious of so many things … of lives unlived, of hopes unfulfilled, of dreams unrealised … of what might – what should – have been.

We Australians grieve, of course, for our young fellow Australians who lie dead. Ours was the land they loved and they were part of us. But equally we grieve for the young people from other countries who have died. They, like the many thousands of other young people who visit Australia each year, often carrying backpacks, were a treasured part of *our* national life. And their deaths are made so much worse by the fact that they were so far away from the lands and the families they loved. We grieve for them not as strangers. For, while they will always belong to their own countries and people, they have become forever part of ours and of us.

May they all rest with God.

Conclusion

[Conc] A Bipartisan Acknowledgment of Deane's Contribution to the Nation

On his last day as Governor-General, Deane concluded his final interview with these words: 'My final word is the one that I've ... been trying to get over to the people of Australia for the whole of my time as Governor-General and that is: The ultimate test of our worth as a nation is how we treat the most vulnerable and disadvantaged of our people.'[1]

About a year after his retirement as Governor-General, Deane was interviewed on the ABC *Encounter* program. He observed: 'There is a century of unbroken democratic rule since our Federation came into being. There are very few countries in the world that can boast such a record. There's the spirit of ordinary Australians, their decency and I think their goodness in times of peace and also in times of war. And most of all, for me, there's what I see as our great national achievement, that is our multiculturalism, or our multicultural inclusiveness, the mutual respect and understanding which has enabled us to take people from all the regions, races, religions and cultures of the world, and come together as a fairly cohesive whole. Now they are wonderful things about Australia, but we're kidding ourselves if at the same time we don't look at our flaws and inadequacies at areas where we haven't achieved as well as we might have. They're the divisions in our society between the haves and the have-nots, and in that context, it seems to me that the disadvantage of Aboriginal Australia and the need for true and lasting reconciliation stands out as a national imperative.'[2]

In this conclusion, I set out the tributes paid him at the end of his term as Governor-General by Prime Minister John Howard, Leader of the Opposition, Kim Beazley, and Tony Stephens, author

---

1 *The Australian*, 29 June 2001.

2 ABA, *Encounter*, 'Sir William Deane', Transcript, 12 May 2002.

of *Sir William Deane: The Things That Matter*. Stephens' book is not a biography but 'an attempt to portray Deane's principles and objectives, to help explain how he arrived at them and to show why his powers of persuasion were such a force in the land.'[3] Eighteen months after Deane's retirement, Stephens completed his book and observed: 'The public interest in what Deane was saying increased the relevance of the office to an Australia at the turn of the century. Deane was striking carefully independent positions in a gently assertive manner, bringing a fresh humanity to public life.' Stephens was convinced that Deane's 'period in office demonstrated clearly that the qualities of the individual person, rather than the formal job description for a governor-general, determine just how worthwhile the job can be.'[4] As Gough Whitlam said, Deane 'was aware of the country's history and society and he was so natural about it ... He unquestionably did a good job and the vast majority of Australians agree.'[5]

Remarks by Mr Kim Beazley, Leader of the Opposition, on the announcement of Sir William Deane's successor, 22 April 2001[6]

Sir William Deane has warmed hearts of every Australian. He is a man who stood for all of us, alongside us in some of the saddest events which have occurred in this country over the last five or six years and as an exemplar on good community relations, particularly with the sympathetic attitude he has had for reconciliation and indigenous issues.

One of the very important roles, I think, that Sir William Deane has played as Governor-General was to express with a generous heart the full character of Australian society and to be an advocate for the tolerance with which we might hope our society functions.

---

3 Tony Stephens, *Sir William Deane: The Things That Matter* (Hodder, 2002), p viii.

4 Ibid, 25.

5 *Canberra Times*, 30 June 2001.

6 Kim Beazley, Australian Labor Party, Transcript, Doorstop Interview, South Perth, 22 April 2001.

And also, to weigh into the developing debate in reconciliation in our community. He is a much loved figure as a result of those interventions. And I would have no problem with a Governor-General who continues to take the view that he should pursue his office in a way that made all Australians feel they were stakeholders in this country.

Address by Prime Minister John Howard at the Farewell Reception for Sir William Deane, Great Hall, Parliament House, 28 June 2001[7]

Your Excellency, Lady Deane, Madam President, Mr Speaker, Mr Beazley Leader of the Opposition, distinguished guests, my parliamentary colleagues, ladies and gentlemen. Tonight is an occasion of mixed emotions. It's an occasion to allow all of us collectively on behalf of the Australian people to express our regard and our gratitude towards Sir William Deane, the retiring Governor-General of Australia. It's also of course an occasion that brings to an end an association between Sir William and Lady Helen Deane and so many of us in a personal sense and also in an institutional sense, the end of his very distinguished term as Governor-General of the Commonwealth of Australia and Commander in Chief of the Armed Forces of the Commonwealth.

When Sir William Deane was appointed as Governor-General of Australia on the recommendation of my predecessor as Prime Minister he capped a very long and distinguished career in the law. He served as an outstanding barrister at the New South Wales Bar taking silk at an early age and then successively on the Federal Court and the High Court of Australia, he left his mark on a profession that he served with such great distinction and he loved so very much. And his appointment to the office of Governor-General was a fitting climax to a very distinguished public career.

It is fair to say that there would be nobody of consequence who

[7] PM Transcripts, ID 12387, 28 June 2001.

would argue with the proposition that he has filled the Office of Governor-General with great compassion, great commitment and great sincerity. He has brought to that office a warmth and a dignity and a concern for the disadvantaged and a capacity to empathise with different sections of the Australian community that I know has won the admiration of people from all walks of life. I would want to say to you Sir William and to Lady Helen Deane on behalf of Janette and myself that in the nature of the two offices that we hold we have a lot of personal contact. And you have on all occasions displayed unfailing courtesy and warmth towards us and on a personal note I record our gratitude.

Sir William has represented the interests of the Office of Governor-General and he has served the people of Australia with particular distinction over the last five and a half years. His evident compassion for and concern for the disadvantaged within the Australian community is something that has been a hallmark and a feature of his time in office. His identification with the cause of reconciliation to which he is very sincerely committed is also something which has been a feature of his term. His understanding of the relationship between the various arms of Government and the institutions of our nation of course is quite unrivalled and his background in the law has made that even more possible.

In so many ways he has been a person who has represented the passion of the nation at times of great sadness. It comes with the responsibility of the beholder of the apolitical office of Governor-General to sometimes say things and to represent feelings on behalf of the nation that perhaps nobody else can. And that's an important character and feature of the office of Governor-General within our system of Government. I don't think any Australian will forget the moving way in which he and Lady Deane represented the feelings of the Australian people at that very tragic service at Interlaken in Switzerland which was a memorial to the deaths of those young Australians who died so very tragically. And that particular event and the way in which the feelings of the Australian people were expressed by him is a metaphor for the way in which in similar situations he has by his words and his deeds and his gesture and his evident decency spoken on behalf of all of us.

It is therefore with a mixture of the happiness of having the opportunity of saying thank you and expressing our affection and admiration but also the sadness of the end of a very positive and very fruitful association that we are gathered here tonight. And gathered here tonight at Sir William's request are not only representatives of the Parliament, of the judiciary, of the diplomatic core, but also of course the representatives of many organisation with which he had a great deal of contact not only in the time that he was Governor-General but also previously.

It is customary for Governments to present the outgoing Governor-General with a gift. On this occasion and in accordance with Sir William and Lady Deane's expressed wishes the Government has decided that a gift be made in their name to Charles O'Neill House in Sydney, one of the charitable projects with which they are associated. Charles O'Neill House is an initiative of the Matthew Talbot Hostel. The building is currently being refurbished to provide long term accommodation for homeless men making the transition back to independent living. The gift from the Government and the people of Australia in the name of Sir William and Lady Deane is for the plants and gardens for the two courtyards of Charles O'Neill House to provide an attractive outdoor area for the residence.

Ladies and gentlemen can I say to you Sir William, Bill as we exchange to each other of course on a personal basis and to Lady Deane can I say to both of you thank you for the service that you have given to the people of Australia. Thank you for the integrity and decency that you have bought to the high office you have occupied, I know that you leave that office with the admiration and the affection and the goodwill of the Australian people. You have done well and faithfully by the oath of office you took five and a half years ago. We wish you good luck, God's blessing and a long life and great happiness in the future.

'Exit Sir William, with a treat for young who know no home' by Tony Stephens, *Sydney Morning Herald*, 29 June 2001

Given the option of a slap-up farewell dinner in Parliament House last night, Sir William and Lady Deane chose a 90-minute reception.

Instead, the main focus of their last day in vice-regal office was on a group of street kids, mostly from Sydney.

The Deanes had 27 young people to lunch of a smorgasbord of roast beef and chicken, vegetables and home-made ice-cream and took them on a cruise of Lake Burley Griffin. Sir William and Lady Deane later went home, while the Right Reverend Dr Peter Hollingworth and his wife, Ann, moved into Yarralumla.

One of the girls at lunch had come, at 13, from a broken home, a drunken mother and sexual assaults. Now she is pursuing her education and wants to look after her mother.

One of the boys lost contact with his family at 12. He was kicked out of home on Christmas Day. He could barely read when Youth off the Streets, the organisation of which Sir William is patron, took him in. Now he is going to school.

Leaving Government House for the last time, Sir William said: 'This is a pretty sad time for Helen and me. We have been extraordinarily happy here at Government House. I would like to say to all Australians, thank you for the immense privilege in being able to serve in this office.'

He and Lady Deane were looking forward to private life, where they would 'try to do something about the matters I've been talking about'. He hoped they would 'achieve a little bit'.

He said: 'The principle I have been trying to get over to people for my whole time as Governor-General is that the ultimate test of our worth as a nation is how we treat the most vulnerable and disadvantaged of our people.'

The Deanes had made a 'very small financial gift' to every street kid. Most immediately gave half to Father Chris Riley, who heads Youth off the Streets.

Sir William said his main disappointment was that Australia had not reached reconciliation by the beginning of the century. 'But great things have been achieved at the grassroots and I am sure we will eventually get there.'

At the reception in the Great Hall of Parliament House, the Prime Minister, Mr Howard, thanked Sir William for his service to Australians and for his integrity and decency. 'You have done well and faithfully by the oath of office you took five and a half years ago.'

He said the Deanes had asked that the customary gift from the people of Australia be plants for Charles O'Neill House, the halfway home in Sydney for men and women trying to re-enter community life.

The Opposition Leader, Mr Beazley, said Sir William had embodied the nation's joys and sorrows and was one of the most loved Governors-General.

'All around Australia, Sir William has been a human face of our Constitution. Countless small communities have felt a sense of connection with the processes of government by his presence.'

Sir William thanked all Australians again. He thanked his wife, Helen: 'You are my rock, my inspiration, my love and my life.' Then the Deanes went home for dinner. A Government House aide thought they would take something from the freezer.

Index

www.ingramcontent.com/pod-product-compliance
Lightning Source LLC
LaVergne TN
LVHW051058210926
848486LV00024B/422/J
9781923568822